WITNESSES TO JESUS

A HISTORY OF THE CATHOLIC CHURCH IN THE FIRST MILLENNIUM

Rev. Rory T. Conley, Ph. D.

Pentecost. *Titian.*

But you shall receive power, when the Holy Spirit has come upon you:
and you shall be my witnesses in Jerusalem,
and in all Judea and Samaria, and to the end of the earth.

Acts 1:8

Christ on the Cross. *Francisco de Zurbaran.*

How can I repay the Lord
for His goodness to me?
The cup of salvation I will raise;
I will call on the Lord's name
My vows to the Lord I will fulfill
before all His people.
O precious in the eyes of the Lord
Is the death of His faithful.

Psalm 116:12-15

May 4, 2017

To my dear friend, Paula,
A wonderful witness to Jesus!
With my prayers
Fr. [Ray T. Conley]

ACKNOWLEDGEMENTS

To my dear friends, Louise Diver, Marian Jenkins and
especially Mary Glaser, whose painstaking proofreading, editing and
encouragement made it possible for this effort to come to fruition.
Many thanks and prayers!

TABLE OF CONTENTS

INTRODUCTION 8

CHAPTER ONE 11

"WE ARE HIS WITNESSES"

THE APOSTOLIC AGE C. 33-155 A.D.

CHAPTER TWO 42

"CITIZENS OF HEAVEN"

APOLOGISTS, VIRGINS & MARTYRS C.155-312 A.D.

CHAPTER THREE 76

"THE CITY OF GOD AND THE CITY OF MAN "

CHURCH AND EMPIRE C. 312-511

CHAPTER FOUR 115

"ORA ET LABORA"

NEW ROUNDATIONS C. 515 TO 750 A.D.

CHAPTER FIVE 143

"TO DEFEND HOLY CHURCH"

THE EARLY MIDDLE AGES C. 750-1050 A.D.

CONCLUSION 182

BIBLIOGRAPHY 184

INDEX 190

INTRODUCTION

The Catholic Church was born on Pentecost when in fulfillment of Christ's promise, the Holy Spirit was poured out upon the twelve Apostles. The Holy Spirit came to the Apostles not only for their own sanctification but also so that they could carry out the great commission that Jesus Christ had given them before His Ascension to the right hand of the Father. The mission Jesus gave them was to be His witnesses "in Jerusalem, throughout Judea and Samaria and to the ends of the earth."

At that first Pentecost the Church had no scriptures of her own, no clearly defined doctrines, no "pastoral plans" and certainly no help from the state. She didn't even have a name. What the Church did have was the experience of having encountered Christ and the conviction that Jesus is Lord. The Church also had some leaders—the Apostles, and the presence of Jesus' mother and foremost disciple, the Blessed Virgin Mary. Most importantly, however, she had the power of the Holy Spirit to guide her. And so it was that with these graces from God that the Church entered the wide-open missionary field of the Greco-Roman world which was ripe to turn from the myths of paganism to the truths of the Gospel.

For the first thousand years of its history the Catholic Church was the one Church. The word "catholic" of course means universal and in the first millennium, whether they lived in the eastern or western half of the Roman Empire, the vast majority of Christians believed themselves to be members of this one Church; having one faith, one baptism and one Lord. For this reason any full history of the Catholic Church must acknowledge the important events which occurred in the East that shaped her development.

I have chosen to present this history of the Catholic Church using a form of historical writing which was common during the first millennium of her existence, the chronology. I believe this form of presentation will provide the contemporary reader with a good overview of the history of the Church without trying their patience with long, detailed narratives.

I also chose the chronological form so that the reader may have a sense of history as it occurred for our forebears, with events and developments taking place concurrently just as they do for us. While historians labor to make the past coherent by arranging the material in seamless narratives, these constructions impose on our ancestors an artificially ordered world that they never knew. Life, history, as it occurs, is chaotic.

Of course, there are drawbacks in presenting the history of the Catholic Church chronologically. Approached this way there are seemingly an infinite number of persons, details and developments to remember; an impossible task. However, the reader need not be overwhelmed by the details but rather focus on how they point to the handful of important issues that the Church must continuously work out.

In every age, the Church, by the grace of God and through the power of the Holy Spirit, seeks to form her members into the **saints** that Jesus calls us to be through her **pastoral practices**. The Church also must carry out the Lord's great commission through the **evangelization** of those who have not yet heard the Gospel of salvation. Internally, the Church grapples with how **authority** is to be exercised by her leaders and the **doctrine** she teaches. Additionally, the Church always has to interact with various governing powers which for the sake of simplicity I call the **state**. Therefore, to assist the reader in understanding historical developments in the Church, each entry in this text will be designated as containing information relevant to one or more of the six constants enumerated above. Many entries will touch on more than one of the six perennial issues and so will have more than one designating symbol.

 Authority. Who has exercised decision making authority in the Church and how has it been challenged?

 Doctrine. What were the various theological questions the Church had to resolve in this era?

 Pastoral practice. How has the faith of the Church been practiced in the daily lives of its members?

 Saints. Who were some of the most notable holy men and women of the time?

 **Evangelization.** The last command that Jesus gave to His Apostles was that they go and baptize the nations. How has the Church responded to this mandate in different times and places?

 State. Jesus instructed His followers to give to Caesar what is Caesar's and to God what is God's. What were Church and State relations like during the period in question? In trying to understand these issues the contemporary reader must remember that the notion of "the separation of church and state" did not develop until the seventeenth century.

At the end of each chapter there is a summary of how these basic issues were faced within the era in question. It is hoped that this form of presentation will provide the reader with both an appreciation of the complexity of the Church's history as well as the constants that reveal the consistent patterns which have emerged in its unfolding.

As much as possible I have tried to provide documentation of the secondary sources I have used in compiling this chronology. I have done this to acknowledge my debt to the historians I have relied on and to demonstrate that the information being given has a sound basis in extant sources. Providing my sources also enables the reader to seek them out if he or she desires more information on a particular subject. I have included this documentation within the text so that it is readily available to the reader rather than leaving it to be searched for at the back of the book.

Finally, readers who are Christians, particularly those of the Catholic faith, should regard the history of the Catholic Church as the history of our family; the family we belong to by virtue of being members of the Body of Christ.

Like our biological families, our Church family has been composed of mostly ordinary men and women who have strived, with God's grace, to be faithful followers of Jesus Christ. Also, like our biological families, our Church family has had its share of heroes and scoundrels.

Our "heroes" are the saints, the thousands of holy men and women who have been outstanding witnesses to our faith in Jesus Christ. Our scoundrels are those members of the Church who by their actions either did not witness to the truth of Christianity or, worse yet, have worked against the Gospel by their evil actions.

We should admire our heroes and seek to imitate their faithful witness to Christ. As for our less than admirable members, we should pray for them and remember that their sinfulness can never overcome the holiness of the Church because she remains the Body of Christ in this world.

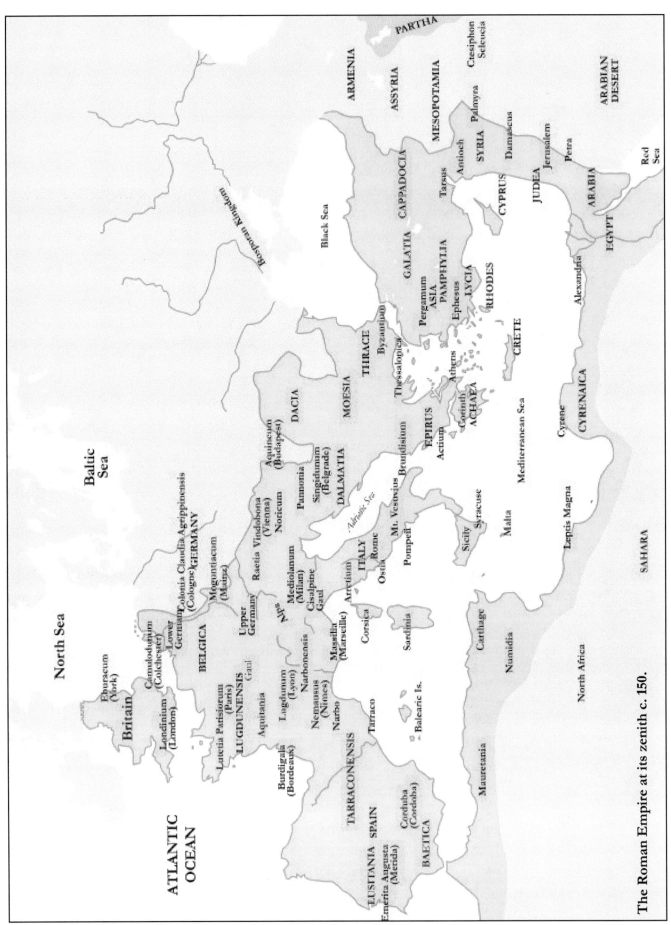

The Roman Empire at its zenith c. 150.

CHAPTER ONE

"WE ARE HIS WITNESSES"
THE APOSTOLIC AGE C. 33-155 A.D.

The first era in the history of the Church is known as the "Apostolic Age" because during this period the Church was led by the apostles and their immediate successors. The Apostolic Age lasted until about the year 150 A.D.

Before His **Ascension, c. 33 A.D.**, Jesus commissioned the apostles to carry on His mission, "…you shall receive power when the Holy Spirit has come upon you; and you shall be my witnesses in Jerusalem, and in all Judea and Samaria and to the end of the earth." The eleven apostles returned to the Upper Room in Jerusalem where, together with the Blessed Virgin Mary and some other women, they devoted themselves to prayer. They were accompanied by other Galilean followers and relatives of Jesus. According to St. Luke, the author of the Acts of the Apostles, "the company of persons was in all about a hundred and twenty." Some scholars speculate that the "Upper Room" may have been in the house of Mary, the mother of St. Mark the Evangelist. *Acts of the Apostles 1:8, 12-15 and 12:12. Paul Barnett, Jesus & the Rise of Early Christianity: A History of New Testament Times (Inter-Varsity Press, 1999) 198-199.*

St. Peter called for the selection of another disciple to replace Judas as one of the twelve apostles and Matthias was chosen. This was the first time that Peter exercised his authority as head of the apostles. *Acts 1:15-26.*

St. Peter is unrivaled in prominence among the followers of Jesus and is mentioned over 200 times in the New Testament. Although the date of his birth is unknown, the Gospels do provide a number of facts about his life. His given name was Simon and he was from Bethsaida. He was also married, as the Gospels mention his mother-in-law. Peter and his brother Andrew were fishermen who worked together with James and John, the sons of Zebedee. These four fishermen were the first to be called by Jesus to be apostles. When the names of the apostles are listed, Peter is always listed first. And he often acts as their spokesmen, such as in the Gospel of John, chapter six, where Peter says that, unlike some other disciples who reject Christ's teaching on "eating his flesh," the apostles will not leave Jesus. *John 6:66-69.*

St. Peter Receives the Keys from Christ.
Jean Auguste Dominique Ingres. 1820. Musee Ingres. Montauban, France

Simon Peter's importance among the Twelve was dramatically confirmed at Caesarea Philippi where, having received a revelation from God the Father, Simon made his confession of faith, "You are the Christ, the Son of the living God." In response, Jesus proclaimed, "And I tell you, you are Peter, and on this rock I will build my Church and the gates of Hades shall not prevail against it. I will give you the keys of the kingdom of heaven, and whatever you bind on earth shall be bound in heaven, and whatever you loose on earth shall be loosed in heaven." *Mt 16:18-19.* The keys signify Peter's authority as the vicar of Christ to open the door to the kingdom to all who wish to belong. The binding authority represents the mandate to protect the community from sin by the excommunication of the erring and the welcoming back of the sinner through reconciliation.

St. Peter's primacy among the apostles is further demonstrated at the Last Supper when Jesus offered a special prayer that, when Peter recovered his cour-

age, he would strengthen the faith of the other apostles. *Lk 22:31-32.* Among the apostles, Peter along with John is the first witness to the resurrection of Christ. *Lk 24:12 & 34. Jn 20:6.*

Following His resurrection, Jesus designated St. Peter as the pastor of His sheep. *Jn 21:15-17.* St. Peter fulfilled his mission by leading the apostles and other disciples after the ascension of Jesus. He is the first to proclaim Jesus as the Christ after Pentecost. Peter was also the first to welcome Gentiles into the Church. *Acts 10:1-11, 18.*

On the Jewish feast of Pentecost the Twelve Apostles were filled with the Holy Spirit and began proclaiming that they were witnesses to the resurrection of Jesus who is "both Lord and Christ" or Messiah. *Acts 2:1-36.*

Peter and the other apostles called the people to repent and to be baptized for the forgiveness of their sins and so they could receive the Holy Spirit. In doing so the apostles fulfilled Jesus' command: "Go therefore and make disciples of all nations, baptizing them in the name of the Father, and of the Son and of the Holy Spirit." *Mt 28:19.* According to St. Luke, about three thousand followers were added to their number that day. It is important to note that in his preaching about Jesus, Peter excused the Jews and their leaders for putting Jesus to death because they "acted in ignorance." *Acts 2:37-41 and 3:17.*

Devotion to Jesus as "Lord," meaning divine, ("Kyrios" in Greek) was at the heart of the Church's proclamation from the very beginning. St. Paul's First Letter to the Thessalonians, written about the year 50 and perhaps the earliest book

Pentecost.
Jean II Restout: Penecote. 1732

of the New Testament, refers to Jesus numerous times as "Lord." In doing so St. Paul simply invoked the "Lord Jesus" without seeing the need to argue the point. While it would take a few centuries and several councils to arrive at a precise doctrinal definition of Jesus Christ as both God and man, from the outset the Church and its members proclaimed, "Jesus is Lord."

Father Benedict Groeschel, C.F.R., *I Am With You Always: A Study of the History and Meaning of Personal Devotion to Jesus Christ for Catholic, Orthodox, and Protestant Christians,* (Ignatius Press, 2010), 20-22.

The growing community of believers in Jerusalem devoted themselves to the teaching of the apostles, to "the breaking of the bread,"—the Eucharist – and to prayer. Thus they fulfilled Christ's command to preach the Gospel and to celebrate the Eucharist. They also shared their goods in common for mutual support. As observant Jews, the first followers of Jesus continued to pray in the Temple. However, because of their already large and ever-increasing numbers, they celebrated the Eucharist in their homes. Although Saturday, the seventh day of

the week, was the Sabbath day for Jews, Sunday, the day Jesus rose, eventually became the "Lord's day" for His followers. *Lk 24:1.Acts 2:42-47.3:1, 20:7-10. Rev.1:10.*

Samuele Bacchiocchi, *From Sabbath to Sunday: A Historical Investigation of the Rise of Sunday Observance in Early Christianity* (Pontifical Gregorian University Press, 1977),183-212.

The "breaking of bread" that St. Luke writes about in Acts probably took place within the context of the traditional weekly Sabbath meal. The first Christians retained the Jewish practice of including prayers of praise, thanksgiving and intercession within their worship of the Lord. Invocations such as "Let us pray," prayers of blessing over the bread and cup, as well as doxologies — "Glory to God" –were adapted from Jewish tradition. The practice of scripture reading was also incorporated into the Christian liturgy.

Keith F. Pecklers, S.J., *Liturgy; The Illustrated History* (Paulist Press, 2012), 16-18.

The Last Supper. *Leonardo da Vinci. c.1495. Santa Maria Delle Grazie, Milan*

The earliest account of how Christians celebrated the Eucharist is found in St. Paul's First Letter to the Corinthians, chapter 11, verses 17-34. Paul's account tells us a number of things about how the first Christians celebrated the liturgy and what they believed about what they were doing. First of all, since St. Paul wrote the First Letter to the Corinthians around the year 54 A.D., he was describing a ritual which had already been celebrated for close to twenty years among the followers of Christ. Secondly, the Eucharist was preceded by a common meal. Thirdly, before repeating the words of Jesus which instituted the Eucharist, St. Paul states that his teaching on the sacrament comes from Christ Himself. Thus, whether Paul received some direct instruction from Christ or simply learned what Jesus said and did at the Last Supper from His followers, as far as Paul was concerned this teaching on the Eucharist came to him from the Lord Himself.

"For I received from the Lord what I also delivered to you, that the Lord Jesus on the night when he was betrayed took bread and when He had given thanks, He broke it and said, 'This is my body which is for you. Do this in remembrance of me.' In the same way also the chalice, after supper, saying, 'This chalice is the new covenant in my blood. Do this, as often as you drink it, in remembrance of me.' For as often as you eat this bread and drink the chalice, you proclaim the Lord's death until he comes."

1 Cor. 11:17-26

St. Paul then goes on to say in verses 27-28:

"Whoever, therefore, eats the bread or drinks the cup of the Lord in an unworthy manner will be guilty of profaning the body and blood of the Lord. Let a man examine himself, and so eat of the bread and drink of the cup."

In these verses Paul is telling us three things. First, that it was customary at that time to receive the Eucharist under both forms. Secondly, St. Paul

14

clearly believes that the consecrated bread and wine of the Eucharist truly become the Body and Blood of the Lord just as Jesus had said at the Last Supper. Thirdly, the Eucharist is not to be received without first examining one's conscience to make sure one does not receive in "an unworthy manner" because of sin. This of course implies that, should a man have a serious sin on his conscience, there must be some means of forgiveness for this sin prior to receiving the Eucharist.

In Acts chapters two, three and ten, we are told that the first Christians continued the Jewish custom of gathering for prayer three times a day: at the third hour, the sixth hour and the ninth hour (9:00 a.m., 12 noon, and 3:00 p.m. respectively). Pecklers, *Liturgy; The Illustrated History*, 19.

As the Christian movement continued to grow, the Jewish religious leaders sought to stop it. Peter and John were arrested for teaching the people about Jesus and proclaiming His resurrection from the dead. However, the authorities let Peter and John go because they had no grounds to punish them and they feared the people. Later all the apostles were arrested for continuing to preach about Jesus and for performing miracles in His name. But once again the authorities released them. The apostles rejoiced that they had been counted worthy to suffer for the sake of Jesus. *Acts 3:2-10, 4:12-16, 5:17-42.*

The early chapters of Acts also record the important place that miracles of healing had in the ministry of the Apostles. The "many signs and wonders" done by the Apostles in the name of Jesus

Martyrdom of St. Stephen. *Adam Elsheimer. The Stoning of St. Stephen. National Galleries Scotland.*

disposed the people to hear their message and put their faith in the Gospel. The combining of works of healing, as well as exorcisms, with preaching continued to be a powerful catalyst in bringing about conversions during the first centuries of the Church. *Acts 3:1-16. 4:13-22, 29-31. 5:12-16.* Ramsay MacMullen, *Christianizing the Roman Empire* (A.D. 100-400) (Yale University Press, 1984), 21-24, 108-112.

The first Christian community in Jerusalem was comprised of diverse groups. Some, like the apostles, were Jews from Galilee who spoke Aramaic. There were also Aramaic-speaking Jews from Jerusalem and other parts of Palestine. And there were Greek-speaking Jews who were originally from different parts of the Roman Empire. Most of these disciples were among the three thousand who were baptized on Pentecost. In the Acts of the Apostles the Aramaic-speaking Jews are referred to as "Hebrews" and the Greek-speakers are called the "Hellenists."

As the community grew there developed a dispute between the two groups over the fair distribution of food for widows. Thus, even in its first days, the Church was never a community of the perfect but of those who were trying to "be perfect as your heavenly Father is perfect" with the help of the Lord's grace. To solve the issue, the twelve apostles asked the community of disciples to choose seven men to assist them so that the apostles could continue to devote themselves to prayer and the ministry of the Word. The seven men chosen all had Greek names as evidently they were chosen to represent the aggrieved Hellenists. After the community chose the seven men, the Apostles consecrated them for ministry by praying over them and imposed their hands on them. (The imposition of hands, a gesture indicating the conferral of authority, has its origins in the Old Testament.) Not long after that, one of these seven men, **Philip**, is described as preaching and baptizing in the name of Jesus Christ. Because of their consecration to serve, to preach and to baptize, these seven men are regarded as the first **deacons** of the Church.
Acts 6:1-7 and 8:5 &12.

Another of the seven men who received the "laying on of hands" from the apostles was Stephen. "Full of grace and power," Stephen preached to Greek-speaking Jews in Jerusalem and aroused the ire of some of them. Like Jesus before him, Stephen was falsely accused of wanting to destroy the Temple. Around the year 35 Stephen was arrested, tried and stoned to death. And also like Jesus before him, **Stephen** prayed for his killers. St. Stephen was the **first martyr** of the Church.
Acts 6:8-7, 60. Barnett, 219-221.

The Conversion of St. Paul. *Pietro da Cortona. Ananias Restoring the Sight of St. Paul.*

The second century Church Father, Tertullian, asserted that the illegal execution of Stephen by the Sanhedrin was reported to the Emperor Tiberius by Pontius Pilate. This may have prompted the Romans to protect the Christians in Palestine from further persecution by Jewish authorities. While many modern historians discount Tertullian's assertion as an apologetic invention, some scholars find his account credible and note that Roman authorities were tolerant of Christians until the reign of the Emperor Nero.
Marta Sordi, *The Christians and the Roman Empire* (University of Oklahoma, 1986), 7-25.

Following the stoning of Stephen, a widespread persecution of the followers of Jesus by their fellow Jews began in Jerusalem. Many of them scattered to the surrounding regions taking the good news of the Gospel with them. As a result, non-Jews began to be converted and were baptized. At this time Christ's disciples referred to their movement as **"the Way."** *Acts 8:1-40, 9:2 & 19:9.*

Among those consenting to the killing of Stephen was another young, Greek-speaking Jew named Saul. By his own account, **Saul** persecuted the followers of Christ with "a raging fury." He imprisoned many, condemned others to death and even pursued them beyond the land of Israel.

On the way to Damascus, where he hoped to arrest more followers of Jesus, Saul, a dedicated Pharisee, encountered Jesus in person and was converted. Saul was originally from Tarsus in Asia Minor (modern day Turkey) and he was a Roman citizen. As a Pharisee, Saul knew the Jewish Law and Scripture well and he could read and write in both Hebrew and Greek. Following his encounter with Jesus, Saul was baptized and received the Holy Spirit through the imposition of hands. Saul, who would change his name to **Paul**, first spent three years in Arabia. *Gal 1:17.*

Then Paul began preaching about Jesus in the synagogues in Damascus and in Jerusalem. *Acts 9:1-31; 22:5-16 & 26:12-18.* Soon Paul and his companions took the Gospel to the Jews living outside of Palestine in the "Diaspora." In fact, by the first century there were more Jews living outside of Palestine than in it. Rejected in some synagogues, Paul extended his mission beyond the Jews and became known as the "Apostle to the Gentiles."

F.L Cross and E.A. Livingstone, eds. *The Oxford Dictionary of the Christian Church.* (Oxford University Press, 1990). Timothy Luke Johnson, *Early Christianity: The Experience of the Divine,* (Great Courses, 2002) course guide book, 39-40.

Arrival of the Apostles. *Duccio.*

Between the years 33 and 47, **St. Peter** carried out his ministry in Palestine. Later he had a prominent role at the Council of Jerusalem and led the church in Antioch. There are two letters from St. Peter in the New Testament. Also, it is widely accepted that St. Mark the Evangelist assisted Peter and based much of his Gospel on the testimony of the Prince of the Apostles.

F.L Cross and E.A. Livingstone, eds. *The Oxford Dictionary of the Christian Church* (Oxford University Press, 1990). Pope Benedict XVI, *The Apostles* (Our Sunday Visitor Press, 2007). Barnett, *Jesus & the Rise of Early Christianity: A History of New Testament Times,* 233-246, 370-372.

The Baptism of Cornelius. *Francesco Trevisani. Peter Baptizing the Centurion Cornelius. 1708*

The followers of Jesus continued to spread His message in the cities and towns of the provinces in the eastern Mediterranean region. It was in the city of Antioch, which is in Syria, that the followers of Jesus began to be known as "Christians" because they proclaimed Him to be the "Christ" which means the one "anointed" or chosen by God. *Acts 11:19-26.*

King Herod Agrippa I, who ruled parts of Palestine from 37-44, launched a persecution of the Church around the year **42** specifically targeting its leaders. **James,** the Apostle and brother of John, was beheaded. He was the first Apostle to be martyred. Peter was also arrested but miraculously escaped and fled Jerusalem for Caesarea. Peter remained away from Jerusalem for a few years and returned only after the death of Herod Agrippa. With Peter in exile, another **James,** known as the "brother of the Lord," became the leader of the Church in Jerusalem.

Acts 12:1-19. Karl Baus, *History of the Church Vol. I, From the Apostolic Community to Constantine Hubert Jedin,* Editor (Crossroad, 1987), 76-77.

A controversy arose in the Church as to whether non-Jewish converts to the Way, "Gentiles," had to take up Jewish practices such as circumcision and dietary restrictions. At the **Council of Jerusalem in the year 49**, it was agreed that the Gentiles did not have to adopt Jewish practices in order to be faithful followers of Jesus. This was tremendously important for the Church's evangelization efforts. It meant that Christianity would not be limited to those willing to accept the religious and cultural practices of the Jews, but would be open to people of all nations. *Acts 15:1-35.*

Having received approval for his work among the Gentiles from the Council of Jerusalem, St. Paul began his first missionary journey with **St. Barnabas.** *Gal 2:7-9.* They went to the latter's homeland of Cyprus. Among their converts was the Roman proconsul or governor of the island, Sergius Paulus. Saul of Tarsus may have taken his Roman name from his prominent Gentile convert. On these journeys he was accompanied at various times by **Mark** and **Luke**, who wrote the Gospels bearing their names, as well as by **Silas, Timothy** and **Titus.** *Acts 13:7-12.* (On the authorship of the four Gospels see Curtis Mitch, *"Introduction to the Gospels,"* in the Ignatius Catholic Study Bible New Testament.)

Paul would preach in the local synagogues, where his proclamation that Jesus is the Messiah was usually rejected by most of the Jews. Paul would then preach to the Gentiles, among whom he had greater success. Some of Paul's Gentile listeners were frequenters of synagogues because they were attracted by Jewish monotheism and ethical standards. However, they had not become Jews, perhaps deterred by the requirement of circumcision. A prominent example is **Cornelius**, the centurion in Caesarea whose conversion by Peter is recounted in chapters ten and eleven of Acts. These "God-fearers," as they were known, were often most receptive to Paul's message of the Gospel covenant which could be entered into without circumcision.

Acts 13:50. Barnett, *Jesus & the Rise of Early Christianity: A History of New Testament Times,* 233-246, 370-372.

After St. Peter proclaimed the Gospel of Jesus Christ to Cornelius he and his "household" were baptized. *Acts 11:14-15* Although the text doesn't explicitly say so, it is assumed that Cornelius' house included children. St. Paul baptized the whole household of Lydia, "the seller of purple goods," *Acts 16:14-15,* and the jailer in Philippi was baptized "with all his family." *Acts 16:33.* Likewise, Paul baptized Crispus, the synagogue ruler "together with all his household" *Acts 18:8* and also "the household of Stephanas." *1 Cor. 1:16.* Again, while these texts do not specifically state that children were being baptized, a "family" and "household" implies the presence of children. The Gospels tell us that parents wanted to have Jesus bless their children. *Mk 10:13-16 & Lk 18:15, 17.* Apparently the first Christians wanted this same desire fulfilled by having their children baptized. While not all agreed with it, the practice of baptizing children and infants was well established in the Church by the beginning of the second century.

Baptism of the Neophytes. *Masaccio. c. 1427*

Various references to **baptism** in the New Testament suggest that it was administered in several ways. These included the full submersion of the person under water, signifying their "burial" with Christ. *Rms 6:3-11* Other methods included the partial immersion of the person in water, and affusion, where water is poured over the person's head. Whichever method was used and however old the recipient, baptism was understood as bringing new life "through water and the Holy Spirit" and union with Jesus Christ in His death and resurrection.

Maxwell E. Johnson, *The Rites of Christian Initiation: Their Evolution and Interpretation,* Revised and expanded edition (Pueblo, 2007), 33-40.

There are **thirteen letters attributed to St. Paul in the New Testament**. Paul's letters are believed to have been written between the year 48 and his death in 64. There is some debate over which was his earliest letter, the Letter to the Galatians, written for the Christians living in a province of what is now Turkey, or his First Letter to the Thessalonians, written for those living in northern Greece.

The Oxford Dictionary of the Christian Church. Barnett, *Jesus & the Rise of Early Christianity: A History of New Testament Times,* 292-294.

There are many opinions as to when **the four Gospels were written**. Some biblical scholars maintain that the Gospels were written between the 40's and 60's while the apostles and other eyewitnesses were still alive. This would explain, among other things, why the *Acts of the Apostles*, which records the martyrdoms of Stephen and the Apostle James, ends with Peter and Paul alive in Rome. Other scholars assert that the Gospels were written between 70 and 90 A.D.

Often it is asserted that, in the first decades of the Church, there was no perceived need for written accounts of Jesus' life and mission as the eyewitnesses were still present. It is also asserted that because the first generation of Christians expected that Jesus would soon return, they saw no point in preserving his memory with written accounts. But these arguments for a later dating of the Gospels ignore the obvious lessons to be drawn from the example of St. Paul. The Apostle to the Gentiles both wrote and preached about Jesus Christ. Why wouldn't the other eyewitnesses have done the same? Obviously, written accounts of the life and teachings of Jesus could spread the message of the Gospel to far more people than could be reached by oral testimonies alone. Based on the historical evidence, all that can be said with certainty about when the Gospels were put into writing is that they were written some time between Christ's Ascension and the end of the first century.

Richard Bauckham, *Jesus and the Eyewitnesses: The Gospels as Eyewitness Testimony* (Eerdmans, 2006).

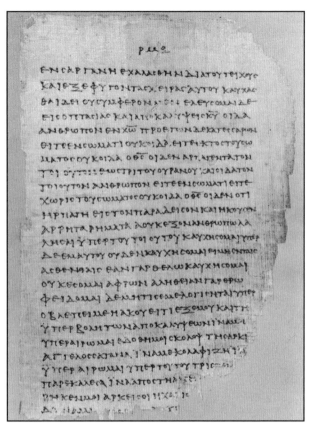

Gospel of Matthew.

The earliest written testimony to Christian writings being regarded as **"Scripture"** comes from the Second Letter of St. Peter 3:15-16. Some biblical scholars say that this letter could have been written in the 60's. This passage acknowledges that the meaning of particular scripture writings is not always immediately understandable.

"So also our brother Paul wrote to you according to the wisdom given him, speaking of this as he does in all his letters. There are some things in them hard to understand, which the ignorant and unstable twist to their own destruction, as they do the other Scriptures."

St. James with Two Children.
Andrea de Sarto.
Uffizi Gallery, Florence.

Just as Pontius Pilate had attempted to stay out of the conflict between the Sanhedrin and Jesus, Roman officials repeatedly declined demands from Jewish leaders that they punish Christians, particularly St. Paul.

Acts 18:12-1, 23:23-35, 25:13-22.

While evangelization efforts were conducted by the apostles and their successors, conversions were also brought about through the daily witness of individual Christians. Their fidelity to the teachings of Jesus Christ prompted their relatives and friends to be open to the Gospel. Indeed, from the beginning it was through the lived Christianity of ordinary believers that others were brought into the Church rather than through any mass movement of conversion.

Rodney Stark, The Triumph of Christianity: How the Jesus Movement Became the Largest Religion in the World (Harper One, 2011), 68-69.

   Christians were present in Rome by the early **40s**. Some of them were Jews who accepted Jesus as the Messiah. Others were Gentiles. Among these Christians, some may have been from the aristocratic class. Two of the Jewish Christians in Rome were Aquila and his wife, Priscilla. A Roman historian of the late first century, Suetonius, wrote that around the year **49** the emperor Claudius expelled the Jews from Rome because they were in constant conflict among themselves over a man named "**Chrestos.**" It is believed by many historians that "Chrestos" is a misspelling of "Christ." Aquila and Priscilla were among those expelled from the city at this time. The couple became coworkers with Paul in Corinth and eventually returned to Rome where they opened their home as a house church for the Christian community.

Acts 18:2 & Romans 16:3-5. Sordi, The Christians and the Roman Empire, 28-29. Bacchiocchi, "Rome and Christianity Until A.D. 62," Andrews University Seminary Studies, Spring 1983, Vol. 21, No.1, 3-25. Baus, History of the Church Vol. I From the Apostolic Community to Constantine, 129, 138-140. Eusebius, The Church History Book II, 18 translation and commentary by Paul L. Maier (Kregel Publications, 2007).

After the Council of Jerusalem, it appears that **St. Peter** continued his evangelization efforts among Jews, continuously moving westward into the heart of the empire. The only thing known for certain about his movements is that according to St. Paul, Peter was in Corinth in the early **50's**. Following the death of the Emperor Claudius in 54, Jews were once again allowed to live in Rome. It is believed that Peter arrived in the imperial capital not long after this and spent the rest of his life ministering there.

1 Corinthians 9:5. Barnett, Jesus & the Rise of Early Christianity: A History of New Testament Times, 301-303.

St. John the Apostle.

Assumption of the Virgin. *Pierre-Paul Prud'hon.*

The Church's earliest **evangelization** efforts were much more successful among the Jews of the Diaspora than they were among the Jews still living in Palestine. This was so because Jews living outside of Palestine had accommodated themselves to the prevailing Hellenistic culture and had given up many Mosaic ritual practices. In addition to the appeal of the Gospel message of Jesus, Christianity promoted the most important teachings of the Old Testament without insisting that its adherents isolate themselves from their pagan neighbors.

Stark, *The Triumph of Christianity*, 71-77.

During the 50's **St. Paul** traveled among the cities of Asia Minor and Greece establishing and visiting small church communities. Like Jesus, Paul most probably traveled with numer-ous companions who shared his evangelization efforts and acted as his scribes. He was often in conflict with Jews who expelled him from their synagogues. He also had to contend with Jewish-Christian "Judaizers," who continued to maintain the necessity of maintaining Jewish customs within the Church. Having returned with funds to support the Church in Jerusalem around 58, Paul was arrested on false charges. As a Roman citizen, Paul insisted on his right to be tried before Caesar and eventually was sent to Rome for trial.

Acts 25-27. Stark, *The Triumph of Christianity*, 66-68.

St. Luke records that St. Paul was under house arrest for two years in Rome,

c. **60-62**. During this time he was able to preach about "the kingdom of God and teach about the Lord Jesus Christ quite openly and unhindered." Acts 28:14-31. Paul's Second Letter to Timothy indicates that after a short period of freedom, he was rearrested. This second imprisonment ended with his martyrdom. It is the faith of all Christians that, while writing his letters to some of the first Christian communities, St. Paul was guided by the Holy Spirit. Therefore his letters were divinely inspired and continue to teach us what it means to be followers of Jesus Christ.

In **62 A.D.**, **St. James**, head of the church in Jerusalem, was martyred. According to the first century Jewish historian, Flavius Josephus, the high priest at the time, Ananus, took advantage of the absence of a Roman procurator to have James and some other Christians stoned to death. When the Roman authorities learned of Ananus' illegal action, they deposed him from office.

Flavius Josephus, Jewish Antiquities, Book 20, Chapter 9,1.

Like Peter and Paul, **St. John** also left Palestine. He became associated with church communities in the eastern cities of Asia Minor (Turkey). According to this tradition, St. John was the only apostle who wasn't martyred and the last of them to die. It is believed that St. John lived near Ephesus in modern day Turkey where, faithful to Jesus' command from the cross, he cared for the **Blessed Mother** until her Assumption. It is thought that St. John died sometime in the 90's. While the New Testament doesn't say what happened to the other apostles, the oral tradition of the early Church recorded the stories of their missionary efforts in Syria, Egypt, Asia Minor, Armenia, Greece and even as far east as India and perhaps as far west as Spain.

Barnett, 309-314, 371. Jean Danielou and Henri Marrou, *The Christian Centuries Vol. One The First Six Hundred Years* (Paulist Press, 1983), 39-53. Pope Benedict XVI, *The Apostles* (Our Sunday Visitor Press, 2007). Herbert Thurston, S.J. and Donald Attwater, eds. *Butler's Lives of the Saints* Vols. I-IV (Christian Classics, 1988). C. Bernard Ruffin, *The Twelve: The Lives of the Apostles After Calvary* (Our Sunday Visitor Press, 1997).

In the year **64** a great fire destroyed much of Rome. The people believed that the fire was deliberately started by the **Emperor Nero** so he could rebuild the city according to his Greek tastes. To deflect the outrage of the populace, Nero made scapegoats out of the Christians in Rome and launched a violent persecution against them. By this time the authorities in Rome were aware that Jews and Christians were not the same. The pagan historian Tacitus, writing about fifty years after the event, described the persecution.

"...Nero fastened the guilt and inflicted the most exquisite tortures on a class hated for their abominations, called Christians by the populace. Christus, from whom the name had its origin, suffered the extreme penalty during the reign of Tiberius at the hands of one of our procurators, Pontius Pilatus, and a most mischievous superstition, thus checked for the moment, again broke out not only in Judaea, the first source of the evil, but even in Rome, where all things hideous and shameful from every part of the world find their center and become popular. Accordingly, an arrest was first made of all who pleaded guilty; then, upon their information, an immense multitude was convicted, not so much of the crime of firing the city, as of hatred against mankind. Mockery of every sort was added to their deaths. Covered with the skins of beasts, they were torn by dogs and perished, or were nailed to crosses, or were doomed to the flames and burnt, to serve as a nightly illumination, when daylight had expired."

The Destruction of Jerusalem. *David Roberts. c. 1850*

These witnesses to Christ are honored as the first martyrs of the Church in Rome. In this period of persecution St. Peter was crucified and St. Paul was beheaded.

"The Annals by Publius Cornelius Tacitus, 15.44," The Complete Works of Tacitus The Modern Library, 1942. Translated by Alfred John Church and William Jackson Brodribb. http://mcadams.posc.mu.edu/txt/ah/tacitus/tacitusabbals15.html

Eamon Duffy, *Saints and Sinners: A History of the Popes* (Yale University Press, 1999), 5.

Evidence suggests that even before Nero's fire, Christians had become unpopular in the city of Rome. According to the First Letter of Peter they were spoken against as "wrong doers" and abused because they would not join their pagan neighbors in "wild debauchery." *1 Peter 2:12 & 4:4.* Also, misunderstandings about the Eucharist led to rumors about cannibalistic practices among Christians. Further, as Nero and some later emperors fostered cults of their own divinity, Christians were persecuted for their suspected disloyalty. Under the Roman imperial government, the persecution of Christians was sporadic although they were always in danger of being persecuted because they refused to participate in pagan rituals which were part of the official religion of the empire. Much depended on the disposition of the reigning emperor. Christians were also a frequent target for discontented citizens in various times and places.

Baus, *History of the Church Vol. I From the Apostolic Community to Constantine*, 125-136.

In **66 A.D.**, the Jews in Judea launched a revolt against Roman rule. Shortly after, the Christian community left Jerusalem for safety and crossed the Jordan where they established themselves in the town of Pella. **The Jewish War** as it became

Supper at Emmaus. *Caravaggio. 1602. Academy of the Arts, Brera, Milan.*

known lasted until the revolt was brutally crushed in the year 70. In retribution for the revolt, the **Romans destroyed the Temple** in Jerusalem. This effectively ended Jewish Temple sacrifices. Synagogue services centered on scripture reading and prayer became the only public form of Jewish worship. Around 73-74 the Jewish Christians returned to Jerusalem and resumed their community life and missionary efforts under their Bishop Simeon, the successor to the martyred James.

Robert Louis Wilken, *The First Thousand Years: A Global History of Christianity* (Yale University Press, 2012), 26-27. Pecklers, *Liturgy; The Illustrated History,* 14-16.

Jewish Christians continued to go to synagogues until around **80 A.D.** when they were for-

mally rejected as apostates. A prayer against the "Nazarenes" became part of the daily synagogue service. This **malediction** effectively forced Jewish Christians to stop attending synagogue services. It also declared them non-Jews and thus unprotected by the toleration Roman authorities had extended to Judaism.

"For the apostates let there be no hope, and uproot the kingdom of arrogance, speedily and in our days. May the Nazarenes and the sectarians perish as in a moment. Let them be blotted out of the book of life, and not be written together with the righteous."

Quoted in Edward Foley, From *Age to Age: How Christians Have Celebrated the Eucharist* (Liturgical Press, 2008), 6. Baus, History of the Church Vol. I From *the Apostolic Community to Constantine,* 77, 205. Samuele Bacchiocchi, From *Sabbath to Sunday: A Historical Investigation of the Rise of Sunday Observance in Early Christianity,* 157-158.

The Jews of Palestine were so opposed to the "apostates" that according to Justin Martyr they sent their own missionaries to Jewish communities of the Diaspora to denounce Christian teachings. Any complete account of the difficult relations between Jews and Christians through history must take into account their origins in the first centuries of Christianity. Also, it appears that Jews who became Christian believers continued to intermingle with unconverted Jews at least until the fourth century. This is not surprising as often they were related.

Justin Martyr, *Dialogue with Trypho*, 17. Flavius Josephus, *The Jewish War* Book 6, chapters 4-9. Rodney Stark, *Cities of God: The Real Story of How Christianity Became an Urban Movement and Conquered Rome* (HarperCollins, 2006), 136-139. Baus, *History of the Church Vol. I From the Apostolic Community to Constantine*, 125-136.

By the end of the first century, **Christian communities** could be found throughout the Mediterranean region: from Alexandria in Egypt; north through Israel to Syria and Turkey; west through Greece; as well as in the capital of the empire, Rome. Although the Church only had approximately 7,400 members, and comprised less than 1% of the empire's total population, Christians could be found in most of the major cities.

Baus, *History of the Church Vol. I From the Apostolic Community to Constantine*, 205-210. Stark, *Cities of God*, 66-73.

Contrary to pagan critics of the time and later historians hostile to the Church, Christianity was not **"a religion of slaves."** While the message of the Gospel certainly found a welcoming audience

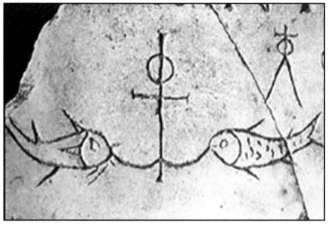

Catacomb showing an anchor, the Christian symbol of hope.

among those at the lower classes of Roman society, it resonated with receptive members of the elite as well. St. Paul himself documented the social diversity among Christians when he wrote to the Corinthians that "...not many were powerful, not many were of noble worth...." Not many were powerful or of the nobility, but at least some were. Otherwise, Paul's assertion makes no sense. Raised in the home of a skilled craftsman, Jesus was neither a slave nor a peasant. According to his own account, Paul himself was the beneficiary of an extensive and expensive education. The New Testament is full of references to individuals who were men and women of means. Thus the Gospel message was not chained to any one social class.

Stark, *The Triumph of Christianity*, 87-104.

Christians gathered in their homes where they continued to reflect on the life and message of Jesus now preserved in the written form of the Gospels. They also followed the inspired teachings of the apostles as recorded in the letters that bear their names. In addition, they continued to celebrate "the breaking of the bread" — in accordance with Christ's instructions to the apostles at the Last Supper, "Do this in memory of me."

Providentially, there were some **social and political factors that facilitated the growth of Christianity.** First, the conquests by Alexander the Great had given the Mediterranean region a common language, Greek, in the centuries prior to the coming of the Christ. Secondly, the dominance of the Roman empire had brought relative peace and stability to the area. Thirdly, although travelers on the Mediterranean Sea faced a very real danger from storms as St. Paul attests, the sea-lanes plied by commercial ships provided an efficient means of transportation for Christian migrants who took the Gospel with them. Fourthly, to ensure that their legions could travel quickly around the empire, the Romans built a system of roads that was unequaled until modern times. These same roads carried Christians to new communities of potential converts.

The **moral character and hopefulness of the first Christians** also attracted others to the Gospel of Jesus Christ. The pagans observed how Christians took care of one another and stood away from the violence and promiscuity of the times. Further, Christianity proclaimed a God of love and mercy who has a plan for His creation and who offered salvation through the sacraments. This was good news for people oppressed by the pagan religious system that forced them to be constantly wary of angering the capricious gods of nature who must be placated with never ending sacrifices. Furthermore, the **charitable works** of ordinary Christians, done not just on behalf of their own but also for those who were ignored and abandoned by pagan society, inspired conversions. Additionally, the heroic witness of Christian martyrs who were usually subjected to terrible tortures testified not only to their sincerity but also to the powerful truth of the Christian faith.

Carl J. Sommer, *We Look For A Kingdom: The Everyday Lives of the Early Christians* (Ignatius Press, 2007), 107-115. Baus, *History of the Church Vol. I From the Apostolic Community to Constantine,* 86-98.

The **hierarchical structure of the Church** gradually emerged during the course of the first century. In addition to the authority of the apostles, the Book of Acts recounts the institution of the first deacons and the existence of "elders" of the church in Jerusalem. *Acts 6:1-6 & 11:30.* Other New Testament books describe how the apostles passed on their authority to their successors, the first bishops. For example, in the letters addressed to them, St. Paul wrote of how he commissioned his young proteges, Timothy and Titus, through the laying on of hands, to lead their local church. Likewise, in his First Letter, St. Peter encouraged the elders of the churches to be good shepherds of the flocks entrusted to their care by Christ, the "chief Shepherd." *2 Timothy 1:6-7. Titus 1:5.* Aidan Nichols, O.P. *Holy Order: Apostolic Priesthood from the New Testament to the Second Vatican Council* (Veritas, 1989), 5-34. Baus, *The History of the Church Vol. I From the Apostolic Community to Constantine,* 86-98.

An important, non-Scriptural document from the first century of Christianity is the **Didache.** The Greek word "didache" means "teaching." Written by an unknown author, the full title of this work is "The Teaching of the Lord Through the Twelve Apostles to the Gentiles." It is thought by most scholars that the Didache was written between 70 and 100. However, others argue that it was written prior to the Jerusalem Council of 49 A.D. If the latter position is correct, it would indicate that both liturgical practices and the hierarchical order of the Church were well established before the canon of the New Testament had taken shape. The *Didache* is the earliest known "church order," which is a sort of manual of Christian practices.

Mike Aquilina, *The Mass of the Early Christians,* (Our Sunday Visitor Press, 2007), 63-68.
Enrico Mazza, *The Origins of the Eucharistic Prayer* (Liturgical Press, 1995), 40-41.

The *Didache* presents teachings on morality citing the "two ways, one of life and one of death." The way of life is comprised of several paraphrases of Jesus' teachings.

"The way of life, then, is this: First, you shall love God who made you; second, love your neighbor as yourself, and do not do to another what you would not want done to you. And of these sayings the teaching is this: Bless those who curse you, and pray for your enemies, and fast for those who persecute you. For what reward is there for loving those who love you? Do not the Gentiles do the same? But love those who hate you, and you shall not have an enemy. Abstain from fleshly and worldly lusts. If someone strikes your right cheek, turn to him the other also, and you shall be perfect..."

The way of death likewise has parallels in both the Old and New Testaments.

"You shall not commit murder, you shall not commit adultery, you shall not commit pederasty (homosexual acts), you shall not commit fornication, you shall not steal, you shall not practice magic, you shall not practice witchcraft, you shall not murder a child by abortion nor kill that which is born. You shall not covet the things of your neighbor, you shall not swear, you shall not bear false witness, you shall not speak evil, you shall bear no grudge. You shall not be double-minded nor double-tongued, for to be double-tongued is a snare of death. Your speech shall not be false, nor empty, but fulfilled by deed. You shall not be covetous, nor rapacious, nor a hypocrite, nor evil disposed, nor haughty. You shall not take evil counsel against your neighbor. You shall not hate any man; but some you shall reprove, and concerning some you shall pray, and some you shall love more than your own life."

The Didache, 1-2, The Roberts-Donaldson Translation, EarlyChristianWritings.com

Among other things, the Didache contains instructions on conducting Baptism which indicates that immersion in "living water" was preferred but that pouring water over the recipient was also permitted. Also, a portion of a **Eucharist prayer** is presented as well as instructions on preparing oneself for the liturgy.

"Now concerning the Eucharist, give thanks this way. First, concerning the cup:
'We thank thee, our Father, for the holy vine of David Thy servant, which You madest known to us through Jesus Thy Servant; to Thee be the glory for ever.'

And concerning the broken bread:

'We thank Thee, our Father, for the life and knowledge which You madest known to us through Jesus Thy Servant; to Thee be the glory for ever. Even as this broken bread was scattered over the hills, and was gathered together and became one, so let Thy Church be gathered together from the ends of the earth into Thy kingdom; for Thine is the glory and the power through Jesus Christ for ever.'
But let no one eat or drink of your Eucharist, unless they have been baptized into the name of the Lord; for concerning this also the Lord has said, 'Give not that which is holy to the dogs.'
But after you are filled, give thanks this way:
'We thank Thee, holy Father, for Thy holy name which You didst cause to tabernacle in our hearts, and for the knowledge and faith and immortality, which You madest known to us through Jesus Thy Servant; to Thee be the glory for ever. Thou, Master almighty, didst create all things for Thy name's sake; You gavest food and drink to men for enjoyment, that they might give thanks to Thee; but to us You didst freely give spiritual food and drink and life eternal through Thy Servant. Before all things we thank Thee that You are mighty; to Thee be the glory for ever. Remember, Lord, Thy Church, to deliver it from

Pope St. Clement I. *Chevalier Artaud de Montor.*
Illustration from The Lives and Times of the Popes. 1842

all evil and to make it perfect in Thy love, and gather it from the four winds, sanctified for Thy kingdom which Thou have prepared for it; for Thine is the power and the glory for ever. Let grace come, and let this world pass away. Hosanna to the God (Son) of David! If any one is holy, let him come; if any one is not so, let him repent. Maranatha. Amen.'

But permit the prophets to make Thanksgiving as much as they desire.

'But every Lord's day gather yourselves together, and break bread, and give thanksgiving after having confessed your transgressions, that your sacrifice may be pure. But let no one who is at odds with his fellow come together with you, until they be reconciled, that your sacrifice may not be profaned."
The Didache, 9-10, 14. *The Roberts-Donaldson Translation,*Early ChristianWritings.com

The instruction above "having confessed your transgressions, that your sacrifice may be pure,"

clearly indicates that the author of the Didache understood the Eucharist as a **sacrificial offering**. The author also encouraged his readers to appoint bishops and deacons. Moreover, he mentions the ministry of apostles and prophets who evidently were not appointed but instead exercised a charismatic ministry. The existence of all four of the aforesaid ministries indicates that church order in the community was still somewhat fluid. The Didache also set aside Wednesdays and Fridays for penitential fasts.
Danielou and Marrou, *The Christian Centuries Vol. One The First Six Hundred Years,* 25-26, 31, 37.

Orthodox Christian authors whose writings guided the Church after the completion of the New Testament are known as the **"Apostolic Fathers."** Among them are St. Clement, St. Ignatius of Antioch, St. Polycarp, Hermas and Papias. Their surviving works provide information on the life of the Church and the challenges that Christians faced in the late first and second centuries.
The Oxford Dictionary of the Christian Church.

The period from about **90-96 A.D.** marked the second time that Christians were persecuted at the express command of the emperor. Because Christians refused to make offerings to the gods or the emperor, Christianity was regarded as a form of "atheism." Under Domitian, Christians were persecuted throughout the empire. His campaign against the Church, which was seen as a threat to social cohesion, took the lives of several members of the Roman aristocracy who were Christians, including his cousin, Flavius Clemens.
Sordi, *The Christians and the Roman Empire,* 44-53. Eusebius, *The Church History V,* 17-20 translation and commentary by Paul L. Maier (Kregel, 2007).

The Christian Martyr's Last Prayer. *Jean-Leon Gerome. 1883. Walters Art Museum, Baltimore.*

 The authority of the successors to St. Peter as the bishops of Rome was recognized in the first century as evidenced by **St. Clement** (+97), the fourth pope, who was elected around the year 88. Approximately a year before his death Pope Clement wrote a letter to the Christians at Corinth. Clement begins his letter by saying he would have written sooner but was prevented from doing so because of "sudden and calamitous events which have happened to ourselves." These "calamitous events" are believed to have been the persecution of Christians and Jews under the Emperor Domitian.

 Although St. Clement's letter to the Corinthians touches on numerous subjects, his main point was to admonish them to end their divisions and to respect the authority of their bishops and deacons as the successors to the apostles. Clement specifically stated that he wrote under the guidance of the Holy Spirit and that he expected obedience to his admonitions from the community in Corinth. Clement's letter was recognized with great respect throughout the Church because of the esteem non-Roman Christians had for the bishop of Rome. In the letter Clement also states that the apostles "appointed bishops and deacons" to carry on their work by leading the Church and "offering the gifts" — the Eucharist. *1 Clement 42:4-5.*

Even as he was suffering under persecution, Clement offered a sincere prayer for "governors and rulers" in imitation of Christ who prayed for His enemies. Tradition holds that not long after writing his letter, St. Clement died a martyr's death.

Pope Benedict XVI, *The Fathers* (Our Sunday Visitor Press, 2008).

 The First Letter of St. Clement also shows the highly **Christocentric spirituality** of the early Church.

"Through Him let us look steadfastly unto the heights of the heavens; through Him we behold as in a mirror His faultless and most excellent visage; through Him the eyes of our hearts were opened; through Him our foolish and darkened mind springeth up unto the light; through Him the Master willed that we should taste of the immortal knowledge Who being the brightness of His majesty is so much greater than angels, as He hath inherited a more excellent name."

The First Letter of Clement to the Corinthians, 1, 36.2. translated by J.B. Lightfoot. EarlyChristianWritings.com

The Christocentric focus of early Christian prayer is further manifested in the recorded prayers of the martyrs which were more often addressed to Jesus than to the Father. In addition to being Christocentric, the spirituality of the early Church was eschatological. They believed that Christ was returning soon and so they lived in active anticipation of the end times, the "eschaton." The first Christians, encouraged by St. Paul and others, tried to imitate Christ by practicing the virtues of charity, humility, chastity and obedience. This cultivation of the virtues was accompanied by ascetical practices such as fasting.

Not surprisingly, given the centrality of the Eucharist in the life of the Church, the spirituality of the first Christians was also **liturgical as well as strongly communal**. As members of an often misunderstood and sometimes persecuted minority, the first Christians supported one another to an impressive degree.

Jordan Aumann, O.P. *Christian Spirituality in the Catholic Tradition* (Ignatius Press, 1985), 22-29. Baus, *History of the Church Vol. I From the Apostolic Community to Constantine*, 302-303.

St. Ignatius of Antioch.

If more Christians in later centuries had been familiar with his reflection on the relationship between faith and works, perhaps St. Clement could have continued to contribute to the unity of the Church.

"And so we, having been called through His will in Christ Jesus, are not justified through ourselves or through our own wisdom or understanding or piety or works which we wrought in holiness of heart, but through faith, whereby the Almighty God justified all men that have been from the beginning; to whom be the glory for ever and ever. Amen.

What then must we do, brethren? Must we idly abstain from doing good, and forsake love? May the Master never allow this to befall us at least; but let us hasten with instancy and zeal to accomplish every good work. For the Creator and Master of the universe Himself rejoiceth in

Early Christian Symbols.

Emperor Trajan. *Head of Trajan from a statue. Rome. 1811.*

His works." 1 Clement 2:4-33:2

By the beginning of the second century **the Eucharistic celebration** was no longer preceded by a meal. As a consequence, in the room where the Eucharist was celebrated, there would now be only one table for the Eucharistic bread and wine. The phrase for identifying the Eucharist celebration found so often in the New Testament — "the breaking of the bread"— was gradually discontinued and replaced by the word "eucharistia." In the same period, since the Eucharist no longer was attached to the evening meal, it began to be celebrated in the early hours of the first day of the week, which of course was when the resurrection of Christ had taken place.

Josef Jungmann, S.J. *The Mass: An Historical, Theological and Pastoral Survey* (The Liturgical Press, 1975), 21-22.

 Around the year **107** Bishop **Ignatius of Antioch** was arrested by Roman authorities and transported to Rome for execution. Along the way, St. Ignatius wrote letters to six Christian communities and one to the bishop of Smyrna, St. Polycarp. In his letters Ignatius upheld both the divinity and the humanity of Jesus Christ. Ignatius also affirmed the Real Presence of Christ in the Eucharist, which he called "the bread which is the flesh of Jesus Christ."

Additionally, Ignatius emphasized **the importance of the bishop** as the head of the Eucharistic community within which the believer was invited into communion with the Lord. The presence of the bishop guaranteed the transmission of authentic apostolic teaching. Ignatius maintained that neither the Eucharist nor matrimony could be celebrated without the permission of the bishop. Along with bishops and deacons, Ignatius refers to priests serving in the churches.

The order of the **priesthood** had developed as the Church grew and bishops needed coworkers to assist them with preaching and the celebration of the sacraments. Our English word "priest" comes from the Greek word "presbyter" which means elder. The hierarchy of bishop, priest and deacon that Ignatius mentions in a number of his letters would be adopted by the whole Church by around the year 150. Wilken, *The First Thousand Years: A Global History of Christianity*, 31-32.

For Ignatius, the Eucharist is essential to salvation since Jesus Christ said that "he who eats my flesh and drinks my blood has eternal life." *Jn 6:54.* Later Church Fathers (Origen and Cyprian) would express this truth in the formula "no salvation outside the Church." St. Ignatius' understanding of the nature of the Church as a community formed by the Eucharist and presided over by a successor to the apostles greatly influenced all subsequent reflections on these matters. Baus, *History of the Church Vol. I From the Apostolic Community to Constantine*, 148-149. John Zizioulas, *"The Early Christian Community,"* in Christian Spirituality: *Origins to the Twelfth Century* edited by Bernarrd McGinn, John Meyendorff, and Jean Leclerq (Crossroad, 1985), 31-35.

 St. Ignatius' Letter to the Smyrnaeans records the earliest known reference to the **Church as "Catholic"** meaning universal. In doing so he was making a distinction between "the great Church" and the partisan sects or "heresies." Ignatius' Catholic principles are neatly summed up in the following passage from his *Letter to the Philadelphians, 4.* "Take care then, to have only one Eucharist. For there is one flesh of our Lord Jesus Christ, and one cup to show forth the unity of his blood; one altar, as there is one bishop, along with his priests and deacons, my fellow servants. All this is so, so that, whatever you do, you may do it according to the will of God." Quoted in Mike Aquilina, *The Mass of the Early Christians*, second edition (Our Sunday Visitor Press, 2007), 80. Phillip Cary, *The History of Christian Theology Course Guidebook* (The Teaching Company, 2008), 25.

St. Ignatius' Letters frequently warned against the dangers of two sets of false teachings or **heresies**. The first was that of the "**Judaizers**." These were Jewish Christians who insisted that all members of the Church must follow the Levitical laws of the Old Testament concerning circumcision and diet. St. Paul had often refuted this heresy in his own letters but its adherents still existed into the second century.

The second heresy that Ignatius warned about was what would later be called "**Docetism**." Docetism, from the Greek word meaning "to seem," was the notion that Jesus Christ only "seemed" to be human, but in fact He was not. Likewise, He never really suffered and died on the cross. The Docetists also taught that Jesus Christ is not really present in the Eucharist. This heresy was addressed in the first Letter of St. John where he warned against false prophets who denied that "Jesus Christ has come in the flesh." St. Paul also warned of this heresy in his letter to the Colossians. *1 John 4:2, Col. 2:8*

 Docetism had its origins in a larger school

of thought known as "**Gnosticism**." This complex religious movement takes its name from the Greek word "gnosis" which means "to know." Gnostics believed that only a certain, enlightened spiritual elite really "knows" God's plan for the world. The rest of humanity lives in ignorance of the truth. Arising first within pagan religious circles, Gnosticism crept into both Jewish and Christian communities and became a real threat to orthodox belief in the second century.

While Gnosticism came in different forms and embraced a wide variety of teachings, a common belief among Gnostics was **dualism**. This is the belief that the spiritual and material realms are completely separate, with the former being good and the latter being evil. They believed that the supreme or "good" God is responsible for the spiritual realm while an inferior, "evil" creator god is responsible for the material world. For Gnostics, salvation meant liberating the spirit from the material world. This liberation took place if you possessed the right knowledge and practiced the proper rituals. Gnostics who professed a belief in Jesus Christ taught that He was a messenger from the supreme God who brought a secret "knowledge" to a chosen few. Since Christ Himself was a divine being, and the divine cannot be contaminated by the material, He only appeared to have a body and to experience death.

Richard M. Hogan, *Dissent from the Creed: Heresies Past and Present* (Our Sunday Visitor Press, 2001), 43-49.

Following the assassination of Emperor Domitian in 96 by his wife, aggressive imperial persecution of Christians ended for a period of almost seventy years. In these decades Christians were not sought out for punishment. But if they came to the attention of the authorities they were

Jesus and the Disciples Going to Emmaus. *Gustave Dore.*

punished.

Around the year **112**, Pliny, the Roman governor of the province of Bithynia, which was near the Black Sea in Asia Minor (Turkey), wrote to the emperor Trajan seeking guidance on how he should treat Christians he had arrested there. Pliny's letter to Emperor Trajan is of great interest as it documents some of the practices of early Christians and the way they were regarded by imperial authorities and other non-Christians.

"It is my custom, Sire, to refer to you in all cases where I am in doubt, for who can better clear up difficulties and inform me? I have never been present at any legal examination of the Christians, and I do not know, therefore, what are the usual penalties passed upon them, or the limits of those penalties, or how searching an inquiry should be made. I have hesitated a great deal in considering whether any distinctions should be drawn according to the ages of the accused; whether the weak should be punished as severely as the more robust, or whether the man who has once been a Christian gained anything by recant-

ing? Again, whether the name of being a Christian, even though otherwise innocent of crime, should be punished, or only the crimes that gather around it?

In the meantime, this is the plan which I have adopted in the case of those Christians who have been brought before me. I ask them whether they are Christians, if they say 'Yes,' then I repeat the question the second time, and also a third -- warning them of the penalties involved; and if they persist, I order them away to prison. For I do not doubt that -- be their admitted crime what it may -- their pertinacity and inflexible obstinacy surely ought to be punished.

There were others who showed similar mad folly, whom I reserved to be sent to Rome, as they were Roman citizens. Later, as is commonly the case, the mere fact of my entertaining the question led to a multiplying of accusations and a variety of cases were brought before me. An anonymous pamphlet was issued, containing a number of names of alleged Christians. Those who denied that they were or had been Christians and called upon the gods with the usual formula, reciting the words after me, and those who offered incense and wine before your image -- which I had ordered to be brought forward for this purpose, along with the regular statues of the gods -- all such I considered acquitted -- especially as they cursed the name of Christ, which it is said bona fide Christians cannot be induced to do.

Still others there were, whose names were supplied by an informer. These first said they were Christians, then denied it, insisting they had been, 'but were so no longer;' some of them having 'recanted many years ago,' and more than one 'full twenty years back.' These all worshiped your image and the god's statues and cursed the name of Christ.

But they declared their guilt or error was simply this -- on a fixed day they used to meet before dawn and recite a hymn among themselves to Christ, as though he were a god. So, far from binding themselves by oath to commit any crime, they swore to keep from theft, robbery, adultery, breach of faith, and not to deny any trust money deposited with them when called upon to deliver it. This ceremony over, they used to depart and meet again to take food -- but it was of no special character, and entirely harmless. They also had ceased from this practice after the edict I issued -- by which, in accord with your orders, I forbade all secret societies.

I then thought it the more needful to get at the facts behind their statements. Therefore I placed two women slaves, called 'deaconesses,' under torture, but I found only a debased superstition carried to great lengths, so I postponed my examination, and immediately consulted you. This seems a matter worthy of your prompt consideration, especially as so many people are endangered. Many of all ages and both sexes are put in peril of their lives by their accusers; and the process will go on, for the contagion of this superstition has spread not merely through the free towns, but into the villages and farms. Still I think it can be halted and things set right. Beyond any doubt, the temples -- which were nigh deserted -- are beginning again to be thronged with worshipers; the sacred rites, which long have lapsed, are now being renewed, and the food for the sacrificial victims is again finding a sale -- though up to recently it had almost no market. So one can safely infer how vast numbers could be reclaimed, if only there were a chance given for repentance."

Trajan to Pliny:

"You have adopted the right course, my dear Pliny, in examining the cases of those cited before you as Christians; for no hard and fast rule can be laid down covering such a wide question. The Christians are not to be hunted out. If brought before you, and the offense is proved, they are to be punished, but with this reservation -- if any one denies he is a Christian, and makes it clear he is not, by offering prayer to our gods, then he is to be pardoned on his recantation, no matter how suspicious his past. As for anonymous pamphlets, they are to be discarded absolutely, whatever crime they may charge, for they are not only a precedent of a very bad type, but they do not accord with the spirit of our age."

William Stearns Davis, ed., *Readings in Ancient History: Illustrative*

Extracts from the Sources, 2 Vols. (Boston: Allyn and Bacon, 1912-13), Vol. II: Rome and the West, 196-210, 215-222, 250-251, 289-290, 295-296, 298-300. Scanned by: J. S. Arkenberg, Dept. of History, Cal. State Fullerton. Prof. Arkenberg has modernized the text. This text is part of the Internet Ancient History Sourcebook. The Sourcebook is a collection of public domain and copy-permitted texts related to medieval and Byzantine history.

According to his letter, Pliny did not know much about Christianity but the fact that Christians met together was in itself viewed as subversive. Pliny knew he could test the beliefs of Christians by requiring them to make offerings to the gods and curse Christ or face execution. Put to this test, some of those in his custody proved to be "really Christians" while others repudiated Christianity. When it became known that Pliny was arresting Christians, accusations, some of them anonymous, were spread by informers.

Pliny attests that in that region the "contagion" of Christian "superstition" was believed by men, women and children in all ranks of society and was found both in the cities and the countryside. The large number of Christians in the area was undermining traditional pagan worship practices. On their part the Christian community met early in the morning on a certain day of the week to worship Christ by singing hymns. They also pledged to follow a moral code. In addition, they met together socially for communal meals.

Pliny's letter also indicates that this Christian community welcomed slaves as it included two women slaves who were "**deaconesses**." These, Pliny had tortured in order to be sure the group was not engaged in subversive activities. In the early Church some women were appointed deaconesses to fulfill certain duties. Most importantly they were involved in the instruction of female catechumens and assisting the clergy in baptizing them. This assistance was necessary because baptism was by immersion and the recipients were naked. The Council of Nicaea in 325 declared that deaconesses were not among the ordained clergy (Canon 19). After the fourth century, when the frequency of adult baptism greatly declined, the need for deaconesses eventually disappeared.

The emperor Trajan's reply is instructive regarding imperial policies toward Christians. While Pliny should not seek to discover Christians, if they came to his attention and were found guilty they should be punished unless they "repent." Pliny was also instructed not to act on anonymous accusations. Even though Christianity was outlawed, Roman officials of the time did not see it as a political threat. In practice they only moved against Christians in response to pressure from the populace.

Sordi, *The Christians and the Roman Empire*, 59-65. Robert Louis Wilken, *The Christians as the Romans Saw Them* (Yale University Press, 2003), 15-30. Danielou and Marrou, *The Christian Centuries Vol. One The First Six Hundred Years*, 50-51. *The Oxford Dictionary of the Christian Church*. Baus, *History of the Church Vol. II The Imperial Church from Constantine to the Early Middle Ages*, 273, 408.

By the beginning of the second century **personal devotion to Jesus Christ** was deeply rooted among Christians. While praying, Christians turned to the east because it was widely held that when Jesus returned he would come from that direction. Concurrently, the customs of making the sign of the cross and of praying before a crucifix both spread.

Baus, *History of the Church Vol. I From the Apostolic Community to Constantine*, 303.

The performance of **works of mercy** was an expectation in the earliest Church communities and Christians were noticed by pagans for how they loved one another. One way that charity was exercised was through the agape meals that accompanied the celebration of the Eucharist. At these communal gatherings those who were better off shared their food with their poorer brethren. Christians also gave to communal funds which were used to aid the poor, orphans, widows and others in need. Almsgiving protected the faithful from becoming enslaved to mammon. Exercising hospitality toward travelers and strangers was embraced. In adherence to Christ's teaching in Matthew 25, the sick were cared for and those imprisoned were visited. Further, as St. Paul's letters indicate, the churches in different communities understood the obligation they had to contribute to the support of their fellow Christians in other places. The practice of slavery in the Roman empire presented the first Christians with a moral challenge that they were unable to surmount. However, while they did not reject the institution outright, they did their best to mitigate its severity and slaves were equally brothers and sisters within the community. Slaves could become bishops and two former slaves became popes. Slaves were also honored among the martyrs.

Sommer, *We Look For A Kingdom: The Everyday Lives of the Early Christians*, 250-274. Baus, *History of the Church Vol. I From the Apostolic Community to Constantine*, 308-313.

From **132-135** the Jews of Palestine once again revolted against Roman authorities. This rebellion, which takes its name from its messianic leader, Bar Cochba, was brutally suppressed by the Emperor Hadrian. The city of Jerusalem was destroyed and a new Roman city, Aelia Capitolina, was built over its ruins. All Jews were expelled and were forbidden to ever re-enter the city. Jews were also forbidden to practice circumcision or observe the Sabbath.

Bacchiocchi, *From Sabbath to Sunday: A Historical Investigation of the Rise of Sunday Observance in Early Christianity*, 159-161.

Following this last failed Jewish revolt and the expulsion of the Jews from Jerusalem, the leadership of the Church in that region passed to Gentile Christians. The final separation of Christian worship and the Jewish Sabbath day may have also occurred at this time. Also, whereas previously Christians sometimes benefitted under imperial policies when they were thought of as a sect of Jews, they now sought to distance themselves from Judaism.

Two of the first **Christian apologists**, Quadratus and Aristides, in tracts addressed to the Emperor Hadrian, emphasized the distinctiveness of Christianity. On their part, Hadrian (117-138) and his successor, Antoninus Pius (138-161), were comparatively benign in their policies towards Christians. Some scholars assert that the need to differentiate themselves from the Jews in the minds of their pagan rulers led some Christian writers to attack Judaism. Coupled with the ongoing struggle within the Church between Jewish Christians and Gentile Christians over practices mandated by Mosaic law, an anti-Jewish polemic began to develop.

Bacchiocchi, *From Sabbath to Sunday: A Historical Investigation of the Rise of Sunday Observance in Early Christianity*, 177-184.

The Apostolic Age ended when **St. Polycarp**, the bishop of Smyrna was martyred at a pagan festival. Because of his long life, (c.70-c.155) Polycarp was an important link between the church of the apostles and the Christian writers like Irenaeus of the second century. The latter in fact asserted that Polycarp had known the Apostle John. Polycarp upheld orthodox teaching throughout his reign as bishop and was energetic in fighting the heresy of Marcion. Polycarp was martyred for refusing to say, "Caesar is Lord" (Kyrios Kaisar) and to make an offering of incense in his honor. Such defiance accompanied by the proclamation of Jesus as "King of kings" was regarded as a treasonous action against the imperial state.

Jaroslav Pelikan, *Jesus Through the Centuries: His Place in the History of Culture* (Yale University Press, 1985),48-49.

The account of Polycarp's martyrdom records that, after he had been burned at the stake, his fellow Christians "took up his bones which are more valuable than precious stones and finer than refined gold, and laid them in a suitable place; where the Lord will permit us to gather ourselves together, as we are able, in gladness and joy, and to celebrate the birthday of his martyrdom for the commemoration of those that have already fought in the contest, and for the training and preparation of those that shall do so hereafter."

This is the earliest documented evidence of the **veneration of relics** although the use of relics is described in both the Old and New Testament. For example, it is recorded in the Acts of the Apostles that handkerchiefs that had been touched by St. Paul were used for healing the sick. *Acts 19:12.*

SUMMARY OF CHAPTER ONE

Authority

By the end of the Apostolic Age, roughly the year 155, the Catholic Church had taken on much of the form and practices that we still know today. First of all, she had attained an internal system of authority which was based on the principal of apostolicity. All her teachings, practices and scriptures could be traced back to the apostles. Additionally, St. Clement's Letter to Corinthians (c.96) demonstrated that, even at an early date, the bishop of Rome had a recognized preeminence in the Church. The New Testament and the letters of St. Ignatius attest to the existence of a three-fold ministry of orders: bishops, priests and deacons.

Doctrine

Certain doctrines were also clearly established during the Apostolic Age. The most important of them is that Jesus Christ is truly God and man and this was firmly held against the heresies of Docetism and Gnosticism. Further, the real presence of Jesus Christ in the Eucharist was repeatedly affirmed in this period in both the New Testament books and in the writings of the Apostolic Fathers. Belief that both the Hebrew Scriptures and the Christian Scriptures were divinely inspired was also established. The principle that Christians did not have to accept Jewish ritual practices was another important milestone.

Pastoral Practice

As for the Church's pastoral practices, the celebration of Baptism and the Eucharist, along with the reading of the books of the New Testament were already being performed much as they are in the twenty-first century. The Lord's Day, Sunday, was established as the day of worship for Christians although Jewish Christians may have continued to honor the Sabbath until the destruction of Jerusalem. St. Ignatius of Antioch provides testimony to the Church's authority over Christian marriages. In addition, Christians established a tradition of not only worshiping together but also performing works of charity for each other and for non-Christians.

Saints

There were several especially noteworthy saints of these centuries apart from the apostles and evangelists. Among them were St. Clement (+c. 99), the third pope, who used his authority to encourage unity in the Church. Another great witness to Christ from this period was St. Ignatius of Antioch (+c107), bishop and martyr. Ignatius wrote seven letters which document faithfulness to scriptural teaching on the real presence of Christ in the Eucharist among first century Christians. Ignatius also testified to the role of the bishop in the local church and the special status of the Church in Rome.

Evangelization

Efforts to bring the Gospel of Jesus Christ to others began with the Pentecost event. The subsequent persecution of Christians in Jerusalem led to their migration and the spread of the Gospel to other parts of Palestine and into Syria. St. Paul was the foremost missionary, traveling extensively along the coastal areas of the eastern Mediterranean and eventually to Rome. St. Peter also went to Rome and tradition records the efforts of the other apostles reaching to Egypt, Arabia & India. While these efforts may not have been as successful as hoped among the Jews, converts to "the Way" were continually being made among the pagan gentiles.

State

Interaction with Roman authorities established a pattern of Church and state relations that would endure until the reign of Emperor Constantine in 312 A.D. For most of this period, the Roman state authorities were indifferent to Christians, although they did take action to prevent the persecution of Christians in Judea by Jewish authorities. However, first Nero and then Domitian engaged in active persecution of the Church. Subsequently, Christians knew that under the laws of the empire they could be arrested at any time, be tortured and put to death simply because of their faith in the one, true, God, Father, Son and Holy Spirit. However, rather than withering under these assaults, the Church continued to grow as the heroic witness of her martyred saints led other men and women to embrace the truth of the Gospel of Jesus Christ.

Martyrdom of St. Polycarp. Church of St Polycarp, Izmir (ancient Smyrna), Turkey.

"And when the proconsul yet again pressed him, and said, 'Swear by the fortune of Caesar,' he answered, 'Since you are vainly urging that I should swear by the fortune of Caesar ... hear me declare with boldness, I am a Christian'.... But again the proconsul said to him, 'I will cause you to be consumed by fire, seeing you despise the wild beasts, if you do not change your mind.' But Polycarp said, 'You threaten me with fire which burns for an hour, and after a little is extinguished. You are ignorant of the fire of the coming judgment and of eternal punishment, reserved for the ungodly. But why hesitate? Bring on what you will...'"

They did not nail him then, but simply bound him. And he, placing his hands behind him, and being bound like a distinguished ram taken out of a great flock for sacrifice, and prepared to be an acceptable burnt-offering unto God, looked up to heaven, and said, "O Lord God Almighty, the Father of your beloved and blessed Son Jesus Christ, by whom we have received knowledge of you, the God of angels and powers, and of every creature, and of the whole race of the righteous who live before you, I give you thanks that you have counted me, worthy of this day and this hour, that I should be numbered with your martyrs, in the cup of Christ, for the resurrection of eternal life, both of soul and body, through the incorruption imparted by the Holy Spirit. Among whom may I be accepted this day before you as a rich and acceptable sacrifice, according as you, the ever-truthful God, have pre-ordained, revealed and fulfilled. Therefore, I praise you for all things, I bless you, I glorify you with the everlasting and heavenly Jesus Christ, your beloved Son, with whom, to you, and the Holy Spirit, be glory both now and forever.Amen.'

When he had pronounced this amen, and so finished his prayer, those who were appointed for the purpose kindled the fire. And as the flame blazed forth in great fury, we, to whom it was given to witness it, beheld a great miracle, and have been preserved that we might report to others what then took place. For the fire, shaping itself into the form of an arch, like the sail of a ship when filled with the wind, encompassed as by a circle the body of the martyr. And he appeared within not like flesh which is burnt, but as bread that is baked, or as gold and silver glowing in a furnace. Moreover, we perceived such a sweet odour [coming from the pile], as if frankincense or some such precious spices had been smoking there."

From the "Martyrdom of St. Polycarp" Roberts-Donaldson translation. Edited & adapted
EarlyChristianWritings.com

CHAPTER TWO

"CITIZENS OF HEAVEN"
APOLOGISTS, VIRGINS & MARTYRS C.155-312 A.D.

"Reason directs those who are truly pious and philosophical to honor and love only what is true, declining to follow traditional opinions, if these be worthless. For not only does sound reason direct us to refuse the guidance of those who did or taught anything wrong, but it is incumbent on the lover of truth, by all means, and if death be threatened, even before his own life, to choose to do and say what is right." - St. Justin Martyr, First Apology, 2.

It is estimated that by the mid-second century there were roughly 40,000 Christians living within the Roman Empire in forty to fifty cities. While they still comprised a small fraction of the total population, because they were concentrated in the major cities and included among their number members of the upper classes, Christians received increasingly negative attention from pagan commentators. One such commentator was a philosopher named "Crescens" who repeated earlier allegations that Christians were atheists. Others alleged that Christians engaged in child sacrifice and sexual immorality. (This was the charge made against the martyrs of Lyons in 177. See below.) To meet such accusations and misunderstandings there arose in the Church of the second century writers who sought to defend Christianity against its critics among both pagans and Jews. Known as "apologists," these writers strove to demonstrate to pagan authorities that Christianity, rather than being a threat to the empire, actually strengthened it by forming citizens with strong moral values. Against Jewish critics, the apologists argued that Jesus Christ was the fulfillment of Old Testament prophesy.

Rodney Stark, *Cities of God,* 67. Robert Louis Wilken, *The Christians as the Romans Saw Them,* 31, 68.
Danielou and Marrou, *The Christian Centuries Vol. One The First Six Hundred Years,* 87.

The greatest of these first apologists was **St. Justin Martyr (c.100-165)**. Justin was born to a pagan family living in Samaria and educated as a philosopher. About the age of thirty Justin was converted to Christianity. His apologetical work, *Dialogue with Trypho,* was written as a debate between himself and a rabbi. By Justin's own account, his journey to faith in Jesus Christ had been facilitated by his encounter with a Jew who had urged him to read the Hebrew Scriptures. Also, as an apologist, Justin needed to not only address the pagans but also the Jews who in the second century may have comprised as much as ten percent of the empire's total population of sixty million.

Wilken, *The Christians as the Romans Saw Them,* 113. J. Lebreton, *"St. Justin Martyr." The Catholic Encyclopedia.* New York: Robert Appleton Company. New Advent: http://www.newadvent.org

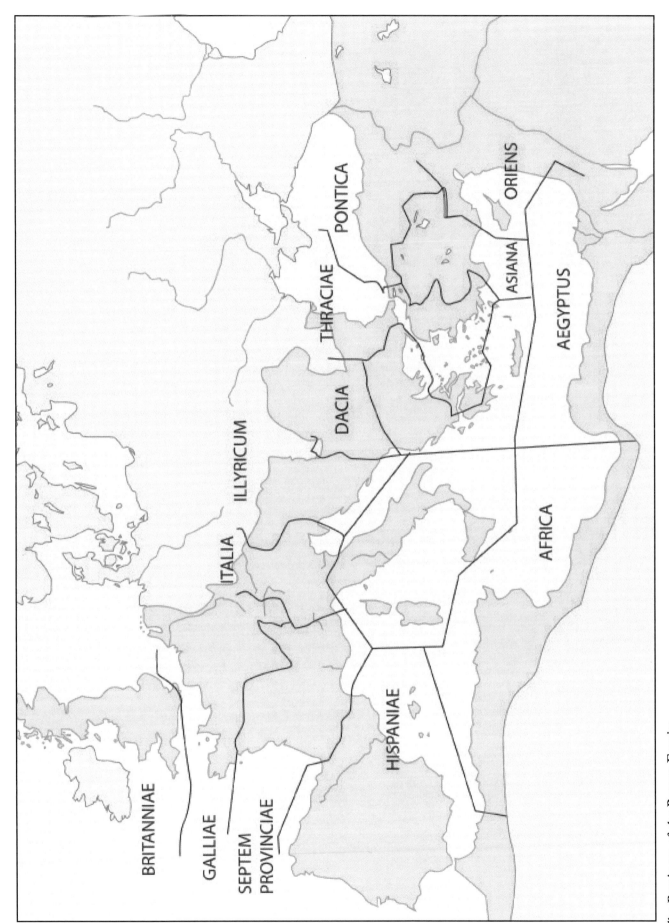

BRITANNIAE

GALLIAE

SEPTEM
PROVINCIAE

HISPANIAE

ITALIA

ILLYRICUM

DACIA

THRACIAE

PONTICA

ORIENS

ASIANA

AEGYPTUS

AFRICA

The Provinces of the Roman Empire.

St. Justin Martyr. *Saint Justin dans André Thevet, Les Vrais Pourtraits et Vies des Hommes Illustres. 1584.*

St. Justin addressed another of his works, his *First Apology*, to the emperor and the people of Rome. The ruling elites despised Christians and saw the new religion as undermining the official cults of Rome. Pagan authors had begun attacking Christianity in pamphlets and speeches. It was this campaign that Justin sought to mitigate. Justin described his apology as a petition on behalf of Christians who were "unjustly hated" on account of "evil rumors that have long been prevalent." Justin then refuted the charge of "atheism" leveled against Christians by explaining that, while they reject the worship of "soulless" idols that "men have formed," they do worship the one, true God who is Father, Son and Holy Spirit. Justin also refuted charges that Christians were immoral and stated that, in fact, because of their moral behavior, Christians make good citizens. They have no political aspirations because

"we look for a kingdom... with God." St. Justin then informed his readers that both the Old Testament and Greek philosophy lead to Christ. St. Justin and some of his disciples were arrested in Rome about the year 165 and when they refused to offer sacrifices to the gods they were beheaded.

Pope Benedict XVI, "St. Justin Martyr," *The Fathers.* Baus, *History of the Church Vol. I From the Apostolic Community to Constantine,* 170-177.

In addition to explaining the non-political nature of Christianity, St. Justin's First Apology also contained important descriptions of how **the sacraments of Baptism and the Eucharist** were celebrated in the early Church. He describes the celebration of the Eucharist as follows:

"And this food is called among us the Eucharist, of which no one is allowed to partake but the man who believes that the things which we teach are true, and who has been washed with the washing that is for the remission of sins, and unto regeneration, and who is so living as Christ has enjoined. For not as common bread and common drink do we receive these; but in like manner as Jesus Christ our Savior, having been made flesh by the Word of God, had both flesh and blood for our salvation, so likewise have we been taught that the food which is blessed by the prayer of His word, and from which our blood and flesh by transmutation are nourished, is the flesh and blood of that Jesus who was made flesh. For the apostles, in the memoirs composed by them, which are called Gospels, have thus delivered unto us what was enjoined upon them; that Jesus took bread, and when He had given thanks, said, 'This do in remembrance of Me, this is My body;' and that, after the same manner, having taken the cup and given thanks, He said, "This is My blood;' and gave it to them alone....

And we afterwards continually remind each other of these things. And the wealthy among us help the needy; and we always keep together; and for all things wherewith we are supplied, we bless the Maker of all through

44

His Son Jesus Christ, and through the Holy Ghost. And on the day called Sunday, all who live in cities or in the country gather together to one place, and the memoirs of the apostles or the writings of the prophets are read, as long as time permits; then, when the reader has ceased, the president verbally instructs, and exhorts to the imitation of these good things. Then we all rise together and pray, and, as we before said, when our prayer is ended, bread and wine and water are brought, and the president in like manner offers prayers and thanksgivings, according to his ability, and the people assent, saying 'Amen;' and there is a distribution to each, and a participation of that over which thanks have been given, and to those who are absent a portion is sent by the deacons.

And they who are well to do, and willing, give what each thinks fit; and what is collected is deposited with the president, who succors the orphans and widows and those who, through sickness or any other cause, are in want, and those who are in bonds and the strangers sojourning among us, and in a word takes care of all who are in need.

But Sunday is the day on which we all hold our common assembly, because it is the first day on which God, having wrought a change in the darkness and matter, made the world; and Jesus Christ our Savior on the same day rose from the dead. For He was crucified on the day before that of Saturn (Saturday); and on the day after that of Saturn, which is the day of the Sun, having appeared to His apostles and disciples, He taught them these things, which we have submitted to you also for your consideration."

St. Justin Martyr, *First Apology*, 65-66. Translated by Marcus Dodds and George Reith. From Ante-Nicene Fathers, Vol. 1. Edited by Alexander Roberts, James Donaldson, and A. Cleveland Coxe. (Buffalo, NY: Christian Literature Publishing Co., 1885.) Revised and edited for New Advent by Kevin Knight. <http://www.newadvent.org/fathers

 From St. Justin's account we learn a number of things about how the weekly liturgy was celebrated in his time. First only those who believe "that the things which we teach are true, and who has been washed" in baptism may participate in the Eucharist. This is necessary because in the Eucharist the participants actually receive "the flesh and blood of that Jesus who was made flesh." Christians know this teaching is true, Justin says, because they received it from the Apostles who had been taught this by Jesus Himself.

Among those gathered for worship, particular roles were carried out by the reader, the presider and the deacons. The worshipers also used different postures at various points in the liturgy. He specifically mentions that they "rise" after listening to the homily. Presumably, they were sitting for the sermon.

The first part of the worship service Justin described was centered on the Word of God with readings from both the Old Testament – "the prophets," and from the Gospels – "the memoirs of the apostles." After this, the "president", meaning the bishop or priest, gave a homily exhorting his listeners to imitate the "good things" they heard in the readings.

The bishop or priest then offered the Eucharistic prayer which included giving thanks to the "Maker of all through His Son Jesus Christ, and through the Holy Ghost." The prayer also included Jesus' words at the Last Supper, "this is My body... this is My blood" to which "the people assent by saying 'Amen.'" After this prayer of blessing, the bread and wine, which became "the flesh and blood of that Jesus who was made flesh," were distributed to the congregation. A portion of the consecrated bread was then taken by the deacons to those who were unable to be present.

The liturgy even included a collection to support those in need. Thus a direct connection was made between the community's worship of the Lord and its service to his least brothers and sisters. The collection was entrusted to the bishop or priest for distribution, indicating the dual responsibility of the clergy to assure that both the spiritual and material needs of their people were being met. Thus the second century liturgy that Justin described had the same elements and proclaimed the same truths as that of the Mass of the twenty-first century.

Annunciation. *James Tissot. 1896. Brooklyn Museum.*

Along with providing an invaluable description of how the Mass was celebrated in the second century and testimony to belief in the real presence of Christ in the forms of bread and wine, Justin was also an early witness to the belief in the Eucharistic celebration as a participation in the **sacrifice** on the cross. This is found in Justin's *Dialogue with Trypho* where Justin wrote that, in the Eucharist, the words of the prophet Malachi are fulfilled.

"I have no pleasure in you, says the Lord of hosts, and I will not accept an offering from your hand. For from the rising of sun to its setting my name is great among the nations, and in every place incense is offered to my name, and a pure offering; for my name is great among the nations, says the Lord of hosts." Malachi 1:10-11

St. Justin Martyr, *Dialogue With Trypho*, chapter 61. EarlyChristianWritings.com

St. Justin was also an early witness to the Church's faith in Christ's birth from the **Blessed Virgin Mary** and her unique role in God's plan of salvation. Defending the faith against Jewish critics, Justin asserted that Jesus Christ is truly the Son of God and that in His humanity He descended from the patriarchs of Israel through Mary, who he depicts as the new Eve.

"... we find it recorded in the memoirs of His apostles that He is the Son of God, and since we call Him the Son, we have understood that He proceeded before all creatures from the Father by His power and will (for He is addressed in the writings of the prophets in one way or another as Wisdom, and the Day, and the East, and a Sword, and a Stone, and a Rod, and Jacob, and Israel); and that He became man by the Virgin, in order that the disobedience which proceeded from the serpent might receive its destruction in the same manner in which it derived its origin. For Eve, who was a virgin and undefiled,

46

having conceived the word of the serpent, brought forth disobedience and death. But the Virgin Mary received faith and joy when the angel Gabriel announced the good tidings to her that the Spirit of the Lord would come upon her and the power of the Highest would overshadow her: wherefore also the Holy Thing begotten of her is the Son of God; and she replied, 'Be it done unto me according to thy word.' And by her has He been born, to whom we have proved so many Scriptures refer, and by whom God destroys both the serpent and those angels and men who are like him; but works deliverance from death to those who repent of their wickedness and believe upon Him."
St. Justin Martyr, *Dialogue with Trypho,* chapter 100. EarlyChristianWritings.com

Still Life With a Bible. *Vincent van Gogh. c. 1885. Van Gogh Van Gogh Museum, Amsterdam.*

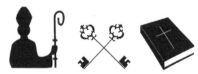 The reign of the Emperor Marcus Aurelius (161-180) was characterized by numerous wars and the resulting economic chaos. Matters only got worse under his son, Commodus (180-192), whose decadent behavior rivaled that of Nero. Several natural disasters also occurred. The discontented populace frequently blamed Christians for their misfortunes and there were numerous instances of local persecutions.
Baus, *History of the Church Vol. I From the Apostolic Community to Constantine,* 159-166.

The Christian movement continued to have its intellectual critics as well as defenders. Around the year 170 a Greek philosopher named Celsus wrote a well-argued attack against Christianity called *True Doctrine.* Celsus' complete work has not survived. However, large portions of it were preserved in the writings of Origen in his response to it, called appropriately, *Against Celsus.* Well acquainted with the Gospels and Christian teachings, Celsus sought to demolish the reasonableness of belief in the incarnation of the Son of God. Besides portraying Christians as ill-educated and gullible, he also demeaned Jesus as a magician and denied the resurrection. According to Celsus the greatest deficiency of Christianity was that it posed a threat to the cohesiveness of the empire. He criticized Christians for their detachment from Roman society and most especially because their religion, having broken away from Judaism, lacked the pedigree bestowed by antiquity. His arguments would provide an intellectual basis for the imperial effort in the following century to eradicate Christianity.
Wilken, *The Christians as the Romans Saw Them,* 94-125. Baus, *History of the Church Vol. I From the Apostolic Community to Constantine Hubert,* Editor, 164-171.

In the middle of the second century the heresy known as **Marcionism** posed a serious challenge to orthodox Christian belief. Marcion's threat to Church unity was particularly acute as he actually set up an organization with bishops and priests. Further, his followers celebrated a ritual which was very much like the Church's Eucharistic liturgy. Originally from Asia Minor and the son of a bishop, Marcion (+160) was excommunicated in Rome in 144 AD for rejecting the Old Testament. Marcion then founded his heretical sect. Basing his teachings on dualism, Marcion taught that the God of the Old Testament was the inferior creator God of the material world. By His coming, Jesus Christ revealed the true God of love. In addition to rejecting the Old Testament, Marcion accepted only ten letters of St. Paul and his own edited version of the Gospel of Luke as Scripture. Marcion's dismissal of most books of the Bible prompted the Church to establish which early Christian writings in circulation should be considered inspired by God and therefore "Scripture." Only those writings which were included on this list, or "canon," could be read during the liturgy. Marcionism continued as a small sect in the empire as late as the fifth century.

Hogan, *Dissent From the Creed*, 44-47. A.A. Stephenson, *"Marcion," The New Catholic Encyclopedia* (Catholic University Press, 2003).

 The word "canon" comes from the Greek term meaning "measuring rod" or "rule." When applied to the Bible it means the writings which are officially considered to be the divinely inspired Word of God. The canon of the Old Testament was for the most part agreed upon by the end of the first century and was limited to books that were originally written in Hebrew. However, Jews who lived outside the Holy Land believed that there were an additional seven books written first in Greek which should also be considered part of the canon. The Catholic Church also accepts these seven books of the Old Testament that were written first in Greek. They are Tobit, Wisdom, Sirach, Baruch, Judith, 1 and 2 Maccabees, as well as parts of Esther and Daniel.

 The majority of the canon of the New Testament was largely settled by about the year 130. It included the Gospels of Matthew, Mark, Luke and John and the thirteen letters written by St. Paul. The oldest surviving list of New Testament books is called the Muratorian Canon. It is named for the archivist Lodovico Muratori who discovered the manuscript in the 18th century. The original manuscript is believed to date from the last half of the second century. It lists all the New Testament books that would eventually be officially accepted as part of the canon with the exception of The Letter to the Hebrews, 1 and 2 Peter and The Letter of James. In 367 St. Athanasius provided a list of all twenty-seven books of the New Testament. A council held in Rome in 382 under Pope Damasus issued a complete list of the 73 books that comprise both the Old and the New Testaments.

Curtis Mitch, *"Introduction to the Gospels"* in the *Ignatius Catholic Study Bible New Testament* and *The Oxford Dictionary of the Christian Church*.

Around 170 a heresy known as **Montanism** began to gain adherents. Named for the self-proclaimed prophet, Montanus, the Montanists, claimed to be under the direct guidance of the Holy Spirit. They asserted that their gifts of prophecy superseded the teaching authority of the bishops. They saw themselves as the spiritual elite who were called to reform the Church before the imminent apocalypse. They practiced a strict moralism that condemned the alleged laxity of other Christians regarding martyrdom, virginity and fasting. The spread of Montanism prompted the bishops in Asia Minor to meet in synods for the first time in order to formulate a united response to the threat. But the strength of Montanism in various forms would continue to exist for centuries.

Baus, *History of the Church Vol. I From the Apostolic Community to Constantine*, 199-205.

One of the women martyrs in this period was St. Blandina (+177). **St. Blandina** was a slave whose mistress was also a Christian. Arrested

during a local persecution of Christians in Lyons, Blandina was a source of encouragement to her fellow martyrs until she herself was executed.

"Last of all, the blessed Blandina, like a noble mother who had comforted her children and sent them triumphantly to the king, rejoiced at her own departure as if invited to a wedding feast. After the whips, the beasts, and the gridiron, she was finally put in a net and thrown to a bull. Indifferent to circumstances through faith in Christ, she was tossed by the animal for some time before being sacrificed. The heathen admitted that never before had a woman suffered so much for so long."

The account of the martyrdom of St. Blandina and the other martyrs of Lyon circulated widely in the early Church.

Eusebius: *The Church History,* translation and commentary by Paul L. Maier (Kregel, 2007), 152-158.

Mike Aquilina and Christopher Bailey, *Mothers of the Church: The Witness of Early Christian Women,* (Our Sunday Visitor Press, 2012) 67-73.

St. Irenaeus of Lyon (130-202) was perhaps the most impor-

tant Church Father of the second century. In fact, he has been called the "first great Catholic theologian". Born in Smyrna, which is the modern day city of Izmir in Turkey, Irenaeus became a priest in the city of Lyon in what was then the Roman province of Gaul and which is now the nation of France. Due to his eastern roots and labors in the West, Irenaeus was a bridge between the Greek and Latin speaking elements of the Church. Irenaeus' presence in Gaul indicates that the number of Christians in Gaul was increasing. He also wrote of Christian communities existing "in the Germanies" and in Spain.

Baus *"The Expansion of Christianity,"* in *History of the Church Vol. I From the Apostolic Community to Constantine,* 210-212.

 In approximately **178,** Irenaeus became the bishop of Lyon after his predecessor and several other Christians, including St. Blandina, had been thrown to the lions at a pagan festival. In his capacity as a bishop, Irenaeus became a prominent defender of the faith against various

heresies. His most important writings are found in *Against the Heresies* and the *Demonstration of the Apostolic Teaching*. As their titles suggest, the first work was concerned with refuting heretical errors about Christianity, while the second sets out to establish the true teaching of the Church. **The Demonstration** is regarded as the oldest catechism of the Catholic Church. Against the dualistic Gnostic heresies, Irenaeus asserted the essential goodness of the material world because it was created by the one, true God. Irenaeus also delineated the characteristics of true Christian teaching. The authentic teaching of the Church is public and can be known by all, not just by a select group of the "enlightened" as in Gnosticism. The true faith is that which was taught by the Apostles and which continues to be taught by their successors, the bishops. The authentic teachings of the faith are also universally believed in the Church. Finally, the Church's authentic teachings, that is the Church's "tradition," are inspired by the Holy Spirit from whom the Church cannot be separated. "For where the Church is, there is the Spirit of God: and where the Spirit of God is, there is the Church and every kind of grace."

St. Irenaeus, *Against Heresies*, Book 3 chapter 24, paragraph 1. EarlyChristianWritings.com

 Irenaeus is also another early witness to belief in the real presence of Christ in the Holy Eucharist as the following passage demonstrates.

"We are his members and we are nourished by creation, which is his gift to us, for it is he who causes the sun to rise and the rain to fall. He declared that the chalice, which comes from his creation, was his blood, and he makes it the nourishment of our blood. He affirmed that the bread, which comes from his creation, was his body, and he makes it the nourishment of our body. When the chalice we mix and the bread we bake receive the word of God, the eucharistic elements become the body and blood of Christ by which our bodies live and grow. ... The slip

of a vine planted in the ground bears fruit at the proper time. The grain of wheat falls into the ground and decays only to be raised up again and multiplied by the Spirit of God who sustains all things. The Wisdom of God places these things at the service of man and when they receive God's word they become the eucharist, which is the body and blood of Christ. In the same way our bodies, which have been nourished by the eucharist, will be buried in the earth and will decay, but they will rise again at the appointed time, for the Word of God will raise them up to the glory of God the Father."

St. Irenaeus, *Against Heresies*, Book 5, chapter 2, paragraphs 2-3. EarlyChristianWritings.com The Oxford Dictionary of the Christian Church. Pope Benedict XVI, "St. Irenaeus," *The Fathers*.

St. Irenaeus, like Justin before him, wrote about the Blessed Virgin Mary as the new Eve, who by her obedience gave birth to the Savior, thus undoing the effects of the first Eve's disobedience. As Irenaeus does not argue the point, it is probable that Mary's status as the new Eve was already widely held by Christian thinkers. Irenaeus was martyred for the faith c. 202.

St. Irenaeus, *Against Heresies*, Book 3, chapter 22, paragraphs 3-4. EarlyChristianWritings.com Jaroslav Pelikan, *Mary Through the Centuries: Her Place in the History of Culture* (Yale University Press, 1996), 42-43.

St. Clement of Alexandria (c.150-215) is another important figure from this period. Of Greek heritage, Clement was much enamored with philosophy which he saw as a gift from God to the Greeks which could prepare them for the Gospel. Clement taught that, through the practice of faith and the exercise of reason, the human person can come to true knowledge of the Word of God, Jesus Christ. Such knowledge leads to the love

Tertullian.

of Christ and transformation into the likeness of God. This transformation depends on both freedom from passions and on love for God. Clement also affirmed that it is through Baptism and the Eucharist that we participate in the immortality of Christ. Like St. Justin before him, St. Clement engaged the teachings of Greek philosophy and affirmed its truths in order to demonstrate the compatibility of the Christian faith and human reason. Additionally, Clement utilized the metrical style of Greco-Roman poetry to write hymns in honor of Jesus Christ.

Pope Benedict XVI, *"St. Clement of Alexandria" The Fathers.*
Foley, From *Age to Age: How Christians Have Celebrated the Eucharist,* 56.

The North African city of Carthage was the home of **Tertullian** (c.160-225). Tertullian was a well-educated pagan who converted to Christianity some time before the year **197**. Eventually becoming a theologian and apologist for Chris-

tianity, Tertullian wrote a number of books in Latin, making him the first of the Church Fathers to use the language of the West. In his works Tertullian explored the great mysteries of the Christian faith such as the Trinity, the Incarnation and the nature of the Church. Against heretics he argued along with Irenaeus that the one, true Church is identified by episcopal succession. Against the political authorities Tertullian defended the teachings and practices of Christians as compatible with good citizenship. The following is perhaps his best known quotation: "refined as it is, your cruelty serves no purpose. On the contrary, for our community, it is an invitation. We multiply every time one of us is mowed down. The blood of Christians is effective seed."

Tertullian, Apologeticus, 50,13. in Pope Benedict XVI, "Tertullian," *The Fathers.*

Unfortunately, Tertullian's moral rigor, and his contempt for his fellow Christians who did not fully share it, led him out of the Church and into the Montanist heresy around the year 206. Although he left the Catholic Church, Tertullian's contributions to theology and apologetics cannot be ignored and that is why he is recognized as a Church Father.

Pope Benedict XVI, "Tertullian," *The Fathers.* Richard M. Hogan, *Dissent from the Creed,* 53-56.
Baus, *History of the Church Vol. I From the Apostolic Community to Constantine,* 248-252.

Of Tertullian's many works one of the most celebrated is his description of Christian marriage. Reflecting St. Paul's teachings in Ephesians 5 and Colossians 3, it discloses what Church leaders hoped Christian couples would aspire to.

"How shall we ever be able adequately to describe the happiness of that marriage which the Church arranges, the Sacrifice strengthens, upon which the blessing sets a

seal, at which angels are present as witnesses, and to which the Father gives His consent? For not even on earth do children marry properly and legally without their fathers' permission. How beautiful, then, the marriage of two Christians, two who are one in hope, one in desire, one in the way of life they follow, one in the religion they practice. They are as brother and sister, both servants of the same Master. Nothing divides them, either in flesh or in spirit. They are, in very truth, two in one flesh; and where there is but one flesh there is also but one spirit. They pray together, they worship together, they fast together; instructing one another, encouraging one another, strengthening one another. Side by side they visit God's church and partake of God's Banquet; side by side they face difficulties and persecution, share their consolations. They have no secrets from one another; they never shun each other's company; they never bring sorrow to each other's hearts. Unembarrassed they visit the sick and assist the needy. They give alms without anxiety; they attend the Sacrifice without difficulty; they perform their daily exercises of piety without hindrance. They need not be furtive about making the Sign of the Cross, nor timorous in greeting the brethren, nor silent in asking a blessing of God. Psalms and hymns they sing to one another, striving to see which one of them will chant more beautifully the praises of their Lord. Hearing and seeing this, Christ rejoices. To such as these He gives His peace. Where there are two together, there also He is present; and where He is, there evil is not."

Ancient Christian Writers translation (ACW 13, 35-36).

For Tertullian, as for St. Paul before him, **the family** was the vocation within which most Christians were called to live out the Gospel. Because married Christians were called to a shared discipleship and spiritual life, some Church leaders were very much opposed to marriages between Christians and non-Christians, whether to pagans or Jews. The indissolubility of marriage was also strongly upheld. Second marriages after the death of a spouse were

discouraged. Adultery incurred severe condemnation and a period of strict penance. Abortion and the abandonment of children, both of which were legal under Roman law, were recognized as murder. Within the marriage the spouses were called to be partners with equal rights. In principle therefore, women enjoyed a greater status under Christianity than among the pagans.

Sommer, *We Look For A Kingdom: The Everyday Lives of the Early Christians*, 296-317. Baus, *History of the Church Vol. I From the Apostolic Community to Constantine*, 307-308.

It has been suggested that the **practice of infanticide**, which was largely directed at female children, had enduring negative consequences for the girls who survived. For example, in Rome the practice created a ratio of boys to girls, men to women of 131 to 100. Fewer women meant they were in greater demand and the expectation that they be virgins at the time they were wed, meant earlier marriages. Indeed, many of the Roman women who are known to history were child brides to much older men. Earlier marriages meant earlier and therefore much more dangerous pregnancies. Women who survived these dangers and outlived their older husbands were not only expected to marry again, they were, if less than fifty years of age, legally compelled to. Taken together, Roman marriage and sexual practices guaranteed that Christian families were much more prolific than their pagan neighbors. Together with evangelization, procreation virtually assured that Christianity would become the majority religion in the empire.

Stark, *The Triumph of Christianity*, 121-136.

It is probable that the tradition of **initiating new members** into the Church at the Easter liturgy became the established practice some time during the second century. The Easter celebration began with a period of fasting of one or more days of Holy Week. In the eastern part of the empire where most Christians lived, they fasted from Monday through Wednesday taking only bread, salt and water. On Thursday and Friday they gave up bread. The celebration began on the vigil of Easter with readings from the prophets, psalms and the Gospels. There followed solemn celebrations of baptism and the Eucharist. By the third century the fifty days after Easter were being celebrated up until the feast of Pentecost. During this joyful season they refrained from fasting and from kneeling during prayer. The practice of celebrating the Eucharist on the death anniversaries of the martyrs was also established by this time starting first in the East. Pope St. Callistus (+222), who was murdered by a mob, was the first martyr to be honored on the Roman calendar.

Baus, *History of the Church Vol. I From the Apostolic Community to Constantine*, 268-274.

An important document that we have from the late second century is the **Epistle to Mathetes of Diognetus.** Written by an anonymous Christian using a pseudonym, the letter is addressed to an unknown inquirer given the name "Diognetus." The first part of the letter seeks to refute the errors of Judaism and paganism. The letter goes on in the passage below to present the author's view point on Christians and their providential role within pagan society. In doing so the author has left us a valuable account of how Christians of this time viewed themselves.

"Christians are distinguished from other men neither by country, nor language, nor the customs which they observe. For they neither inhabit cities of their own, nor employ a peculiar form of speech, nor lead a life which is marked out by any singularity. The course of conduct which they follow has not been devised by any specula-tion or deliberation of inquisitive men; nor do they, like some, proclaim themselves the advocates of any merely human doctrines. But, inhabiting Greek as well as barbarian cities, according as the lot of each of them has determined, and following the customs of the natives in respect to clothing, food, and the rest of their ordinary conduct, they display to us their wonderful and confessedly striking method of life. They dwell in their own countries, but simply as sojourners. As citizens, they share in all things with others, and yet endure all things as if foreigners. Every foreign land is to them as their native country, and every land of their birth as a land of strangers. They marry, as do all [others]; they beget children; but they do not destroy their offspring. They have a common table, but not a common bed. They are in the flesh, but they do not live after the flesh. They pass their days on earth, but they are citizens of heaven. They obey the prescribed laws, and at the same time surpass the laws by their lives. They love all men, and are persecuted by all. They are unknown and condemned; they are put to death, and restored to life. They are poor, yet make many rich; they are in lack of all things, and yet abound in all; they are dishonored, and yet in their very dishonor are glorified. They are evil spoken of, and yet are justified; they are reviled, and bless; they are insulted, and repay the insult with honor; they do good, yet are punished as evil-doers. When punished, they rejoice as if quickened into life; they are assailed by the Jews as foreigners, and are persecuted by the Greeks yet those who hate them are unable to assign any reason for their hatred. To sum up all in one word— what the soul is in the body, Christians are in the world. ..."

Epistle of Mathetes to Diognetus, 5-6. Translated by Alexander Roberts and James Donaldson. From Ante-Nicene Fathers, Vol. 1. Edited by Alexander Roberts, James Donaldson, and A. Cleveland Coxe. (Buffalo, NY: Christian Literature Publishing Co., 1885.) Revised and edited for New Advent by Kevin Knight. <http://www.newadvent.org/fathers

Pope Victor (c. 189-199) tried to establish throughout the Church the Sunday after

Origen.

Passover as the day for the celebration of **Easter**. In some places in Asia Minor, Easter was celebrated on the day of the Jewish Passover, the 14th day of Nissan, regardless of what day of the week it was. Victor called bishops to synods in order to get them to go along with his proposal and threatened to excommunicate those that didn't. While he was challenged for his severity by some, including St. Irenaeus, no one questioned his authority to declare excommunication. This was a major step in the assertion of papal primacy as the authority of the pope to excommunicate someone was not contested by contemporaries.

Eusebius, *The Church History V, 25* translation and commentary by Paul L. Maier.
Baus, *History of the Church Vol. I From the Apostolic Community to Constantine,* 269.

 In the year **202**, the Emperor Severus declared that Christians were forbidden to make converts. In a change from the earlier policy established under Trajan of not seeking out Christians, imperial authorities targeted Christian schools and particularly catechumens. It is thought that Severus took this step out of concern that some of the heretical sects like the Marcionites and the Montanists were teaching their followers to reject marriage and service in the imperial army. One of the victims of this new outbreak of violent persecution was a catechist in Alexandria named Leonidas. Leonidas was succeeded in his role as catechist by his son Origen, who was only about 17 years old. As the persecution continued it took the lives of many men and women who were in the process of preparing for baptism. Some were beheaded, others like Potamiene and her mother Marcella, were burned to death in boiling pitch. It was a very dangerous time to be a catechist or to seek conversion.

Danielou and Marrou, *The Christian Centuries Vol. One The First Six Hundred Years,* 141-143. Baus, *History of the Church Vol. I From the Apostolic Community to Constantine,* 217-219.

The emperor Caracalla enacted a law in **212** which granted citizenship to virtually all the inhabitants of the empire who were not slaves. Citizenship bestowed legal privileges. It also brought in more revenue and enabled more non-Romans to serve in the military, as citizens were taxed at a higher rate than noncitizens and only citizens could join the legions.

During the third and fourth centuries the Roman army became less and less Roman.

Although the young **Origen** longed for martyrdom, he lived to be an old man. Origen's youthful zeal led him to interpret Christ's words in Mt 19:12 literally and he castrated himself. Having rendered himself a eunuch, Origen became prolific in another way through his writings and is recognized as one of the early Church Fathers. Origen was one of the first great Scripture scholars of the Church and promoted lectio divina, the reading of Scripture as a form of personal prayer. Origen emphasized the common priesthood of the faithful noting that all members of the Church are to give their lives in service to the Lord. Origen's intellectual gifts were even recognized by pagans. So much so that around the year 224 he was summoned to Antioch by Julia Mamaea, the mother of Emperor Severus Alexander, to acquaint her with the teachings of Christianity. During the thirteen year reign of Severus Alexander (222-235), Christians were tolerated and were even numbered among his associates. The Christian communities of Asia Minor grew in size and there are no documented instances of martyrdom during the period of his rule.

Baus, *History of the Church Vol. I From the Apostolic Community to Constantine*, 220-221.

While Christianity remained an illegal religion under Roman law, some Church Fathers refrained from being very specific about the celebration of the Eucharist and practiced what is called the **"discipline of the secret."** This self-censorship was thought needed to protect the sacred mysteries from misunderstanding and attack from the Church's enemies. It was also held by some that the sacraments of Baptism and the Eucharist could only be rightly understood after one had experienced them. Tertullian put it this way, "Silence is due to the sacred mysteries." (Apology 7) Still, adherence to the teaching of Jesus could not be denied as the passage below from Origen indicates.

"What people are accustomed to drinking blood? In the Gospel, the Jews who followed the Lord heard and were offended, and they said: 'Who can eat flesh and drink blood?' But the Christian people, the faithful people, hear these things and embrace them, and follow him who says: 'Unless you eat my flesh and drink my blood, you have no life in you; for my flesh is food indeed, and my blood is drink indeed.'"

Origen, *On Numbers, 16.8* Cited in Aquilina, *The Mass of the Early Christians*, 154.

Origen's writings also provide the earliest known instance of devotion to Jesus Christ as the "Divine Physician." Devotion to Christ as the healer of soul and body became quite popular in North Africa and was promoted there by St. Cyprian and St. Augustine.

Groeschel, *I Am With You Always: A Study of the History and Meaning of Personal Devotion to Jesus Christ for Catholic, Orthodox, and Protestant Christians*, 37-43.

Along with Clement of Alexandria, Origen was among the first Greek Church Fathers to write extensively about **prayer and the spiritual life**. For both of them the Christian was called to thank God daily in personal prayer for His many gifts. Each day and every thought, word and action should be consecrated to the Lord through prayer. The believer needs to pray for growth in the virtues and for the forgiveness of sins. Furthermore, Christians are called to intercede for each other and to pray for their enemies. Clement and Origen both commented on the distinction between vocal prayer and interior mental, or contemplative prayer which is wordless. According to them, this contemplative prayer unites the soul to God and enables the believer to become "divinized." Origen must also be remembered for promoting prayer not just to the Father but also to Jesus. His teaching on prayer had a tremendous influence on the Eastern Church and his devotion to

Jesus, passed along by St. Ambrose, St. Bernard and St. Francis of Assisi, helped shape the Western mystical tradition.

Origen's zeal led him to promote a spirituality centered on the struggle of individual Christians for union with Christ by the purification of their hearts and minds by ascetical practices. This spiritual "athleticism" strongly influenced early monasticism and has appealed to countless Christians into the present. However, in its immoderate forms it has at times undermined the Eucharistic centered spirituality of the community articulated so well by St. Ignatius of Antioch. The history of Christian spirituality has largely been the story of how these two visions have complimented and competed with each other.
John Zizioulas, *"The Early Christian Community,"* in *Christian Spirituality: Origins to the Twelfth Century* 41-42.

Origen was eventually granted his wish to suffer for Christ. He was imprisoned and tortured and eventually died four years later in 254. However, because some of his theories about the Trinity, the nature of the soul, and the afterlife were later judged to be heretical, not to mention his self-castration, Origen is not recognized as a saint of the Church.
Pope Benedict XVI , "Origen," *The Fathers*. H. Crouzel, *"Origen and Origenism," New Catholic Encyclopedia*.
Baus, *History of the Church Vol. I From the Apostolic Community to Constantine*, 234-240.

Tertullian and St. Cyprian wrote extensive commentaries on the Our Father which focused on the practical aspects of prayer. In addition to praying when they rise and go to sleep, Tertullian, citing Scripture, encouraged the faithful to pray at the third, sixth and ninth hours of the day (in modern terms — 9 a.m., 12noon and 3p.m.). Except on Sundays and during the Easter Season, when the resurrection is celebrated, prayers should be offered while kneeling, with hands humbly raised in imitation of the penitent tax collector. Tertullian added that it "becomes believers not to take food, and not to go to the bath, before interposing a prayer; for the refreshments and nourishments of the spirit are to be held prior to those of the flesh, and things heavenly prior to things earthly."

In addition to the Our Father, the faithful had long been accustomed to praying the Psalms both liturgically and privately. And they did so from a typological perspective meaning that, depending on the content of the particular psalm, they viewed the speaker as either Christ addressing the Father or the Church addressing Christ. By the third century it was customary for prayers addressed to Christ to be offered while facing east because, like the rising sun, the Lord was expected to return from there. Even before this development, praying before a crucifix had become common and the making of the sign of the cross was a frequent practice. Among his many contributions, Tertullian left an account of the Catholic practice of making the sign of the cross. In doing so it is clear that he is describing a longstanding custom and not some new development. Tertullian wrote the following in his work *De corona militis* around the year 204: "In all our travels and movements, in all our coming in and going out, in putting on our shoes, at the bath, at the table, in lighting our candles, in lying down, in sitting down, whatever task occupies us, we mark our forehead with the sign of the cross."
Cited in Scott Hahn, *Signs of Life: 40 Catholic Customs and Their Biblical Roots* (Doubleday, 2009), 26.
Baus, *History of the Church Vol. I From the Apostolic Community to Constantine*, 299-300.

The practice of **fasting** as a regular spiritual exercise increased during the third century. Wednesday and Friday became the weekly fast days as these were the days on which Jesus was betrayed by Judas and then crucified. Fasting was seen as both a penitential practice and a spiritual discipline which disposed one to pray and to submit to the guidance of the Holy Spirit.

Baus, *History of the Church Vol. I From the Apostolic Community to Constantine*, 299-305.

Martyrdom, meaning laying down one's life rather than giving up the Faith, was seen as the perfect imitation of Jesus Christ. "Martyr" means "witness" in Greek and those men and women who died rather than renounce their Faith made the ultimate sacrifice. Those who were martyred under the Romans were usually subjected to horrific physical and mental tortures before actually being killed. Because of their faith and courage, martyrs were heroes to their fellow Christians. At every martyrdom it was believed, St. Cyprian said, that "Christ was there to wage his own battle." The anniversary of a martyr's death, which was regarded as his birthday into heaven, was celebrated with a Mass at the martyr's tomb. The heroism of the martyrs identified them as having truly been "temples of the Holy Spirit." Therefore, their bones were venerated as relics through which the Lord may choose to work miracles for petitioners through the intercession of the martyr. When Christianity was no longer outlawed, churches were built over the tombs of the martyrs, as in the case of both St. Peter and St. Paul. The veneration that the Church initially showed for martyrs was eventually applied to all the saints.

Baus in *History of the Church Vol. I From the Apostolic Community to Constantine*, 292-295. Groeschel, *I Am With You Always: A Study of the History and Meaning of Personal Devotion to Jesus Christ for Catholic, Orthodox, and Protestant Christians*, 24. F.X. Murphy// W.F. Dicharry, *"Martyrdom," New Catholic Encyclopedia*.

In 203 in Carthage a local persecution claimed the lives of numerous Christians, among them were **Perpetua**, and her servant, **Felicity**. The account of their imprisonment, torture and execution in "The Passion of St. Perpetua," some of which was written from prison by St. Perpetua herself, was greatly revered in the early Church and is the oldest known document written by a Christian woman. St. Perpetua was twenty-two years old when she died for the faith.

Herbert Thurston, S.J. and Donald Attwater, eds. *Butler's Lives of the Saints Vols. I-II.*

"After a few days there prevailed a report that we should be heard. And then my father came to me from the city, worn out with anxiety. He came up to me, that he might cast me down, saying, 'Have pity my daughter, on my grey hairs. Have pity on your father, if I am worthy to be called a father by you. If with these hands I have brought you up to this flower of your age, if I have preferred you to all your brothers, do not deliver me up to the scorn of men. Have regard to your brothers, have regard to your mother and your aunt, have regard to your son, who will not be able to live after you. Lay aside your courage, and do not bring us all to destruction; for none of us will speak in freedom if you should suffer anything.'

These things said my father in his affection, kissing my hands, and throwing himself at my feet; and with tears he called me not Daughter, but Lady. And I grieved over the grey hairs of my father, that he alone of all my family would not rejoice over my passion. And I comforted him, saying, 'On that scaffold whatever God wills shall happen. For know that we are not placed in our own power, but in that of God.' And he departed from me in sorrow."

A few days later Perpetua and Felicity were placed in the arena bound in nets where they were trampled

Church at Dura-Europas.

by a "fierce cow." Having survived this ordeal they were finally stabbed to death by soldiers to the delight of the crowd.

The Passion of the Holy Martyrs Perpetua and Felicitas, EarlyChristianWritings.com

Mike Aquilina and Christopher Bailey, *Mothers of the Church: The Witness of Early Christian Women,* 60-67.

The introduction of **Latin** as a language of the Roman liturgy occurred during Pope Victor's pontificate. Prior to this time the Mass had been celebrated solely in Greek. For the next one hundred and fifty years the Roman liturgy mixed languages, with the Scripture in Latin and the prayers in Greek.

Pecklers, *Liturgy: The Illustrated History,* 27.

Early in the third century two **Trinitarian heresies** arose. The first was "Adoptionism" which maintained that Jesus Christ was simply an ordinary man until he was "adopted" by God at his baptism. The second heresy was "Modalism" which denied that there were three persons in God. According to Modalism the Father, Son and Holy Spirit are simply three ways or "modes" that God manifests Himself. Fortunately, neither of these heresies gained many adherents and quickly died.

From the very beginning **widows** had a special status in the Church. They were to be taken care of by the community if in need. At the same time widows were called to be role models for other women in living the Christian Faith. The special status of widows included a call to minister to others through works of charity. In this capacity widows would come to know much about the personal lives of others in the community. This explains the frequent admonitions in early Christian writings that widows not be gossips.

1 Timothy 5, 3-16. Sommer, We Look For A Kingdom: The Everyday Lives of the Early Christians, 210-213.

On account of Christ's teaching in Matthew 10 and St. Paul's advice in First Corinthians 7:25-38, many early Christians regarded **celibacy** or **virginity** superior to the married state. The example of Christ Himself and His mother also inspired some Christians to embrace life-long virginity. Testimony to the practice of celibacy and consecrated virginity in the early Church comes from a number of sources. For the first centuries of the Church bishops, priests and deacons were permitted to be married but they were not to marry again if they were widowed. They were also expected to abstain from marital relations for a period of time prior to celebrating the sacraments.

As **consecrated women**, virgins were seen to comprise a semi-official status in the Church even though religious orders would not be founded until after Christianity became officially tolerated. Virgins were to be models of prayer and workers of charity. However, given the challenge of pursuing life-long virginity within a promiscuous culture and without the support of the community life later to be found within religious orders, a number of early Church leaders including Pope Clement and Clement of Alexandria cautioned aspiring virgins to recognize the challenge they were undertaking.

In his *Apology* St. Justin Martyr pointed to the number of Christian men and women living celibate lives as proof of Christianity's moral superiority over paganism. A bit later Tertullian wrote that virgins were "the most illustrious portion of the flock of Christ" and "the spouses of Christ." In the third century St. Cyprian and Methodius of Olympia both extolled consecrated virginity as the most excellent witness to Christ after martyrdom itself. Indeed, numerous Church Fathers spoke of the "white martyrdom" of consecrated chastity. Until the middle of the fourth century men and women consecrated themselves as virgins through personal vows. The increasing number of Christians embracing consecrated virginity as the ideal life contributed to the growth of monasticism and clerical celibacy.

Baus, History of the Church Vol. I From the Apostolic Community to Constantine, 295-298. Sommer, We Look For A Kingdom: The Everyday Lives of the Early Christians, 213-217. Christian Cochini, S.J., The Apostolic Origins of Priestly Celibacy (Ignatius, 1990) 245-254.

As Christian communities grew so did the desire for places of worship which could accommodate larger congregations. The earliest written evidence for the existence of an actual **church** is from around 205 when a government official recorded that a flood in the town of Edessa had destroyed "the temple of the Christians." Archaeologists have uncovered another of these early churches in the ruins of Dura-Europos, a Roman garrison town on the Euphrates River. The building was originally a private home. However, internal walls were removed to create a worship space decorated with frescoes of the Good Shepherd and Jesus walking on the water. The floor is also raised on one end probably for the altar. Documents from the second half of the third century record that churches existed in Palestine and Sicily. Eusebius reported that in the years just before Diocletian's persecution "mass meetings gathered in every city, and congregations worshiped in new, spacious churches that replaced the old."

Baus, History of the Church Vol. I From the Apostolic Community to Constantine, 286-287. 8. Sommer, We Look For A Kingdom: The Everyday Lives of the Early Christians, 138-140. Eusebius, The Church History VIII, 1 translation and commentary by Paul L. Maier (Kregel Publications, 2007).

The Apostolic Tradition is an important compilation of documents from the early third century which have been attributed to **St. Hippolytus of Rome (c.170-236)**, although some scholars dispute his authorship. In any case, the document describes the ordination rites of bishops, priests and deacons as well as the ritual for baptizing catechumens and children. St. Hippolytus also encouraged the use of the sign of the cross in prayer and in times of temptation as part of the apostolic tradition. The *Apostolic Tradition* had great influence throughout the Church and ancient copies exist not only in Latin but also in Coptic, Arabic and Ethiopic.

Sommer, *We Look For A Kingdom: The Everyday Lives of the Early Christians*, 116-121.

Pecklers, *Liturgy: The Illustrated History*, 35-37.

Furthermore, the *Apostolic Tradition* preserves an early Eucharistic Prayer which was used as the basis for the composition of Eucharistic Prayer II after the Second Vatican Council (1962-1965). This Eucharistic prayer did not include the Sanctus, or "Holy, holy," and the Holy Spirit is invoked after Christ's words of institution are prayed, "Take, eat, this is my body..."

"The Lord be with you. And with your spirit.

Lift up your hearts. We have lifted them up to the Lord.

Let us give thanks to the Lord. It is meet and just.

We render thee thanks, O God, through thy beloved child Jesus Christ, whom in these last times thou hast sent us as Savior, Redeemer and messenger of thy will; who is thine inseparable Word, through whom thou madest all things, and in whom thou were pleased. Thou didst send him from heaven into the womb of the Virgin, where he

Martyrdom of St. Hippolytus. *Dirks Barts. c. 1475.*

was incarnate of the Holy Spirit and the Virgin; fulfilling thy will and acquiring for thee a holy people, he extended his hands in his Passion, in order to deliver from suffering those who have believed in thee. And when he was betrayed voluntarily to his passion, in order to destroy death, break the chains of the devil, tread hell under his feet, enlighten the just, fix a term, and manifest the resurrection, taking bread and giving thanks to thee he said, 'Take, eat, this is my body which is broken for you.' And likewise the chalice, saying 'This is my blood, which is shed for you: when you do this, you make a memory of me.' We, therefore, remembering his death and resurrection, offer to thee the bread and the chalice giving thee thanks that thou hast deigned to allow us to appear before thee and to serve thee. And we beg thee to send the Holy Spirit upon the oblation of thy holy Church and, gathering all together in one, grant to all the saints who partake to be filled with the Holy Spirit and to be strengthened in the faith in truth, so that we may praise and glorify thee by thy child Jesus Christ, through whom be glory and honor to thee, Father and Son with the Holy Spirit, in thy holy Church, now and for ever and ever. Amen."

Quoted in Josef Jungmann, S.J. *The Mass: An Historical, Theological and Pastoral Survey* (The Liturgical Press, 1975), 31-32.

CALISTVS·I·PP·ROMANVS

Left: **Pope St. Clement I.** *Chevalier Artaud de Montor. Illustration from The Lives and Times of the Popes. 1842.*
Right: **"Jesus as Teacher,"** *Catacomb of Domitilla, Rome.*

Information gleaned from the Apostolic Tradition and Tertullian's many writings indicate that the main features of the **Eucharistic celebration** had become uniform by the third century. The gifts of bread and wine were provided by the faithful for the sacrifice. The Eucharistic prayer was addressed to the Father through the Son. When the words of consecration are spoken the bread and wine become Christ's Body and Blood. The Eucharist was distributed under the forms of both bread and wine. And, somewhat surprisingly, the faithful could take the consecrated bread home to receive privately when they could not attend the liturgy. In Tertullian's community, the Mass was offered in the early morning before sunrise.
Baus, *History of the Church Vol. I From the Apostolic Community to Constantine,* 281-285.

The *Apostolic Tradition's* instructions regarding **catechumens** indicate that by the early third century the Church had a well established program of instruction and evaluation of new converts. The potential convert had to be presented to the Church by a practicing Christian who would attest to their sincerity. After an initial inquiry by a teacher of catechumens into the moral suitability of the candidate, they were received into the catechumenate for a period of instruction that normally lasted three years. Instruction was based on the Bible and training in spiritual practices and charitable work. When the period of instruction was completed the candidate was once again examined and then submitted to the rites of exorcism conducted by the bishop. Finally, on the night of the Easter vigil, the catechumen professed the baptismal promises and received the sacraments from the bishop or priest who was assisted by the deacons.
Baus, *History of the Church Vol. I From the Apostolic Community to Constantine,* 275-281.

The *Apostolic Tradition* included a list of forbidden occupations that a potential convert must leave before being received into the Church. For most of the occupations listed it is easy to understand why they are forbidden (pagan priests, prostitutes, etc.). Interestingly, while he says catechumens who want to become soldiers should be rejected, men who are already in the military may be accepted as long as they promise not to take part in executions. Hippolytus' position on Christians being in the Roman army reflects the ambiguity of the early Church as a whole on the question. Some Church Fathers were essentially pacifists while others apparently had no problem with Christians being soldiers as long as they neither executed anyone nor were involved in pagan practices. It is unclear how many Christians served in the Roman legions but certainly some did and their numbers increased with time. Also of note, the document says that both "a military governor" or "a ruler of a city who wears purple" must resign their posts before being received into the Church. This admonition is testimony to the fact that members of the ruling classes were being converted to Christianity.

Sommer, *We Look For A Kingdom: The Everyday Lives of the Early Christians*, 275-295. Baus, *History of the Church Vol. I From the Apostolic Community to Constantine*, 277.

In addition to his various writings, St. Hippolytus is remembered as the first "anti-pope." Around **218** there was a disputed papal election in Rome and Hippolytus was the loser. He and his followers subsequently refused to recognize the election of his rival, **Pope St. Callistus** (218-223), or the latter's two successors. In 235 both Hippolytus and the reigning pope, Pope Pontian, were arrested and sent to work in the salt mines in Sardinia. They both died soon afterwards but not before Hippolytus was reconciled with the Church. Their remains were returned to Rome for reburial and both were honored as martyrs and saints. The historian Karl Baus asserts that there is no evidence in the sources for Hippolytus' election as an anti-pope.

Baus in *History of the Church Vol. I From the Apostolic Community to Constantine*, 244-245. Michael J. Walsh, *Consultant editor Lives of the Popes: Illustrated Biographies of Every Pope From St. Peter to the Present* (London, 1998), 27-28.

Pope Callistus is remembered for establishing the **catacomb** in Rome which bears his name. The construction of this underground cemetery was in accord with contemporary Jewish burial practices. Jews and Christians alike rejected the pagan practice of cremation as the desecration of the body. At times Masses were offered in the catacombs for the deceased but, contrary to popular myth, Christians did not live in them during persecutions.

Wilken, *The First Thousand Years: A Global History of Christianity*, 47-48.

Manichaeism, named for its Persian founder, Manes (c.216-276), was a Gnostic heresy that incorporated elements of Christianity, Buddhism and Zoroastrianism. It spread through the empire during the second half of the third century. In Manes' version of "dualism" there were two gods, one good and the other evil. Hating the material world as evil, the Manichaeans practiced a strict asceticism which they believed would release the particles of light which were imprisoned in all matter, which was evil and polluted. The Manichaeans claimed that their religion was the true Christianity and were aggressive missionaries. After the year 400 its influence declined although it endured in India and China.

Hogan, *Dissent from the Creed: Heresies Past and Present*, 61-66. Baus, *History of the Church Vol. I From the Apostolic Community to Constantine*, 261-268.

During the third century the Roman Empire experienced a **three-fold crisis**. The first came from outside forces when the Persians in the east and Germanic tribes along the Danube River were increasingly successful at penetrating the empire's borders. In order to protect itself the empire required ever larger armies and during the middle decades of the third century, the army doubled in size to 600,000 troops. A larger army required more revenue, so taxes were raised and the coinage devalued. This led to the second crisis as poor economic conditions caused social upheaval. Military defeats combined with social unrest yielded the third crisis which was political instability. From 235 until 284, the Roman Empire was wracked by civil war. During these fifty years there were more than twenty emperors and virtually all of them died violently; either in battle, from mob violence or by assassination.

Philip Daileader, *The Early Middle Ages* (Great Courses, 2004) Course Guide Book, 7.

The violence of this period included two **imperial persecutions** of the Church. The persecution which claimed the lives of Saints Hippolytus and Pontian was ordered by the Emperor Maximinus in 235. Fortunately, Maximinus' reign did not last long. Prior to his reign, Christians had enjoyed twenty-five years of tolerance and even held positions in the imperial court. However, the laws against them were still on the books and violent persecutions in various places broke out from time to time. These local persecutions were usually the result of resentment of Christians among the populace. In 244 Phillip the Arab came to the imperial throne. Some have speculated that Philip may have been a Christian although others dispute this. In any case, during his five-year reign, Christians were once again tolerated. The emperor even corresponded with the Christian theologian, Origen.

Sordi, *The Christians and the Roman Empire*, 80-82, 96-100.
Baus, *History of the Church Vol. I From the Apostolic Community to Constantine*, 295-298.

It is estimated that the **Christian population of the empire** around the year 250 was 1,120,246, about 1.9% of the total population. In Rome, the Church owned numerous properties, had forty-six priests, seven deacons and over 1,500 widows. Total church membership in Rome may have been as high as 50,000 adherents. About this time Origen reported that some pagans were saying that there were far too many Christians and that the government should do something about it.

Sordi, *The Christians and the Roman Empire*, 100. Stark, *Cities of God: The Real Story of How Christianity Became an Urban Movement and Conquered Rome*, 67. Duffy, *Saints and Sinners: A History of the Popes*, 14.

By the third century, Christians could be found throughout the Roman Empire. Not surprisingly, their numbers were particularly large in the East as it was the most populous half of the empire. Although the importance of Jerusalem had waned, there were large Christian communities in Alexandria and Antioch. Egypt, Syria, Asia Minor and Armenia were well populated with Christians. Small bands of missionaries had also extended the Church's presence outside the empire into Ethiopia, Arabia and Persia. The Latin West was always less populated and less urban than the East. In the western provinces the largest concentrations of Christians were found, from greatest to least, in Italy, North Africa, Spain, Gaul, the Balkans and Britain. The success of the Church in spreading the message of Jesus Christ to all corners of the empire and beyond is testimony to the seriousness with which the first Christians answered the great commission to "go out to all the world."

Baus, *History of the Church Vol. I From the Apostolic Community to Constantine*, 367-388.

Phillip the Arab was killed in 249 by **Decius** who, as the new emperor, was determined to restore Rome's ancient religion. His policies resulted in the first **universal persecution** of Christians and the most serious attack on the Church up to that time. In an effort to enlist the help of the gods and to enforce religious uniformity, Decius declared that every inhabitant of the empire must make a public sacrifice to the gods which would be documented by government officials. Those who refused were to be thrown into prison and tortured. One of the first persons to be executed was **Pope Fabian** who was martyred in January 250. Many Christians, in fear for their lives, made the required sacrifices. Those who conformed to the law included a few bishops. Some submitted after being tortured. Others avoided the requirement to make sacrifices by bribing government officials and some simply fled. Still, many Christians refused to offer sacrifices to the gods. Of these, thousands died. Some were immediately executed while others died in prison. A few were eventually released. This systematic persecution was a catastrophe for the Church but ended in June 251 when Decius was killed in battle by the Goths.

Baus, *History of the Church Vol. I From the Apostolic Community to Constantine*, 222-226. Sordi, *The Christians and the Roman Empire*, 101-105.

At the time that Decius sought to re-establish traditional Roman religious practice the empire was under attack in Spain, Italy and along the Danube by various barbarian peoples. Concurrently, the Persian Empire was pressing in from the East. From 251 to 266 the empire was racked internally by a plague.

One of the most courageous leaders of the Church during this persecution was **St. Cyprian of Carthage** (c.210-258). Cyprian was a wealthy pagan rhetorician who converted to Christianity when he was about 35. Having distributed his wealth to the poor, Cyprian dedicated himself to the study of Scripture and the writings of his North African predecessor, Tertullian. Soon after his conversion, Cyprian was or-

St. Cyprian.

dained a priest and then Bishop of Carthage. Within months of his consecration the Decian persecution of the Church broke out and Cyprian went "underground." When the persecution ended, Church leaders were confronted with the dilemma of what to do with the large number of Christians who had lapsed from the faith during the persecution.

Cyprian, along with Pope Cornelius, took the position that those who had actually offered the pagan sacrifices could only be readmitted to Communion after performing appropriate penance. A more rigorist faction in the Church, led in Rome by the antipope Novatian, insisted that those who denied the faith could never be readmitted. This led to the Novatianist schism with these heretics setting up their own churches. When converts from paganism who had been baptized by Novatianist clergy then sought membership in the Catholic Church, Cyprian insisted that they must be re-baptized. The new pope, Stephen, took the more moderate view that every baptism using water and the prayer invoking the Holy Trinity was valid. This was and remains the teaching of the Church. However, at the time it was rejected by Cyprian and other African bishops. **Pope Stephen**, invoking Matthew 16, demanded compliance. This was the first documented instance of a pope asserting his primatial authority over other bishops specifically as the successor to St. Peter. Renewed persecution of the Church left the dispute over "re-baptism" unsettled and the issue of what makes for the validity of the sacraments would come up again in the next century.

Baus, *History of the Church Vol. I From the Apostolic Community to Constantine*, 252-254.

The Oxford Dictionary of the Christian Church. Duffy, *Saints and Sinners: A History of the Popes*, 14-16.

"The Good Shepherd," *Catacomb of Priscilla, Rome.*

Jesus entrusted the Church with His mission of **reconciling sinners** through the forgiveness of sin. This was accomplished first and foremost through Baptism. However, Baptism did not guarantee that the believer would not later commit serious sin. The letters of Paul, Peter, James and John all testify to fallen members, who had confessed their sins, being reconciled through penance and prayer. During the first centuries of the Church, when many members were tempted or coerced to fall away from their profession of faith, leaders struggled to find the right balance between upholding firm standards and extending the Lord's mercy. Being barred from receiving Holy Communion, "ex-communication," was the penalty for such offenses. Intense debates among bishops took place as to whether and how many times such offenses could be forgiven. In addition to apostasy and heresy, violations of sexual morality were also grounds for excommunication.

Baus, *History of the Church Vol. I From the Apostolic Community to Constantine*, 318-345.

St. Cyprian's writings provide accounts of the process through which serious sinners were reconciled to the Church. First, they were given pre-scribed penances of prayer, fasting, and almsgiving. They might also have been required to wear penitential garments. After the prescribed period of penance was completed they would have to publicly request, in the presence of the bishop and congregation, re-admission to the community. The penitent was then reconciled when the bishop imposed hands on them. After that, they could once again participate in the Eucharist. While the process varied in some details in different regions, the core principle, that all repented sins could be forgiven by the Church in the name of Christ, was universal.

The fashioning of **Christian art** objects was slow to develop. This was due in part to the fact that some Christians subscribed to the Old Testament prohibition against the use of idols. The use of art in pagan worship also discouraged the development of Christian art forms. Additionally, prior to the establishment of actual church buildings there was little demand for Christian art. Still, the early Christians harbored the desire to express their faith in art and they often did this by borrowing from traditional Roman forms. Writing around the year 200, Clement of Alexandria suggested that Christians use images of the dove, fish, ship, anchor and fisherman on their signet rings. His contemporary, Tertullian, noted that some Christians used drinking cups with images of the Good Shepherd on them. Christians also decorated the tombs of their loved ones with various religious symbols.

This was particularly true when they began to establish their own burial places in the catacombs of Rome. Among the earliest depictions found in the catacombs are Adam and Eve, Noah and his Ark, Jonah and the whale, the sacrifice of Isaac, Moses, Daniel and the lions and Lazarus raised from the dead. There are images of Jesus depicted at his birth, baptism and performing miracles. He is also often found painted as the Good Shepherd. The general theme of these images was to show how the promises of the Old Testament were fulfilled with the coming of Christ. A fresco in the catacomb of Priscilla in Rome, dating to around 200, features the earliest surviving depiction of the Blessed Virgin Mary.

Wilken, *The First Thousand Years: A Global History of Christianity*, 49-54.

Baus, *History of the Church Vol. I From the Apostolic Community to Constantine*, 285-288.

Pecklers, *Liturgy; The Illustrated History*, 31-32.

During the second and third centuries the Church's offices continued to develop. The particular responsibilities of bishops, priests and deacons were more clearly differentiated. The requirements for admission to each order also became more demanding. This was especially true for bishops. Ongoing controversies with various heretical groups as well as with the pagan culture at large necessitated that bishops have sound theological training. Among the writings of the Fathers, both Origen in the East and St. Cyprian in the West, showed special solicitude for the proper formation of bishops. They also agreed that the men chosen to be bishops should be well vetted by the bishops of the province and that the churches that they belong to concur with their selection.

A church order from Syria written in the mid-third century, **the Didascalia Apostolorum**, provides the most detailed description of the episcopal office that exists prior to the time of Constantine. According to the *Didascalia* the bishop was the leader of his church and as such he is "the mouth of God." Therefore, the bishop must be quite knowledgeable about Scripture because he would be its interpreter for his people. He should also be a model to his flock of the highest moral behavior. To better insure that a bishop had these qualities, they should normally be chosen only from mature men who are at least fifty years old, married only once and whose families reflect positively on their character.

Baus, *History of the Church Vol. I From the Apostolic Community to Constantine*, 346-349.

Along with their other responsibilities, bishops are charged with reminding the faithful of the **obligation to come to church on the Lord's Day**. That such admonitions were deemed necessary as early as the third century reminds us, alas, that truly, there is nothing new under the sun.

"Now when thou teachest, command and warn the people to be constant in assembling in the Church, and not to withdraw themselves but always to assemble, lest any man diminish the Church by not assembling, and cause the body of Christ to be short of a member. For let not a man take thought of others only, but of himself as well, hearkening to that which our Lord said: 'Everyone that gathereth not with me, scattereth.' Since therefore you are the members of Christ, do not scatter yourselves from the Church by not assembling. Seeing that you have Christ for your head, as He promised ... for you are partakers with us... be not then neglectful of yourselves, and deprive not our Savior of His members, and do not rend

and scatter His body. And make not your worldly affairs of more account than the word of God; but on the Lord's day leave every thing and run eagerly to your Church; for she is your glory. Otherwise, what excuse have they before God who do not assemble on the Lord's day to hear the word of life and be nourished with the divine food which abides forever?"

The Catholic Didascalia That is the Teaching of the Twelve Holy Apostles and Disciples of our Savior, Trans. R. Hugh Connolly (Clarenddon Press, 1929) Chapter XIII, ii, 59.

With the increasing number of Christians the responsibilities of **priests** also grew. The tradition of having a bishop for every church community had to be adapted. In villages where bishops could not be present, priests acted for them in celebrating the Eucharist and preaching. Deacons were also appointed by the bishop. A letter of St. Cyprian indicates that, in times of persecution, priests and deacons were expected to stand in for bishops who may have been martyred or forced to flee.

The growth of the Church also led to the development of other clerical ministries ranking below the order of deacon. These were subdeacons, acolytes, lectors and doorkeepers. These "minor orders" had specific liturgical roles and would assist priests and deacons with non-liturgical tasks. Then there were the "exorcists" who ministered to the mentally ill and epileptics.

The clergy received their basic training by going through the catechumenate. This would be followed by private study under the tutelage of an experienced Christian teacher. Liturgical roles were gradually learned through participation in the community's celebration of the Eucharist. The development of the "minor orders" provided progressive levels for training although advancement to higher orders was neither a requirement nor automatic.

Baus, *History of the Church Vol. I From the Apostolic Community to Constantine*, 350-352.

As church communities grew both in size and in number, they gradually organized themselves into provinces following the pattern of the imperial organization of towns, cities and provincial capitals. Local churches retained their links to their "mother churches" and bishops gathered periodically in local and regional synods to address issues of mutual concern. In the eastern, and more densely populated, half of the empire synods were a well established custom by the beginning of the third century. In the less populated Latin West, Carthage in North Africa and Rome in Italy were recognized as the mother churches of all the communities around them. So when synods were necessary in these regions they were called by the bishop of Carthage or the bishop of Rome. Additionally, the Church of Rome and therefore its bishop continued to exert preeminence over all local and provincial churches because of its connection to St. Peter and St. Paul.

Baus, *History of the Church Vol. I From the Apostolic Community to Constantine*, 352-365.

After several years of relative peace, the Church was attacked again under the **Emperor Valerian in 257**. Unlike his predecessors who sought to integrate Christians within the culture of the empire, Valerian's plan was to destroy the Church as an institution by forcing all bishops, priests and deacons to offer sacrifices to the gods. If they refused they were executed. The following year a similar edict targeted prominent lay Christians. Christians holding government posts were threatened with forced labor and confiscation of their property. The aim of these decrees was to eliminate both the ordained and lay leadership of the Church. Having been subject to numerous natural and military disasters, much of the populace warmly supported these persecutions as they believed that the "impiety" of Christians was bringing ill fortune upon the empire. This time Christians faced the persecution with greater courage than eight years before and very few lapsed. There were many martyrs among both the clergy and the laity.

Baus, *History of the Church Vol. I From the Apostolic Community to Constantine*, 226-228.

Among the first martyrs under Valerian's persecution was **Pope Sixtus II**, who was executed along with four of his deacons on August 6, 257. St. Cyprian wrote an account of Sixtus' death.

In the twelve years from his conversion until his martyrdom, St. Cyprian wrote numerous pastoral letters to his flock which shed light on the life of the church in Carthage at that time. His most important works were "On the Unity of the Church," which strongly asserted papal primacy, and his "Treatise on the Lord's Prayer," which continues to inspire readers.

Pope Benedict XVI,"St. Cyprian," *The Fathers.*

In his "Treatise on the Lord's Prayer" St. Cyprian makes an explicit connection between its fifth petition, "Give us this day our daily bread..." and the Eucharist. He also records the fact that at least some Christians received Communion daily.

"When he says that whoever eats of this bread shall live forever, he makes clear that those who partake of his body and receive the Eucharist, by the right of that Communion, are living. On the other hand, we must fear and pray for anyone withheld from Communion and separated from Christ's body, lest they should remain at distance from salvation. He himself threatens: 'Unless you eat the flesh of the Son of man and drink his blood you have no life in you.' (Jn. 6:53) So we ask that our bread—that is, Christ—may be given to us daily, that we who abide and live in Christ may not depart from his sanctification and body."

On the Lord's Prayer, 18 Cited in *Aquilina, The Mass of the Early Christians*, 168.

St. Cyprian is also another early witness to the common understanding of the Eucharist as a participation in Christ's sacrificial death on the cross.

"Because we make mention of his passion in all sacrifices (for the Lord's passion is the sacrifice we offer), we ought to do nothing else but what he did. For Scripture says, 'For as often as you eat this bread and drink this cup, you proclaim the Lord's death until he comes' 1 Cor 11:26. As often, therefore, as we offer the cup in commemoration of the Lord and of his passion, let us do what we know the Lord did."

Letter to Cecilius. Cited in *Aquilina, The Mass of the Early Christians*, 179.

At the height of the persecutions some communities were substituting water for wine at their early morning Eucharistic celebrations lest the smell of wine on their breath in the morning give them away as Christians. St. Cyprian was aghast. Manifesting both his concern for fidelity to the tradition and courage in the face of persecution he wrote: "How can we shed our blood for Christ, who blush to drink the blood of Christ?" St. Cyprian himself was beheaded just over a year later on September 14, **258**. The persecutions abruptly stopped in 259 when Valerian was killed in a battle with the Persians.

Cited in Paul Bradshaw and Maxwell E. Johnson, *The Eucharistic Liturgies: Their Evolution and Interpretation* (Liturgical Press, 2012), 35.

St. Anthony of Egypt. *Piero di Cosimo. c. 1489.*

♔ The Emperor Valerian was succeeded by his son, **Gallienus**, who had a benign view of Christians. Shortly after taking the imperial throne in **260** he issued a **decree of toleration** and ordered the restoration of all confiscated church property. These actions resulted in the de facto recognition of the Church. The succession of Gallienus to the imperial throne initiated a forty year period during which Christians were free to practice their faith and even to build churches.

Baus, *History of the Church Vol. I From the Apostolic Community to Constantine*, 226-228.

During this time of toleration, about the year 269, **St. Anthony of Egypt** (c.251-356) renounced his possessions and began living a strict ascetical life. Sixteen years later he went into the desert to live the life of a hermit. As his reputation for holiness grew, others followed him into the desert and he organized them under a proscribed rule of life. Thus St. Anthony is considered the father of Christian monasticism.

The Oxford Dictionary of the Christian Church.

Eusebius of Caesarea (c. 260-c.340), the "father of Church History," describing the years of toleration wrote:

"Before the persecution of my day, the message given through Christ to the world of reverence to God was accorded honor and freedom by all men, Greeks and non-Greeks alike. Rulers granted our people favors and even permitted them to govern provinces, while freeing them from the agonizing issue of [pagan] sacrifice. In the imperial palaces, emperors allowed members of their own households—wives, children, and servants—to practice the faith openly...All governors honored the church leaders, mass meetings gathered in every city and congregations worshiped in new, spacious churches that replaced the old. This all progressed day by day, the divine hand protecting its people from jealousy or plot so long as they were worthy. But greater freedom brought with it arrogance and sloth."

Eusebius attributed the persecution that followed to the "divine judgment" upon the Church which was rent with factionalism while "unspeakable hypocrisy and pretense reached their evil limit."

Eusebius, *The Church History VIII*, 1 translation and commentary by Paul L. Maier (Kregel Publications, 2007).

 Between 280 and 290 **St. Gregory the Illuminator,** a convert to Christianity who had been living in exile, returned to his native Armenia and converted the Armenian ruler, King Tiridates III. The aristocracy followed suit and soon the populace as well. **Armenia** can rightly claim to be the first Christian state. Local tradition claims that the Apostles Bartholomew and Thaddaeus had brought the Gospel to Armenia and there had been Christian missionaries there before this time. However, it was only with the coming of St. Gregory that the continuous history of Christianity in Armenia began. St. Gregory became the first bishop, titled "Catholicos," of Armenia and was succeeded in office by his son, Aristaces. The latter would attend the first ecumenical council at Nicaea.

Danielou and Marrou, *The Christian Centuries Vol. One The First Six Hundred Years,* 283-284. N. M. Setian, *"The Catholic Church in Armenia," New Catholic Encyclopedia.*

Emperor Diocletian.

 An army general, **Diocletian,** became the emperor of Rome in 284. In an effort to restore imperial power he tried to organize the empire along military lines. Diocletian divided the empire into eastern and western halves and created the tetrarchy, or rule of four. Under this system the burden of leadership would be shared and imperial succession would be systematized. Accordingly, there would be an "Augustus" in both East and West. They would each have a "Caesar" as an assistant and heir apparent. Diocletian also greatly expanded the imperial bureaucracy and sought to double the size of the army. To accomplish the latter, more barbarians were incorporated into the army. To finance these initiatives Diocletian increased taxes. Diocletian also attempted to further divinize the office of the emperor along Persian lines by demanding that he be addressed as "lord and god."

 It was under Diocletian that **the great persecution** of the Church began. Diocletian's persecution had an intellectual defender, the philosopher **Porphyry** (c.232-305). As a young man Porphyry had listened to the catechesis of Origen in Alexandria but remained unconvinced by the Christian claim. Later he went to Rome where he was a protégé of the Platonic scholar, Plotinus. Although a defender of traditional pagan devotions to the gods as part of the Roman civic cult, Porphyry, like many of the elite at this time was a monotheist. Along with Diocletian, Porphyry believed that Christians were undermining the unity of the empire. Porphyry acknowledged the wisdom of some of Christ's teaching but held that teaching that Jesus was fully divine was an affront to the one, true God. With erudition and scholarship Porphyry attacked the credibility of the Gospels and the consistency of the Bible in general. Because of his stature as a philosopher, Porphyry's attacks could not be ignored and several early Church Fathers, including Eusebius, Jerome and Augustine responded to his criticisms of Christianity in their works. That

they deemed it necessary to do so and recorded his arguments in their own writings is the only reason Porphyry's writings survive. In 448 the Emperor Theodosius II ordered that Porphyry's writings against Christianity be destroyed.

Baus, *History of the Church Vol. I From the Apostolic Community to Constantine*, 389-396. Wilken, *The Christians as the Romans Saw Them*, 126-163.

♔ The systematic persecution of the Church by Diocletian stunned its first victims. For years Diocletian had tolerated Christians and they were found at all levels of the imperial government. There was even a church within eyesight of his palace. Evidently Diocletian believed that having strengthened the empire's borders, and reformed the government and the economy, the one last task of insuring Roman greatness was to restore conformity to the ancient religion. Diocletian believed that Christianity was divisive and that Christians could not be counted on to serve the empire. It is estimated that, at the time of the persecution, Christians constituted almost 10% of the empire's population.

Stark, *The Triumph of Christianity*, 144-150, 157.

♔ The persecution began in **300** when Diocletian ordered that all soldiers were required to offer sacrifices to the gods. Christians who refused to do so were purged from the military. In 303 Diocletian's deputy and successor, Galerius, launched an all out assault on Christians in order to restore traditional pagan religion. The son of a priestess, Galerius was ruthless in his campaign. Churches were destroyed, scriptures burned and Christians purged from government posts. Other edicts followed requiring that all priests and deacons be executed if they would not make sacrifices to the gods. Christians in the imperial government who refused to make sacrifices were tortured and then burned alive or drowned.

St. Marcelnus. *Chevalier Artaud de Montor. Illustration from The Lives and Times of the Popes. 1842.*

♔ In 304 an edict was issued which required all Christians to offer sacrifices. Eusebius, who lived through this last persecution, remarked, "how could one number the host of martyrs in each province...?" The only provinces of the empire that did not witness violent persecutions of Christians were Gaul (France) and Britain. That is because they were under the leadership of Constantius, the "caesar" in the West, who was favorably disposed toward Christians. Where he ruled, Christian buildings were destroyed but the Christians themselves were not attacked. In 305, Diocletian retired and was succeeded by his deputy Galerius, who became emperor in the East. Meanwhile Constantius became emperor in the West. Constantius died a year later and was succeeded by his twenty-six year old son, Constantine. Under Galerius the persecution of Christians continued in the East. While it is impossible to know just how many

Christians were martyred during the last and worst Roman persecution of the Church, based on contemporary reports their number must have been in the thousands.

Baus, *History of the Church Vol. I From the Apostolic Community to Constantine*, 396-404.

Pope St. Marcellinus (296-304) is the first bishop of Rome for whom there is an extant inscription referring to him as "papa" or pope. Pope Marcellinus is also a controversial figure as some early sources, particularly Donatist ones, assert that he lapsed during the great persecution. St. Augustine, among others, denied this charge. There are also accounts that allege that he did indeed lapse but then repented of his apostasy and was martyred.

Baus, in *History of the Church Vol. I From the Apostolic Community to Constantine*, 401. Walsh, *Lives of the Popes*, 34. Duffy, *Saints and Sinners: A History of the Popes*, 16.

Even in a time of persecution, church order remained a concern among its leaders. At the **Council of Elvira,** ca. 305 in Spain, the assembled bishops approved eighty-one canons regulating the moral behavior of Christian clergy and laity. It also established boundaries for interactions with pagans, heretics and Jews. The penalty for each infraction was to be barred from receiving Holy Communion for various lengths of time and sometimes for life. Included among these decrees is the oldest known church legislation mandating continence within marriage for bishops, priests and deacons. "We declare that all bishops, priests and deacons in the service of the ministry are entirely forbidden to have conjugal relations with their wives and to beget children; should anyone do so, let him be excluded from the honor of the clergy." As the bishops did not regard it as necessary to explain the reasons for the decree, especially considering the severity of punishment for infractions, it is likely that they were not introducing a new clerical discipline but rather maintaining an existing one.

Roman Cholij, *"Priestly Celibacy in Patristics and in the history of the Church,"* www.vatican.va/roman_curia/nongregations/clergy/documents.

SUMMARY OF CHAPTER TWO

Authority

By the year 200 a defined system of authority in the Church had developed based on a hierarchy of bishops, priests and deacons. Additionally, the Canon of Scripture was largely agreed upon although it would not be officially defined until the fourth century. In the middle of the third century, Pope Stephen, invoking Matthew 16, asserted his primatial authority over other bishops specifically as the successor to St. Peter. The Church of Rome was honored by Christians elsewhere because it was the place of the martyrdom of Peter and Paul and the capital of the empire. The fact that Roman Christians supported other churches materially added to its prestige. The second and third centuries saw the emergence of Antioch, Alexandria and Jerusalem as patriarchates honored regional authorities.

Doctrine

During the second and third centuries, the Church had to ward off various Gnostic heresies which promoted dualistic theologies. Because they maintained that the material world is evil, they con-tended that Jesus Christ was not a true man. Instead, the Son of God only appeared to have a body. The greatest threat to orthodox Christianity in this period came from Marcionism which arose in the second half of the second century. This heresy posited the existence of both a good and an evil god. It rejected the Old Testament books and accepted only the letters of Paul and an edited version of Luke's Gospel. The success of this heretical movement prompted the Church to begin defining the canon of Scripture by deciding which written works were in fact divinely inspired. Also during this period, baptismal creeds were formalized as statements of orthodox Christian faith. One of these creeds would serve as the basis of the Nicene Creed approved by the whole Church in 325.

Pastoral Practice

The Sacrament of Baptism as conversion from sin and initiation into the Church became more formalized. Baptism was observed with great solemnity at the Easter Vigil. The celebration of the Eucharist in houses and later in church settings occurred weekly and in some places daily. Presided over by bishops and priests and assisted by deacons, the liturgy attained its enduring structure centered around the liturgy of the Word and the liturgy of the Eucharist. Eucharistic prayers were composed and the rituals were formalized. Participants were taught that they were sharing in Christ's sacrifice and that Holy Communion was truly His Body and Blood. Communicants received under both forms and the Eucharist was taken to the sick in their homes. Men were consecrated as bishops, priests and deacons through the imposition of hands during the celebration of the Mass. While there are no extant marriage rituals from this period, the faithful were urged to have their marriages blessed by a bishop.

Saints

St. Justin Martyr was a pagan philosopher in the second century who embraced the Gospel and became a noted apologist for Christianity. St. Irenaeus was the bishop of Lyons (France) and the first great Catholic theologian. Irenaeus wrote against the errors of the Gnostics. In doing so he reaffirmed the humanity of Christ and stressed the importance of the Apostolic succession of bishops and the Canon of Scripture. St. Cyprian of Carthage was another important leader and defender of the faith during this period.

Evangelization

The collapse of faith in the pagan gods created a spiritual void. Most pagans regarded Christianity as just another cult in a time of religious pluralism. However, some were attracted to the new and hope-filled message of the Gospel and the Christian way of life. The refusal of Christians to participate in the rites of civil religion was regarded by many with suspicion. For this reason, Christians were often blamed for natural disasters and social unrest.

State

Christianity remained illegal throughout this period. However, when active persecution of Christians did occur it was usually on a local level. The exceptions to this were the periods of persecution which occurred in the years 250 to 251, 257 to 259 and from 300 to 312. These persecutions, initiated by emperors, were intended to strengthen the empire by purifying it from the "impiety" of the "godless" Christians. This goal would be accomplished by destroying the Church. Thousands of Christians were martyred during these persecutions.

St. Perpetua and Felicity.

The day of their victory shone forth, and they proceeded from the prison into the amphitheatre, as if to an assembly, joyous and of brilliant countenances; if prechance shrinking, it was with joy, and not with fear. Perpetua followed with placid look, and with step and gait as a matron of Christ, beloved of God; casting down the luster of her eyes from the gaze of all. Moreover, Felicity, rejoicing that she had safely brought forth, so that she might fight with the wild beasts; from the blood and from the midwife to the gladiator, to wash after childbirth with a second baptism...O most brave and blessed martyrs! O truly called and chosen unto the glory of our Lord Jesus Christ! whom whoever magnifies, and honours, and adores, assuredly ought to read these examples for the edification of the Church, not less than the ancient ones, so that new virtues also may testify that one and the same Holy Spirit is always operating even until now, and God the Father Omnipotent, and His Son Jesus Christ our Lord, whose is the glory and infinite power for ever and ever. Amen.

From the "Passion of the Holy Martyrs Perpetua and Felicity" Roberts-Donaldson English translation. www.EarlyChristianWritings.com

CHAPTER THREE

"THE CITY OF GOD AND THE CITY OF MAN "
CHURCH AND EMPIRE C. 312-511

"We see then that the two cities were created by two kinds of love: the earthly city was created by self-love reaching the point of contempt for God, the Heavenly City by the love of God carried as far as contempt of self. In fact, the earthly city glories in itself, the Heavenly City glories in the Lord." - St. Augustine, The City of God (XIV, 28)

After being proclaimed emperor by his troops in York, England in **306, Constantine (c.280-337)** spent the next few years campaigning against other imperial contenders. His great victory came in **312** at the Milvian Bridge outside of Rome when he defeated his rival in the West, Maxentius. Eusebius, in his biography of Constantine, recorded that before the battle the emperor received a vision of the Christian Chi-Rho symbol, XP, and heard the words "In this sign, conquer." So he had the symbol painted on the shields of his soldiers and did indeed conquer. The following year, Constantine and the emperor of the East, Licinius, met in Milan and agreed on a policy of religious toleration. This policy was implemented through a decree, the so-called **"Edict of Milan" of 313**, which granted "to Christians and all others the freedom to follow whatever form of worship they pleased, so that all the divine and heavenly powers that exist might be favorable to us and all those living under our authority." Licinius would later turn on the Church so Christians in the East did not experience a final respite from persecution until Constantine deposed Licinius in 324. Finally, after nearly three centuries of on again off again persecution, the Church was at peace with the Roman Empire.

Eusebius, *The Church History X,* 5.
Peter J. Leithart, *Defending Constantine: The Twilight of an Empire and the Dawn of Christendom,* (IVP Academic, 2010), 73-74. Cameron, *The Later Roman Empire,* AD 284-430, 50-56. Brown, *The World of Late Antiquity,* AD 150-750, 87-89.

Constantine's conversion has been dismissed by some historians. They assert that the reports of his vision at the Milvian Bridge are based on legends and that his support of Christianity was politically motivated. However, while the story of Constantine's vision may have been embellished, the evidence suggests he had some sort of religious experience before the battle. Indicative of this is the fact that it was no small thing for Constantine to change the emblems on his battle standards. Such symbols were quasi-religious objects for ancient warriors. Additionally, while there may have been nine million Christians living in the empire at the time

Emperor Constantine.

of Constantine's conversion, they made up no more than fifteen percent of the population, and they were a persecuted minority. Supporting Christianity hardly improved Constantine's popularity with the pagan majority. It is true that Constantine's understanding of Christianity was most probably rudimentary. He could also be just as violent as his pagan predecessors. For example, in 326 he had his son, Crispus, and second wife, Fausta, executed for allegedly having an affair. Still, Constantine's words and actions display a genuine sense of loyalty to the God of the Christians whom he saw as the god of his victory.

Leithart, *Defending Constantine*, 79-86. Vasiliev, *History of the Byzantine Empire Volume One* (University of Wisconsin Press, 1952 & 1980), 45-50. Stark, *Cities of God: The Real Story of How Christianity Became an Urban Movement and Conquered Rome*, 68.

 While Constantine was bringing political unity to the West in **312**, a serious religious division was occurring in North Africa.

The **Donatist Schism** began in the province of Numidia, which is part of modern day Algeria. Taking its name from one of its leaders, Donatus, the Donatists maintained that a local bishop who had handed over sacred books to imperial authorities during the last persecution, a "traditor," could no longer be considered a true bishop. By refusing martyrdom, a traditor lost his sacred character and could not confer the sacraments. Therefore, they considered his ordination of Caecilian as Bishop of Carthage in 311 invalid. Subsequently, the Donatist faction consecrated their own bishop. When neighboring bishops refused to recognize this action, the Donatists appealed to Constantine. That they would do so was out of character as they regarded imperial power itself as evil.

This was the first time that a Roman emperor became involved in an ecclesiastical conflict and it set a precedent for future imperial interventions in Church affairs. Constantine instructed Pope Miltiades to convene a synod of bishops to settle this dispute. This synod in Rome in 313 ruled against the Donatists. However, Donatus and his followers refused to accept the ruling. Seeking religious unity, Constantine then called for a synod himself.

 The **314 Synod of Arles** was a council of bishops held in southeastern France. Convened by Constantine to deal with the Donatist heresy, it foreshadowed the Emperor's role at the Council of Nicaea. Despite its rulings, the Donatist faction continued to reject Caecilian as Bishop of Carthage. A third synod on the matter reached the same conclusion. But still the Donatists resisted. Constantine then issued an edict in 317 ordering the arrest of Donatist leaders and the closure of their churches. This led to a revolt against imperial authority. A violent group of Donatists known as Circumcellions terrorized local Catholics, particularly the clergy. Constantine was forced to back down and in 321 effectively recognized the Donatists as a le-

gitimate body. The Donatists, who considered themselves the true "elect," had become a parallel church in parts of North Africa with their own clergy and churches. In some places they outnumbered orthodox believers. Christians in the western regions of North Africa continued to be divided into Catholic and Donatist camps for the rest of the fourth century.

Baus, *History of the Church Vol. II The Imperial Church from Constantine to the Middle Ages*, 136-146. Danielou and Marrou, *The Christian Centuries Vol. One The First Six Hundred Years*, 243-246.

The Synod of Arles also concerned itself with issues of clerical discipline. The synod decreed that clerics who loaned money at interest would be "excluded from fellowship," that is, excommunicated. There were two decrees aimed at preventing clergy from moving from place to place without official permission. Wandering clergy would remain a perennial problem for the Church as they evaded discipline and often preyed on unsuspecting congregations. The Synod of Arles issued two decrees on the relationship of priests and deacons. Deacons were admonished to "not presume too much for themselves, but reserve honor for the presbyters, so that they do nothing of importance without the presbyter's knowledge."

Roman Cholij, *"Priestly Celibacy in Patristics and in the history of the Church,"* www.vatican.va/roman_curia/congregations/clergy/documents.

Constantine not only legalized Christianity, he favored it by inscribing its morality into the laws of the empire, building churches, and enhancing the social position of its clergy. In 321 he declared Sunday, the "Lord's Day," a legal day of rest. Execution by crucifixion ended and the practice of killing unwanted children through exposure to elements was outlawed. Constantine revised marriage and family laws so that they were more equitable to women. Bishops were entrusted with judicial functions and supported in their work of founding hospitals and orphanages. Under Constantine's patronage great churches were built such as St. Peter's in Rome and the church of the Holy Sepulcher in Jerusalem. Before his death Constantine requested baptism and accounts of the event record his sincere repentance and devotion.

Leithart, *Defending Constantine*, 299-300. Brown, *The Rise of Western Christendom: Triumph and Diversity, A.D. 200-1000* Second edition. (Blackwell Publishing, 2003), 60-64. Vasiliev, *History of the Byzantine Empire*, 52-54.

The church that Constantine built in Rome over the tomb of St. Peter utilized the traditional architecture of Roman civic buildings. The construction of **"Old St. Peter's,"** which measured approximately 400 by 200 feet, took over twenty years. Completed in the 340s, St. Peter's was built in the traditional style of a Roman basilica. A basilica was a long rectangular building which had a curved "apse" at one or possibly both ends. Basilicas served as meeting halls for civic functions. St. Peter's also had short transepts which gave it a cruciform shape. St. Peter's was unusual among early churches in that the apse with the altar was on the western end of the building. The apse was usually erected on the eastern side of the building to accommodate the Christian tradition of praying and offering the Mass facing east in honor of the risen Son of God.

Foley, *From Age to Age: How Christians Have Celebrated the Eucharist*, 84-86. Pelkers, *Liturgy: The Illustrated History*, 44-47.

 **St. Pachomius (c.290-346)** was an Egyptian monk who founded the first monastery where the monks lived a communal (cenobitic) life. Pachomius believed that by their daily interactions

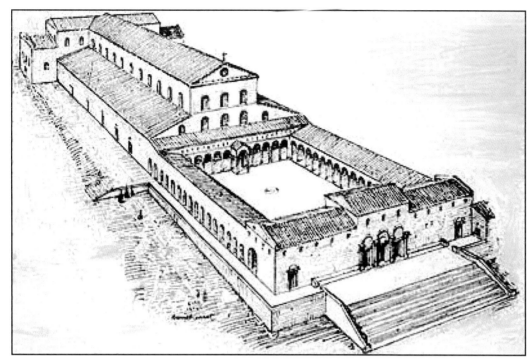

Old St. Peter's Church.

the monks both challenged and inspired each other to grow in virtue. By the time of his death Pachomius was overseeing eleven monasteries, including two for women. The "rule" he wrote for his monks established the role of the abbot as head of the monastery and outlined the supreme importance of obedience in monastic life. Pachomius' Rule would later influence monastic leaders like St. Basil and St. Benedict.
Jordan Aumann, O.P., *Christian Spirituality in the Catholic Tradition*, (Ignatius Press, 1985), 40-42.

Around **318** a theological controversy broke out in Alexandria. A priest there named Arius began teaching that although Jesus Christ was the greatest of all God's creations, he was a creature nonetheless and therefore not equal to God. Arianism sought to preserve strict monotheism by asserting that the Son did not always exist and is subordinate to the Father. When confronted by his bishop, Arius refused to recant his opinions and was eventually excommunicated by a synod of Egyptian bishops. He then sought and gained episcopal allies in Palestine.

In a letter circulated in **319** about this growing Arian heresy Bishop Alexander of Alexandria referred to the Blessed Virgin Mary as **"Theotokus."** Theotokus means the "God-bearer," or more precisely, "the one who gave birth to the one who is God." This is the earliest documented use of this title for Mary. However, it was probably already in use in popular devotion. Bishop Alexander's successor, St. Athanasius would also employ the term in his writings against Arianism.
Jaroslav Pelikan, *Mary Through the Centuries: Her Place in the History of Culture*, 55-61.

After taking control of the eastern provinces of the empire in **324**, Constantine became aware of the division that Arianism was causing in the Church. He sent his ecclesiastical advisor, Bishop **Hosius of Cordova** (256-358), to Alexandria to reconcile Arius with his bishop, Alexander. When this effort failed, Arius' teaching was

The Council of Nicea. *Pvasiliadis. 1590.*

condemned again at a synod in Egypt and at another synod in Antioch presided over by Hosius. However, Arius and his allies persisted in their dissent. So Hosius advised Constantine that a general council of the Church should be called to resolve the issue.

V. C. De Clercq, *"Arianism," New Catholic Encyclopedia,* Second edition, 2003.

 The first ecumenical council, a synod to which all the bishops of the Church were called to attend, was held at **Nicaea** in **325**. According to Eusebius of Caesarea, the Council, as well as local synods, used the procedures of the Roman Senate. The emperor was present but did not vote. Bishop Hosius presided over the council and only bishops voted. A place of honor was given to two priests representing Pope Sylvester. Besides these priests, only a handful of bishops from the West were among the approximately three hundred bishops present for the Council.

V. C. De Clercq, *"Arianism," New Catholic Encyclopedia,* Second edition, 2003. F. Dvornik/EDS. *"Councils, General History of," New Catholic Encyclopedia.* Leithart, *Defending Constantine,* 147-153.

 Arianism had wide support in the eastern half of the empire. However, following the leadership of St. Athanasius, who attended the council as a deacon, all but two of the approximately three hundred bishops present supported the traditional teaching that Jesus Christ is indeed divine, being "consubstantial," that is, of one substance with the Father. The council endorsed a baptismal creed that had long been in use in Palestine and declared it the basic creed of the universal Church. This Creed, known as the **Nicene Creed,** was later elaborated by the Council of Constantinople. It presents Christianity's core beliefs regarding the nature of the Holy Trinity, the Church and resurrection from the dead.

The Council of Nicaea also passed several canons which related to church order. The decrees of the council were confirmed by Constantine as binding on all Christians in the empire. He also issued a decree banning gatherings by heretics and confiscating their buildings. Setting a precedent that would be followed in future doctrinal controversies, books deemed heretical were banned. However, even though they had endorsed the decrees of Nicaea, after the council there were some bishops who continued to support Arianism. Perhaps influenced by the wide support for Arianism in the East, Constantine himself seems to have softened his stance towards the heresy.

The Oxford Dictionary of the Christian Church. Hogan, *Dissent From the Creed,* 79-88. V. C. De Clercq, *"Arianism,"* New Catholic Encyclopedia.

 In the same year that the council was held at Nicaea, Constantine began to construct his new capital in the East at Byzantium. Strategically located on an almost impregnable site between the Black and Mediterranean Seas, the new city was also at the center of important trade routes between Asia and Europe. Formerly dedicated in 330, the "City of Constantine" bore his name. Constantine's establishment of his new capital of **Constantinople** in the center of Hellenistic culture also facilitated the preservation of Greek language, philosophy and art.

Vasiliev, *History of the Byzantine Empire,* 58-60. Judith Herrin, *The Formation of Christendom,* (Princeton University Press, 1987), 24-25.

St. Athanasius.

 **Eusebius of Caesarea** (260-340) is regarded as the "Father of Church History." He was an eyewitness to the persecution under Diocletian and had been imprisoned himself. Eusebius became the bishop of Caesarea in Palestine in 315 and in this capacity he participated in several important church councils including Nicaea. His **Ecclesiastical History** recounts the history of the Church from Pentecost until its legalization under Constantine. Eusebius' history preserves the content of many important documents that are no longer extant. The same is true of his Life of Constantine. In his biography of Constantine, Eusebius asserted that the emperor was directly chosen by God and thus his regent in the world. Acceptance of the sacred status

of the emperor and his primacy in all matters had a tremendous influence on the relations of church and state in the East for as long as the Byzantine Empire endured.

Pope Benedict XVI, *"Eusebius of Caesarea,"* The Fathers. Cameron, *The Later Roman Empire,* AD 284-430, 50-56. Jaroslav Pelikan, *Jesus Through the Centuries: His Place in the History of Culture,* 54-55.

 **St. Athanasius (c. 296-371)** was the bishop of the important see of Alexandria for almost fifty years during the tumultuous fourth century. As a young deacon at the Council of Nicaea, Athanasius was a spokesman for the orthodox cause and his unyielding assertion of the full divinity of Christ earned him the enmity of the Arian faction. With the support of various emperors, Athanasius'

enemies succeeded in having him driven from his see five times and he spent a total of seventeen years in exile. During these years he spent much of his time in Rome. Although he was from the Greek-speaking East, Athanasius was honored in the West as the defender of the faith against the Arian heresy.

Athanasius' most important theological work is *De Incarnatione* and in it is found a well-known statement that sums up his theology. The Word of God "was made man so that we might be made God; and he manifested himself through a body so that we might receive the idea of the unseen Father and he endured the insolence of men that we might inherit immortality." (54,3). Based on the core message of the Gospel, the central point of Athanasius' theology is that in Jesus Christ, the Son of God, God has made himself accessible to the faithful.

Some modern commentators on Arianism suggest that it wasn't really a heresy at all but just another form of Christianity. However, Christianity is specifically about Jesus Christ, so having a correct understanding of who He is as God and man is essential. Unlike twenty-first century relativists, both Arius and St. Athanasius understood this.

A close friend of the founder of monasticism, **St. Anthony of the Desert**, Athanasius contributed to the spread of the monastic ideal through his biography of the saint which he wrote while in exile. The Life of Anthony was popular into the Middle Ages and introduced the new literary form

known as hagiography, which were idealized lives of the saints.

Charles Kannengiesser, *"The Spiritual Message of the Great Fathers,"* in *Christian Spirituality: Origins to the Twelfth Century*, Bernard McGinn, John Meyendorff and Jean Leclercq eds. (Crossroad, 1985) 63-67. *The Oxford Dictionary of the Christian Church*. Pope Benedict XVI, *"St. Athanasius,"* The Fathers.

Sometimes referred to as "the Athanasius of the West," **St. Hilary of Poitiers** (c. 310-367) was one of the most notable defenders of the divinity of Jesus Christ against the incorrect teaching of the Arian heretics. According to his own autobiographical account, Hilary was not raised as a Christian. He came to faith in Christ as the result of an intellectual quest. Baptized at age thirty-five, married and a father, Hilary was elected bishop of his native city around 355. A few years later, Hilary's opposition to the Arian faction then dominating the Church led to his forced exile in Asia Minor at the insistence of the emperor Constantius. During his five years in exile Hilary wrote his most important theological work, "On the Trinity." This defense of the Trinitarian creed is founded on the baptismal formula left to the Church by Jesus Christ himself. St. Hilary was declared a Doctor of the Church in 1851. His feast day is January 13th.

Charles Kannengiesser, *"The Spiritual Message of the Great Fathers,"* in *Christian Spirituality: Origins to the Twelfth Century*, 77-79. *The Oxford Dictionary of the Christian Church*. Pope Benedict XVI, *"St. Hilary,"* The Fathers.

St. Hilary is recognized as one of the earliest composers of hymns in the West. His hymn writing was motivated at least in part by the desire to counter Arius and the Gnostics who promoted their heretical views with simple hymns.

Paul Westermeyer, *Te Deum: The Church and Music* (Augsburg Fortress Press, 1998), 66, 84, 101.

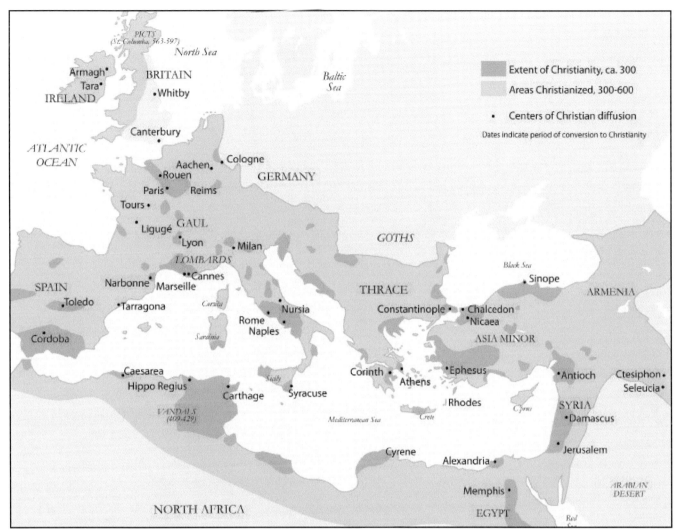

Map of the Spread of Christianity.

Following the legalization of Christianity and strengthened by the emperor's patronage, the Church grew rapidly during the fourth century. This can be seen in the increased number of bishops. For example, the number of bishops in northern Italy increased from five to about fifty in this period. The number of bishops in Gaul (France) increased from twenty-two to seventy. Similar growth was seen in Spain, Britain and in the Roman towns in the Germanic lands. Although Christians in the Greek-speaking eastern half of the empire had always been more numerous than those in the West, even there the Church continued to gain new adherents. The final end of persecution in the East brought the willing embrace of Christianity by the majority of the population. Although Constantine practiced toleration towards paganism, his sons enacted laws restricting its practice. Pagan sacrifices were banned in 341 and all temples were ordered to be closed in 356. In this atmosphere some Christians took it upon themselves to destroy pagan temples.

Stark, *Triumph of Christianity*, 178-180.

At the beginning of the fourth century **Egypt** had one of the largest Christian populations in the empire. Under St. Athanasius, bishop of Alex-

83

andria, a determined effort was made to evangelize the peasants who remained largely pagan. Additionally, missionaries were sent into southern Egypt.

Constantine's erection of numerous shrines in the **Holy Land** and the subsequent arrival of pilgrims did much to facilitate evangelization efforts in Palestine. By the late fourth century Jerusalem was largely a Christian city with numerous churches, monasteries and hospices for pilgrims. Caesarea and other Roman towns also were majority Christian. However, Judaism still prevailed among the rural residents of Palestine.

In **Arabia** the Roman provincial capital was at Bostra, which currently is the city of Bosra, located on the border between Syria and Jordan. An episcopal see had been established there some time before Constantine. Between 325 and 451, the number of bishoprics in this area increased from five to eighteen. In southern Arabia, which was outside the empire, Christian monks established communities at Zafar, Yemen and on the Persian Gulf in the late fourth century. A Christian community was also established at Negran in Arabia around the year 500. However, this Christian community was destroyed in 523 by the Jewish Sabean king, Masruq.

The province of **Syria**, which included modern day Lebanon, was one of the first areas to experience evangelization as recounted in the New Testament. Following the legalization of Christianity, the Church grew rapidly and achieved majority status both in rural areas and the capital of **Antioch** by the beginning of the fifth century. Around the year 390, St. John Chrysostum reported that there were 100,000 Christians in Antioch. The church in Syria also sent missionaries into the Persian Empire and as far as India and China.

Baus, *History of the Church Vol. II The Imperial Church from Constantine to the Middle Ages,* 184-187.

When the persecution of Christians ended and they no longer had to hide their faith, it was evident that the majority of the Greek and Hellenized population of **Asia Minor** (Turkey) were already Christians. The evangelization of the peasantry proceeded rapidly during the fourth century. The church in the region of **Cappadocia**, which is in the center of modern Turkey, sent many missionaries to surrounding regions and had an important role in the establishment of the church in Armenia.

Even before Constantine was proclaimed emperor in the West in 306, Christians were quite numerous in the cities and towns of southern Greece. However, paganism remained strong into the fifth century. After toleration was granted, missionaries from Greece proceeded north into Macedonia and evangelized the Gothic tribes along the Danube.

Baus, *History of the Church Vol. II The Imperial Church from Constantine to the Middle Ages,* 181-217.

At the time of Constantine's victory, there were bishops in the towns of Trier, Cologne, Mainz and Augsburg serving the Romanized German peoples.

H. Tuchle, *"The Catholic Church in Germany," New Catholic Encyclopedia*

Emperor Constantine and Helena.

By the year **350 Christians constituted a majority of the population** in the empire. It is estimated that there were more than thirty million Christians at that time, which was about 53% of the population. Undoubtedly, many of them were only nominally followers of Christ. On the other hand, while paganism was receding, it continued to have its adherents and some of them continued to be appointed to prominent imperial offices.

Stark, *The Triumph of Christianity*, 156-157, 184-198.

Christianity was also practiced beyond the borders of the Roman Empire. Lying between the Roman and Persian Empires, Armenia was often caught in the long running war between them. However, as mentioned in the previous chapter, Christianity had become the state religion there by the year three hundred and remained strong.

Christians in **Persia** struggled to persevere in the face of government persecution. The reigning Sassanid Dynasty sought to maintain religious uniformity by imposing the national religion, Mazdaism, on everyone. The fate of Persian Christians became even more precarious when the Roman Empire adopted Christianity as its official religion, as they were suspected of being enemy collaborators. In 344 a major persecution of Christians began with the beheading of five bishops and a hundred priests. The persecution lasted for several decades and it is estimated that sixteen thousand Christians living within the Persian Empire were martyred.

Danielou and Marrou, *The Christian Centuries Vol. One The First Six Hundred Years*, 282-283. Stark, *The Triumph of Christianity*, 180-181. Philip Jenkins, *The Lost History of Christianity: The Thousand Year Golden Age of the Church in the Middle East, Africa, and Asia and How it Died* (New York, 2008) 57.

The conversion of **Georgia** in the Caucasus Mountains took place in the middle of the fourth century and is unique in that the catalyst was a woman whom the tradition calls "St. Nino." Brought to Georgia as a slave, St. Nino succeeded in converting first the queen and then the king of Georgia. The latter then sent word to the Emperor Constantine requesting clergy to be sent to organize the Church in his country.

Around the year 350 St. Athanasius sent Syrian monks to evangelize the "Kingdom of Axum" (**Ethiopia**). He also consecrated St. Frumentius to be the first bishop of **Ethiopia**. Frumentius succeeded in converting the king and the evangelization effort continued. The church in Ethiopia remained firmly united to the church in Egypt.

Baus, *History of the Church Vol. II The Imperial Church from Constantine to the Middle Ages*, 181-184. F.X. Murphy, *"Ethiopia," New Catholic Encyclopedia*.

During the fourth century the vellum or parchment codex replaced scrolls as the most common form of producing written works. This revolutionary development was a great boon for Christianity as now not only Bibles but also liturgical books and theological tracts could be more easily reproduced and disseminated in various languages. The translation of the Bible from Hebrew, Greek and Latin to the other languages greatly facilitated evangelization efforts.

Brown, *The Rise of Western Christendom: Triumph and Diversity*, A.D. 200-1000 Second edition, 23. *"Book"* Britannica Online Encyclopedia.

The growth of Christianity affected every aspect of the Church including the liturgy. By way of analogy, before official toleration the celebration of the liturgy could have been likened to a simple hymn of praise to the Triune God, which often could only be sung quietly by small groups. With toleration and state support the liturgical celebration became like a symphony with many players and greater complexity. Unfortunately, unintended consequences of these developments included the loss of the intimacy enjoyed by small groups and the diminishment of total communal involvement in the rites.

St. Cyril of Jerusalem

On a very basic level, increased numbers and the freedom to worship publicly meant that Christians no longer worshiped secretly. House chapels were replaced by churches, some of which were former temples. As with St. Peter's, the traditional Roman public building style, the basilica, was adapted for liturgical use. Larger numbers and larger spaces encouraged grander rituals within the Mass. Accouterments and actions, such as vestments, incense and processions, which would have been difficult if not impossible to accommodate in house chapels during the era of persecution, could now be included in the liturgy to give it greater solemnity.

Bradshaw and Johnson, *The Eucharistic Liturgies: Their Evolution and Interpretation*, 61-62. Foley, *From Age to Age; How Christians Have Celebrated the Eucharist*, 102-103.

Separate buildings for performing baptisms, "baptistries," were erected. Often they were octagons, their eight sides representing the "eighth day" which was one day more than the "perfect" number seven. In the center of the baptistry was a pool for full immersion of the recipients.

Candidates continued the practice of removing their clothes before entering the pool and being robed in the white garments of their new life afterwards. Because they would be disrobing, the baptistries often had separate changing rooms for men and women.

Pecklers, *Liturgy: The Illustrated History*, 33.

Constantine himself is credited with donating numerous silver patens for use at the Lateran Basilica in Rome. Large chalices made with precious stones and metals also came into use. Additionally, there is evidence that what would later be called "tabernacles" began to be used at this time to contain the consecrated bread of the liturgy.

Foley, *From Age to Age; How Christians Have Celebrated the Eucharist*, 116-119 and 125-128.

The theological controversies of the fourth century necessitated that the liturgical prayers be standardized and that they clearly express the orthodox faith. Thus, improvised prayers gave way to written ones which were gradually compiled into books. Additionally, there were changes in the prayers that were used which reflected developments in the theological understanding of the Mass itself. In the first three centuries of the Church descriptions of the liturgy tended to describe it as an act of thanksgiving. The Church Fathers wanted to be clear that the Christian liturgy was completely different from the rituals of pagans and Jews which involved material sacrifices. Fourth century writers were less concerned about making this distinction and wrote of Christ's sacrificial death being made present through the liturgy. Also, the miraculous nature of the real presence of Christ in the Eucharistic elements, through the work of the Holy Spirit, received greater elucidation by various Church Fathers including Cyril of Jerusalem, Ambrose and Augustine.

Foley, *From Age to Age; How Christians Have Celebrated the Eucharist*, 120-123. Bradshaw and Johnson, *The Eucharistic Liturgies: Their Evolution and Interpretation*, 129-132.

Belief in the power of the liturgy as a form of intercessory prayer also grew stronger. St. Cyril of Jerusalem wrote that prayers of intercession are offered following the consecration "for we believe that it will benefit immensely the souls for whom we pray when the holy and awe-inspiring Victim lies before us." In the first centuries there was no hard and fast rule as to whether the priest faced the people or whether they all faced east. However, as the sacrificial nature of the liturgy was increasingly emphasized the "ad orientum," facing the east, arrangement became almost universal. The "ordinary" parts of the Mass like the "Kyrie" and "Sanctus" were now standard. Furthermore, the fourth century saw the introduction of hymns into the liturgy to accompany the already mostly chanted readings and prayers.

Josef Jungmann, S.J., *The Mass: An Historical, Theological and Pastoral Survey*, 44-63. Foley, *From Age to Age; How Christians Have Celebrated the Eucharist*, 96-100, 111-112.

Many of the new adherents to Christianity lacked the knowledge and fervor of their predecessors who had literally risked their lives to be Christians during times of persecution. To form these new believers, liturgical prayers sought to impress upon the assembly the solemnity of the Mass and catechesis emphasized the humility with which the Eucharist was to be received.

"Therefore when you approach, do not come with arms extended or with fingers spread, but making the left [hand] a throne for the right, as if it is about to welcome a king; and cupping the palm, receive Christ's body, responding 'Amen.'"

St. Cyril of Jerusalem, Mystagogical Cathechesis, 5:21 cited in Bradshaw and Johnson, *The Eucharistic Liturgies: Their Evolution and Interpretation*, 65.

Fourth century preachers emphasized the necessity for the proper moral and spiritual disposition required for the reception of Christ's Body and Blood. However, rather than reforming their lives, some Christians either abstained from receiving Communion or absented themselves from the Mass altogether. For those not receiving Communion it was easy to lose a sense of their own role in the Eucharistic celebration. This phenomenon raises the question as to just how well these Christians were formed in the first place.

Bradshaw and Johnson, *The Eucharistic Liturgies: Their Evolution and Interpretation*, 66-68.

By the end of the fourth century Sunday was the regular day for the principal celebration of the Mass. The Eucharist was also celebrated on other days of the week and even daily in some places. The frequency varied in different parts of the empire.

Bradshaw and Johnson, *The Eucharistic Liturgies: Their Evolution and Interpretation*, 68-69.

The yearly **liturgical calendar** was greatly enhanced during the course of the fourth century. Easter remained the most important feast and its importance was accentuated with the addition of the forty day season of Lent which preceded it. Begun as a period of penance for adults coming into the Church, Lent became a penitential season of renewal for everyone. The celebration of Easter was extended for fifty days concluding with the celebration of the Ascension on the fortieth day and Pentecost on the fiftieth day.

The first record of the celebration of Christ's birth on December 25 dates from the year 336 in Rome. It is likely that the feast of the birth of the Son was fixed in December to supplant a pagan feast in honor of the sun-god. The celebration of **Christmas** was soon adopted by Christians in eastern regions while the feast of the **Epiphany**, which began in the East, was taken up in the West. The four week preparatory season of **Advent** was added to the calendar in the middle of the fifth century. In addition to these observances, feasts in honor of the Apostles and well-known martyrs were also added to the general liturgical calendar. Additionally, there were local feast days that were eventually adopted by the universal Church. For example, the feast of the Purification of Mary which began in Jerusalem around 350 gradually spread to the whole Church.

As in modern times, the size of the congregations that crowded the churches on feast days underlined the fact that many Christians were not coming to Mass on ordinary Sundays, a dereliction which was condemned by preachers of the day.

Foley, *From Age to Age; How Christians Have Celebrated the Eucharist*, 96-100. L. E. Boyle/Eds., "Liturgical Calendar," I: Catholic, *A New Catholic Encyclopedia* Second edition, 2003. Baus, *History of the Church Vol. II The Imperial Church from Constantine to the Middle Ages*, 302-305, 311. Johnson, *The Rites of Christian Initiation: Their Evolution and Interpretation*, 201-218.

During the course of the fourth and fifth centuries the **roles of the clergy** within the Church evolved. Bishops, who alone could ordain other bishops as well as presbyters (priests) and deacons, became increasingly involved in the affairs of the universal Church through synods and councils. Bishops were the leaders of local churches with the deacons serving as their close collaborators. In addition to their liturgical functions, deacons were much involved in the administration of church property. They were also involved in the selection of candidates for ordination and at times they represented their bishops.

As the Church grew and bishops took on more responsibilities for the larger church, elders or presbyters were ordained to serve in parishes as delegates of the bishop. In this capacity presbyters administered baptism, celebrated the Eucharist and preached. In the East some bishops even delegated to presbyters the authority to administer confirmation. The earliest evidence for the use of the term "priest" as applied to presbyters comes from funeral memorials in Asia Minor around the year 360. The practice spread rapidly and "priest" largely supplanted the use of "presbyter" within fifty years. Gradually, as the number of priests leading local congregations increased, the leadership role of deacons in the Church was diminished. While there were changes in the roles of bishops, priests and deacons, the Catholic Church, unlike some heretical groups, only admitted men to Holy Orders.

Baus, *History of the Church Vol. II The Imperial Church from Constantine to the Middle Ages*, 269-271.

Nichols, *Holy Order: Apostolic Priesthood from the New Testament to the Second Vatican Council*, 47-52.

Early Germanic Warriors.

During the fourth century the criteria for admission into Holy Orders were more formally defined by the Church. The Council of Nicaea declared among other things that men who have castrated themselves cannot be clerics. Nor should newly baptized "heathens" be admitted to Holy Orders. Later guidelines set minimum ages for admission to the three major orders: for deacons it was twenty-five and for priests thirty years of age. It was recommended that bishops be at least forty-five. But the fourth century guidelines were very flexible. For example both St. Hilary (315-367) and St. Ambrose (340-397) were ordained bishops before the age of thirty-five. By way of comparison, under the 1983 Code of Canon Law, candidates for ordination to the priesthood must be at least twenty-five and bishops must be thirty-five. Married men who are ordained permanent deacons must also be at least thirty-five.

Candidates for Holy Orders were also subject to a probationary period to evaluate the strength of their faith and moral life. Numerous authors of the period stressed the importance of clerics receiving proper pastoral and theological training. A few theological schools existed in the major cities of the empire which served the educated elite. However, most of those training to enter clerical life were apprenticed in scripture studies, the liturgy and pastoral practice by their local clergy. Knowledge of scripture was considered the most important aspect of clerical training. Familiarity with Church doctrine and adherence to it were other expectations, especially for bishops.

Baus, *History of the Church Vol. II The Imperial Church from Constantine to the Middle Ages*, 273-277.

Not long after the Council of Nicaea the bishops who supported **Arianism** sought to undermine the Council's teachings on the consubstantiality of the Father and the Son by securing the deposition of the bishops who supported the orthodox position. Using their access to Constantine, they reported to him that bishops such as St. Athanasius were to blame for the continued unrest in the eastern empire. They asserted that Athanasius and other bishops were provoking discontent by their tyrannical treatment of their theological opponents. Athanasius was also accused of treason by his enemies among the episcopate. It is unclear whether Constantine believed these charges against Athanasius or whether he just used them as an excuse to get rid of the controversial bishop of Alexandria. In any case, in 335 Constantine banished Athanasius to Trier in Germany on the northern boundaries of the empire. This was the first of five banishments Athanasius endured because of his fidelity to orthodox teaching. With Athanasius out of the way, the Arian faction was now dominant in the East and they successfully had other orthodox bishops banished. They almost succeeded in having Arius reinstated as a priest by Constantine himself. Only the death of Arius prevented this from happening.

Baus, *History of the Church Vol. II The Imperial Church from Constantine to the Middle Ages*, 29-33.

 Just prior to **his death in 337, Constantine** was baptized by a bishop known for his Arian leanings. Following Constantine's directives his three sons, Constantine II, Constantius II and Constans divided the empire among themselves. Even though they had been raised as Christians, they soon entered into bloody struggles with each other which resembled the dynastic conflicts of their pagan predecessors. Eventually Constantius II, whose designated portion of the empire was the East, was the sole survivor.

Constantius II favored the Arian faction in the Church and was persuaded by them that Athanasius was the instigator of conflict. When he could not persuade Pope Liberius to condemn Athanasius he had the pope exiled to Thrace in 355 and installed "Felix II" in his place. However, the moral standing of Liberius was such that the emperor was not satisfied with his exile. The emperor needed his acquiescence. Pressure continued to be exerted against Liberius, and after two years of exile he gave in to the emperor's demand and condemned Athanasius. Pope Liberius was then allowed to return to Rome to serve jointly with Felix. The people rallied to Liberius and Felix was largely ignored until his death in 365. Following the death of Constantius II, Pope Liberius attempted to rehabilitate his reputation for orthodoxy. However, his contemporaries could not overlook his vacillation and he was the first pope not regarded as a saint. Liberius was also the first pope of many who would be persecuted by a Christian emperor.

Baus, *History of the Church Vol. II The Imperial Church from Constantine to the Middle Ages*, 39-50, 248-250. Duffy, *Saints and Sinners*, 24-25. *Walsh, Lives of the Popes*, 37-38.

The Cappadocian Fathers.

In **361** Constantius II died in battle attempting to quell a rebellion led by his cousin, Julian. His death left Julian, the great nephew of Constantine the Great, as the sole claimant to the imperial throne. As a young man, Julian had secretly renounced Christianity for the mystery cults of paganism. Known to history as "Julian the Apostate," the thirty year old emperor tried to revive pagan practice in the empire and viciously attacked Christianity in his writings. In an attempt to undermine the prophecies of Jesus found in the Gospels, he invited the Jews to rebuild the Temple in Jerusalem. Julian also tried to provoke conflict in the Church by reinstating unorthodox bishops who had been deposed. There is even evidence that Julian planned to launch a persecution of the Church. Hoping to raise his popularity, Julian began a war against the Persians but his death in battle in 363 snuffed out his effort to restore paganism.
Wilken, *The Christians as the Romans Saw Them*, 164-196. Vasiliev, *History of the Byzantine Empire*, 68-78.
Baus, *History of the Church Vol. II The Imperial Church from Constantine to the Middle Ages*, 50-59.

Following Julian's brief reign, the contest between orthodoxy and Arianism in the Church resumed. Valentinian, who reigned as emperor in the West from **364 to 375**, gave nominal support to the orthodox Nicene party. His brother Valens, emperor in the East from **364-378**, was a strong supporter of the Arian faction.

In the early fourth century **Goths** living along the Danube in an area stretching from modern day Hungary to the Ukraine began to be harassed by raiding Huns. To escape these attacks, in **376** the Goths requested that they be allowed to live within the boundaries of the Roman Empire in exchange for providing military service.

These Germanic peoples were evangelized by Ulphilas, the "Apostle to the Goths" (c.311-383). Ordained a bishop in Constantinople in 341 by one of the leading Arians, Ulphilas translated the Bible into the Gothic language. He was largely responsible for the Goths loyalty to Arianism for the next few centuries.
Christopher Dawson, *The Making of Europe: An Introduction to the History of European Unity* (New York, 1932), 81-87. Herrin, *The Formation of Christendom*, 25-26, 31-32.

The adherence to Arianism by the barbarian peoples coming into the empire was an important way they distinguished themselves from the Latinized, Catholic peoples they were conquering. By upholding Arianism the Germanic kings signaled

91

their independence from imperial control. It was perhaps this aspect of Arianism more than anything else that retained the allegiance of the Visigoths, Ostrogoths, Vandals, Lombards and Burgundians.

H. Tuchle, *"The Catholic Church in Germany," New Catholic Encyclopedia.*

 In **378**, oppressed by famine and exploitation at the hands of the Romans, the Goths rose up against the imperial government. They defeated and killed the eastern emperor, Valens, at the battle of Adrianople. Upon the death of Valens the orthodox teaching of the Council of Nicaea received its strongest imperial ally when **Theodosius**, a Roman general from Spain and a Catholic, came to rule in Constantinople.

Daileader, *The Early Middle Ages,* 27-28. Baus, *History of the Church Vol. II The Imperial Church from Constantine to the Middle Ages,* 61-67.

St. Macrina the Younger.

The **Cappadocian Fathers** are named for the province of Asia Minor where they lived. They were **St. Basil the Great** (c. 330-379), his brother, **St. Gregory of Nyssa** (c. 335-395) and their friend, **St. Gregory of Nazianzus** (329-389). After St. Athanasius, they were the chief spokesmen for the orthodox position against the Arians. In addition to holding fast to the doctrines on the full divinity of Jesus Christ and the Holy Spirit, each of these three made their own contribution to the life of the Church. St. Basil, besides being eloquent and a great organizer, was known for his personal holiness. He wrote a rule for monks which became the basis of monasticism in the East. In Basil's vision, monasteries were to serve the larger Christian community. Basil was also greatly interested in the liturgy and promoted frequent, even daily communion. St.

Gregory, bishop of Nyssa, was renowned as a powerful preacher and his sermons often included admonitions to help the poor. His spiritual writings include works on Christian perfection through the imitation of Christ and on consecrated virginity. St. Gregory, bishop of Nazianzus, like his friend Basil, embraced the monastic life and only reluctantly agreed to be ordained a priest and later a bishop. St. Gregory is remembered particularly for his doctrinal writings on the Holy Spirit.

The Oxford Dictionary of the Christian Church. Pope Benedict XVI, The Fathers. Aumann, *Christian Spirituality in the Catholic Tradition,* 44-50.

In writing about consecrated virginity Gregory used as an example his older sister, **St. Macrina** (c.327-379). Named after her grandmother, who was a revered Christian woman herself, "Macrina the Younger," had formed a religious community of women. For this she is sometimes referred to as the "Mother of Eastern Monasticism." She had a strong influence on her younger brothers. It was Macrina who inspired Basil to leave a secular career and enter the priesthood. And her brother, Gregory of Nyssa, credited Macrina with helping him with his own theological ideas. Gregory wrote a moving account of his sister in his "Life of Marcina" shortly after her death. St. Macrina was credited with performing several miracles in her own lifetime. Her feast day is July 19th.

Charles Kannengiesser, *"The Spiritual Message of the Great Fathers, in Christian Spirituality: Origins to the Twelfth Century,"* 67-74. *The Oxford Dictionary of the Christian Church.*

As the fourth century progressed, more and more bishops in Egypt, Italy and eastern Europe were practicing **celibacy**. They had either never married or had left their wives prior to their consecration. Many priests and deacons, on the other hand, were married men. However, there was a growing consensus in the Latin West that they were obliged to abstain from sexual relations after ordination. This belief was codified in a decretal Pope Siricius sent to other bishops in 386. The sending of decretals was an assertion of papal primacy over the whole Church. This particular decretal informed bishops in other provinces that a council in Rome of eighty bishops ruled that married men admitted to the clerical state must practice absolute continence.

Citing 1 Corinthians 7:5, where St. Paul tells married couples "do not refuse one another except per-haps by agreement for a season, that you may devote yourselves to prayer," Pope Siricius asserted priests were to be men of prayer so the Apostle's admonition was binding on them at all times. By about the year 400 the ideal of absolute continence by bishops, priests and deacons, including married ones, was virtually universal. While the requirement for continence was based partly on Old Testament notions of cultic purity, there were other reasons offered as well.

First and foremost, the priests were called to imitate Christ who was celibate. Further, they were to exercise a spiritual fatherhood over their flock and were called to model the virtues of chastity and virginity which they preached. Additionally, the Church Fathers considered it an inappropriate mingling of the things of earth and the things of heaven for a priest to go from the marriage bed to the altar of the Lord. Regional councils held in Carthage (390 & 419), Turin (398), Orange (441) and Tours (461) followed Popes Damasus, Siricius, Innocent I and Leo the Great in calling for complete continence among bishops, priests and deacons. Concurrently, the practice of requiring vows of continence for married clergy before ordination was implemented.

Christian Cochini, S.J., *The Apostolic Origins of Priestly Celibacy,* 11-12, 247-254. Duffy, Duffy, *Saints and Sinners: A History of the Popes,* 31. P. Delahaye, *"Celibacy,"* The New Catholic Encyclopedia Second edition, 2003.

In addition to the major orders of bishop, priest and deacon, the fourth century saw the emergence of what became known as the "minor orders." These included subdeacon, acolyte, exorcist, porter and lector. While men admitted to these orders were considered clerics they were not ordained through an essential rite – the sacramental laying on of hands.

The Oxford Dictionary of the Christian Church. Nichols, *Holy Order: Apostolic Priesthood from the New Testament to the Second Vatican Council,* 53-54. Baus, *History of the Church Vol. II The Imperial Church from Constantine to the Middle Ages,* 272-273.

Pope Damasus.

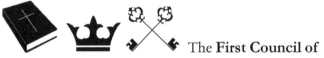 The **First Council of Constantinople** was convened in **381** by the eastern Emperor Theodosius with the support of his counterpart in the West, Gratian. Its purpose was to end the conflict over Arianism which had racked the Church in the East for sixty years. Although no western bishops or delegates from the pope participated in the council, its decisions were eventually accepted as ecumenical; that is, as applying to the whole Church. At the council, the creed of Nicaea, with the addition of a statement on the full divinity of the Holy Spirit, was reaffirmed and Arianism was condemned. The decrees of the council were promulgated by Theodosius in July 381 at the bishops' request. At the same time he decreed that all churches in the empire must be under the authority of bishops who upheld the orthodox Trinitarian formula of the equality of Father, Son and Holy Spirit. Still, even after the Council of Constantinople, Arianism continued to be a problem in some regions. A number of barbarian tribes had been converted by Arian missionaries and they held fast to this form of Christianity for some time. This council also declared that Constantinople was second only to the see of Rome in importance. However, this assertion was not accepted by the papacy.

Baus, *History of the Church Vol. II The Imperial Church from Constantine to the Middle Ages*, 59-61.
Cameron, *The Later Roman Empire, AD 284-430*, 69-71.

The following year, at the Synod of Rome in **382, Pope Damasus** declared that the pope's primacy was based on his status as the successor to St. Peter. The same synod approved as official the seventy-three books which comprise **the canon of Scripture**. About this time Damasus commissioned St. Jerome to provide a new Latin translation of the Bible. Jerome's translation became known as the Vulgate version. It was also during the pontificate of Damasus that Latin became the principal language used in the liturgy in Rome as so few there understood Greek.

M. R.P. McGuire, *"Pope St. Damasus,"* New Catholic Encyclopedia.
Pecklers, *Liturgy: The Illustrated History*, 27.

In **383** the imperial court in the West withdrew from the increasingly vulnerable northern town of Trier to Milan. Not since the time of Constantine had an emperor lived in Rome for an extended period. The city was dominated by the senate whose members remained largely pagan.

Herrin, *The Formation of Christendom*, 31-32.

Around the year 384 a woman named "Egeria" completed her three year pilgrimage from her home in Gaul (or perhaps Spain) to Egypt, Palestine, Syria, Asia Minor and Constantinople. Her account of her journey, commonly known as "The Pilgrim-

St. Cyril of Jerusalem.

age of Egeria," which she wrote in Latin, provides a wealth of information about geography, travel conditions and the religious communities which hosted her. About half of the book is a detailed description of liturgical practices in Jerusalem including Lenten practices, Holy Week liturgies and the rites of initiation. Egeria was the first Christian woman to author a book-length text in Latin. Her written Latin is of great interest to philologists for what it discloses about the evolution of Latin into the Romance languages of French, Italian and Spanish. Lost for centuries, Egeria's book was "found" in 1884 in the library of a convent in Tuscany.

George E. Gingras, *"Itinerarium of Egeria," New Catholic Encyclopedia.* Pecklers, *Liturgy: The Illustrated History,* 51-52.

 **St. Cyril of Jerusalem (c.315-386)** became the bishop there in 349. Like Athanasius, Cyril suffered banishment from his see because of his adherence to the orthodox position regarding the true divinity of Christ. Shortly after becoming bishop of Jerusalem, St. Cyril wrote a series of twenty-four sermons addressed to candidates for the Easter sacraments. Cyril's writings shed light on liturgical and sacramental practices in Jerusalem in the fourth century. In these sermons Cyril emphasized the importance of baptism and the real presence of Christ in the Eucharist.

The Oxford Dictionary of the Christian Church. Pope Benedict XVI, St. Cyril of Jerusalem, The Fathers.

In Cyril's catechesis on the liturgy we have another written testimony to the belief in the early Church that the substance of the bread and wine of the Eucharist truly become Christ's body and blood. "Since he himself declared of the bread, 'This is my body,' who shall dare to doubt any longer? And since he himself affirmed, 'This is my blood,' who shall ever hesitate, saying that it is not his blood? ... Even though your senses tell you otherwise, let faith strengthen you. Do not judge the matter from taste, but be fully confident, from steady faith, that the body and blood of Christ have been given to you."

Mystagogical Lecture 4. Cited in *Aquilina, The Mass of the Early Christians,* 225-226.

Manifesting the deepening of theological reflection which followed the legalization of Christianity, in his fifth Mystagogical Catechesis, St. Cyril provides a detailed account of how the liturgy was celebrated in Jerusalem in the middle of the fourth century. St. Cyril was also the first theologian to attribute to the Holy Spirit the change that takes place in the Eucharist when ordinary bread and wine become the body and blood of Christ. "...we call upon the merciful God to send the Holy Spirit upon our offerings so that he may make the bread

Christ's body, and the wine Christ's blood; for clearly whatever the Holy Spirit touches is sanctified and transformed..."

Mystagogical Catechesis c.348, 5.7 Quoted in Foley, *From Age to Age: How Christians Have Celebrated the Eucharist*, 121-122. Aquilina, *The Mass of the Early Christians*, 220-233.

St. Cyril also beautifully defined what it means to say that the Church is "catholic."

"The Church is called catholic or universal because it has spread throughout the entire world, from one end of the earth to the other. Again, it is called catholic because it teaches fully and unfailingly all the doctrines which ought to be brought to men's knowledge, whether concerned with visible or invisible teachings, with the realities of heaven or the things of earth. Another reason for the name catholic is that the Church brings under religious obedience all classes of men, rulers and subjects, learned and unlettered. Finally, it deserves the name catholic because it heals and cures unrestrictedly every type of sin that can be committed in soul or in body, and because it possesses within itself every kind of virtue that can be named, whether exercised in actions or in words or in some kind of spiritual charism."

Catechetical Instruction 18, 23: PG 33, 1043.

St. Martin (316-397) became the bishop of Tours in Gaul (France) in 372. He had been a Roman soldier until he was blessed with a vision of Christ in the appearance of a beggar. After leaving the army he established the first monastery in Gaul in 360. From their monastery Martin and his monks set out to evangelize the rural inhabitants. Known for his holiness in his own time, Martin became one of the most popular saints of the Middle Ages and the patron of France.

The Oxford Dictionary of the Christian Church.

St. Martin of Tours. *Anthony Van Dyck. 1618. Royal Collection, Windsor Castle, London.*

St. Ambrose (c.339-397) was born in the town of Trier on the northern frontier of the Roman Empire. Trained as a lawyer, Ambrose was named a provincial governor in northern Italy at the age of thirty. When the bishop of Milan died in 374 the laity demanded that Ambrose succeed him. Since he was only a catechumen at this time, Ambrose reluctantly agreed to become bishop. He was promptly baptized and ordained. Although well educated, until this time Ambrose had little knowledge of Scripture or theology. He diligently applied himself to the study of both. He is credited with mediating the theology of Origen to the West as well as the Greek father's practice of lectio divina. A great preacher, Ambrose was instrumental in St. Augustine's conversion in 386 and his teachings greatly influenced his protégé.

St. Ambrose wrote on the sacraments and on ethics. He is also credited with bringing to the

St. Jerome. *Paulo Veronese. Saint Jerome in the Wilderness. 1580.*

West teachings regarding the role of the Blessed Virgin Mary that were already well known in the East. In particular, his treatise, "Concerning Virgins" portrayed Mary as the model of Christian discipleship. He also composed a number of hymns.

Emperor Theodosius. *Anthony van Dyck. Saint Ambrose barring Theodosius I from Milan Cathedral. 1619-1620.*

The introduction of hymns in the liturgy caused controversy in the Church. Many Church leaders believed that only the actual words of Scripture in the form of psalms and canticles should be chanted during divine worship. As for musical instruments, there was universal agreement that they should not be used during the liturgy because of their association with pagan worship and the disreputable theater.
Westermeyer, *Te Deum: The Church and Music,* 74-100.

St. Ambrose was firm in his conviction that all members of the Church must live by Christ's teaching and he publicly chastised Emperor Theo-

dosius twice for his sinful actions. Frustrated by Ambrose's fearlessness, the emperor was forced to accept his corrections and to do public penance for having ordered the massacre of men, women and children in Thessalonica in retaliation for the killing of some officers. St. Ambrose's willingness to stand up to the emperor set an example for later bishops and popes. However, they did not all have the same success that Ambrose did.
Charles Kannengiesser, *"The Spiritual Message of the Great Fathers,"* in *Christian Spirituality: Origins to the Twelfth Century,* 79-82. *The Oxford Dictionary of the Christian Church. Pope Benedict XVI* "St. Ambrose," *The Fathers.* Pelikan, *Mary Through the Centuries: Her Place in the History of Culture,* 80.

St. Jerome (c.342-421) was a priest, monk, and biblical scholar. A native of Dalmatia, Jerome was educated at Rome and after a randy youth was baptized in his late twenties. Jerome was one of the great scholars of the early Church. His greatest achievement was his translation of the Bible from their original languages into the Latin "Vulgate" edition. Jerome's great love for the Word of God is captured in his aphorism: "Ignorance of Scripture is ignorance of Christ."

Jerome's translation of the *Rule of Pachomius* into Latin was instrumental in the development of monasticism in the West. Jerome was involved in a number of the controversies of his day and was a fierce defender of orthodoxy against Arianism, Origenism and Pelagianism. Having alienated many with his irascible temper and seeking a more contemplative life, Jerome left Rome and spent his last thirty-five years in a monastery he founded near Bethlehem. In addition to his works on the Bible, Jerome is remembered for his contributions to Mariology and the spirituality of vowed religious life. St. Jerome is one of the four great Latin Fathers of the Church along with Ambrose, Augustine and Gregory the Great.

Aumann, *Christian Spirituality in the Catholic Tradition*, 57-59. Kannengiesser, *"The Spiritual Message of the Great Fathers,"* in *Christian Spirituality: Origins to the Twelfth Century*, 82-84. *The Oxford Dictionary of the Christian Church*. Pope Benedict XVI, *"St. Jerome," The Fathers*. Jaroslav Pelikan, *Mary Through the Centuries: Her Place in the History of Culture*, 116-119.

Emperor **Theodosius**, who reigned from **379 to 395**, sought to complete the work that Constantine started by making Christian-

St. John Chrysostom.

ity the official religion of the empire. He vigorously clamped down on the Arian heresy among citizens of the empire although large numbers of Germanic Arians staffed his armies.

Theodosius also put ever stricter limitations on paganism. During his reign a number of pagan temples were either closed or destroyed. In 392 Theodosius banned every form of pagan worship whether public or private. Concurrently, a rebellion supported by some prominent pagans was launched against the emperor. When the revolt failed paganism was further discredited. Government subsidies to pagan temples and clergy ended. There were also numerous occasions of Christian mobs attacking pagans and their temples. However, paganism persisted particularly in the large cities of the East for another two centuries and known pagans continued to hold high offices in the imperial government. Evidently the emperors declined to actively persecute pagans because they wished to maintain the peace of the empire.

Vasiliev, *History of the Byzantine Empire*, 79-83. Stark, *Cities of God*, 183-208. Cameron, *The Later Roman Empire*, AD 284-430, 73-76.

In the fourth and fifth centuries there were some small scale efforts to evangelize and convert Jews. These met with little success and Christians and Jews competed for converts from among the pagans. Bishops of the time were also concerned about the number of Christians who continued to share in Jewish feasts and to observe the Sabbath. Gradually, imperial laws put greater restrictions on the freedom of Jews to worship and choose professions. There were also instances of Christian fanatics attacking synagogues.

Baus, *History of the Church Vol. II The Imperial Church from Constantine to the Middle Ages*, 221-224.
Brown, *The World of Late Antiquity*, AD 150-750, 104. *Cameron, The Later Roman Empire*, AD 284-430, 76-78.

St. John Chrysostom (c.349-407) was born in Antioch (Turkey) and was educated in philosophy and rhetoric. Baptized at nineteen, he then spent six years as a hermit during which time he studied the Gospels and the Letters of St. Paul. Forced by illness to return to Antioch, John was ordained a deacon in 381 and a priest in 386. John was renowned for his great preaching and close to three hundred of his sermons are still extant. ("Chrysostom" means "golden tongue".)

Among St. John's surviving homilies are eight that he preached in 386 and 387 against Jews. Incensed that some in his congregation were also frequenting synagogues and celebrating Jewish feast days, the "Golden Tongue" unleashed a torrent of vitriol against the Jews and their practices. In point of fact, many of his condemnations were culled from the prophets of the Old Testament and some from Jesus himself.

John and other bishops were especially perturbed that some who entered the Church saw no incompatibility between the Christian faith they professed and practicing the rites of their Jewish and pagan neighbors. Religious syncretism has always been a challenge for the Church and indicates that some of its members have not experienced full conversion to Jesus Christ. That Jews and Christians were still intermingling in Antioch at the end of the fourth century is also a testimony to the enduring bonds of family and friendship in spite of official condemnations of fraternization.

John Chrysostom: "Eight Homilies Against the Jews" [Adversus Judeaus], Patrologia Greaca, Vol 98, 1.
Cohen, *Under Crescent & Cross: The Jews in the Middle Ages*, 19-20.
Paula Fredriksen, *Augustine and the Jews: A Christian Defense of Jews and Judaism* (Doubleday, 2008), 90-102.

John's reputation as a preacher led to his appointment, against his will, as patriarch of Constantinople in **398**. There he set about the reform of the clergy, imperial court and people. Fearless in denouncing vice and challenging the wealthy to help the poor, John alienated many among the elite. Resistance to John's reform efforts, the schemes of his rivals and the hatred of the Empress Eudoxia led to his ruin. Despite the support of the pope and the people of Constantinople, John was banished from his see and worked to death on a forced march. St. John is remembered for sermons, Scripture commentaries, and liturgical reforms. St. John Chrysostom is a doctor of the Church and the patron saint of preachers.

Pope Benedict XVI, *The Fathers*. Charles Kannengiesser, "The Spiritual Message of the Great Fathers," in *Christian Spirituality: Origins to the Twelfth Century*, 67-74.

With the Church firmly established in the cities, by the end of the fourth century Christian missionaries were evangelizing rural areas. Some missionaries were monks; others were bishops sent out to establish new Christian centers in regions that heretofore had not heard the Gospel. The missionaries would begin instructions for the locals and then destroy the pagan sanctuaries, replacing them with churches. According to extant sermons from the period, the lay faithful were expected to play an active part in evangelizing potential converts. While the externals of the pagan cults could quickly be replaced, catechizing the people took much longer and elements of the old religion were sometimes kept along with the new practices. Paganism continued for a time to be strong among rural peasants and the established aristocracy of Rome associated with the Senate as well as within intellectual circles. Among these social groups the persistence of paganism was a matter of traditionalism. There was also an elitism that scorned the whole notion of worshiping the carpenter from Nazareth. This would give way as Christianity produced its own intellectual giants.

Danielou and Marrou, *The Christian Centuries Vol. I The First Six Hundred Years*, 291-299. Baus, *History of the Church Vol. II The Imperial Church from Constantine to the Middle Ages*, 181-221. Brown, *The World of Late Antiquity AD 150-750*, 104.

Following the death of Emperor Theodosius in **395** he was succeeded by his two young sons. Arcadius, age seventeen, ruled in the East (395-408) and Honorius, age eleven, ruled in the West (395-423). Unfortunately, they and the emperors who followed them, whether in Rome or Constantinople, were distinguished only by their incompetence. The imperial bureaucracy in the East could compensate for the intelligence and spine that the eastern emperors of this period lacked. However, this did not happen in the West as, in the midst of the decline, the elites that could have provided leadership looked more and more to their own interests while imperial institutions grew steadily weaker. Without strong leadership, the western empire was increasingly under pressure both from within and from without by various Germanic tribes.

Vasiliev, *History of the Byzantine Empire*, 90-98. Kenneth W. Harl, *The World of Byzantium Transcript Book* (The Great Courses, 2001), 117-119.

Because it was easier to defend, the city of **Ravenna** on the Adriatic coast became the home of the imperial court in the West in **402** and remained so until the fall of the western empire in 476. As resources were expended on enhancing Ravenna, the city of Rome went into decline losing population as well as prestige. Increasingly the popes filled the leadership vacuum in the ancient capital and its environs.

In the winter **406-407** the Rhine River froze and large numbers of barbarians were able to cross over into the empire. They overran Gaul (France) and rampaged their way into Spain and North Africa.

Concurrently, in the East, Alaric, a Visigothic ruler was plundering the Balkans. Eventually he entered Italy. Alaric was just one of the many barbarian leaders who had formerly served in the Roman army. His attack on Italy came after the authorities in the East refused him a leading role in the government there. So, with their apparent blessing, he fought his way west. **Alaric sacked the city of Rome in 410** after the imperial court in the West refused his demands for official recognition.

Philip Daileader, *The Early Middle Ages Course Guidebook* (The Teaching Company, 2004), 27-29.

St. Augustine.

St. Monica. *Benozzo Gozzoli. c. 1464. Aspidale Chapel, St. Augostino, San Girigrano, Italy.*

♛ Although Alaric's sacking of Rome was comparatively restrained and there was not a lot of death and destruction, it was a terrible blow to general morale. Some pagans attributed the fall of Rome to the empire's abandonment of traditional religion in favor of the God of the Christians. It was to counter this accusation that St. Augustine wrote his great philosophical and theological treatise on history, the *City of God.*

Harl, *The World of Byzantium.* 120-21. Herrin, *The Formation of Christendom,* 25-27.

♛ Alaric died soon after sacking Rome and the Visigothic tribes he had led eventually settled in southern France and accepted the nominal rule of the emperor. Most of these tribes practiced the Arian form of Christianity. There were also some pagan tribes that settled within the empire at this time, most importantly the Franks who entered northeast-

ern Gaul.

The mounting incursions of barbarians into the empire led to the withdrawal of all imperial forces from northwest Gaul. Roman troops left Britain by **410**. The Roman society there was left to its fate at the hands of Germanic invaders, the Angles and Saxons. Unlike other barbarians, these invaders were pagans and by the end of the century Christianity had been relegated to the remote Celtic areas of the island.

Dawson, *The Making of Europe,* 87-91. Brown, *The Rise of Western Christendom,* 47-48, 86. Harl, *The World of Byzantium,* 117-127.

At the time of the sack of Rome in 413, Innocent I (+417) was the pope. The son of the previous pope, Anastasius I, Innocent had been elected pope in 401 and was known for his abilities and strong moral character. He was also influential in establishing the papacy's primacy over the Church. As pope, "the head and summit of the episcopate," Innocent maintained that he exercised the authority of Peter himself and asserted that all major disputes in the Church must be submitted to papal judgment. He also insisted that all the churches in the West should follow the liturgical rites of Rome and that the conferral of Confirmation was reserved to bishops. Innocent's "Letter to Decentius" contains the earliest magisterial reference to the Sacrament of Anointing of the Sick. A strong supporter of St. John Chrysostum and his struggle against imperial power, Innocent chastised the bishops of Alexandria, Antioch and Constantinople for acquiescing to John's deposition.

Baus, *History of the Church Vol. II The Imperial Church from Constantine to the Middle Ages*, 256-258. Walsh, *Lives of the Popes*, 41. P.T. Camelot, *"Pope St. Innocent I," The New Catholic Encyclopedia*.

St. Augustine (354-430) was born in Thagaste, which is in North Africa (Algeria). He studied rhetoric for the purpose of practicing law. Gifted with tremendous intellectual abilities, Augustine, as he would later confess, was a restless seeker of truth in philosophy and religion. At nineteen Augustine abandoned Christianity for Manichaeanism. He also lived with a mistress for fifteen years and together they had a son. Augustine became disillusioned with Manichaeanism and gave up its practice. Throughout his years of spiritual wandering Augustine was followed by his mother, **St. Monica** (332-387), who never gave up hoping for her son's conversion. After much study, the influence of St. Ambrose, and the prayers of his mother, Augustine was baptized in 387 in Milan. The following year Augustine returned to Thagaste to establish a monastery. Along the way, outside of Rome, Monica died. Later Augustine would write a moving account of her death and a tribute to her influence in bringing him to conversion. Augustine was ordained a priest by popular demand in 391 and a bishop in 395. The following year he became the bishop of Hippo and was soon recognized as the leading voice of orthodox teaching in the West.

Around the year 397 St. Augustine wrote *Confessions*, the world's first autobiography. In it he recounts his spiritual journey to conversion. But the title of his autobiography carries a double meaning. In addition to being the confession of his failings it is also his confession of faith in the Lord. This dual aspect of Augustine's Confessions is beautifully presented in the work's most well-known passage.

"Late have I loved you, beauty so old and so new; late have I loved you. And see, you were within and I was in the external world and sought you there, and in my unlovely state I plunged into those lovely created things which you made. You were with me, and I was not with you. The lovely things kept me far from you, though if they did not have their existence in you, they had no existence at all. You called and cried out loud and shattered my deafness. You were radiant and resplendent, you put to flight my blindness. You were fragrant, and I drew my breath and now pant after you. You touched me, and I am set on fire to attain the peace which is yours."

St. Augustine, *Confessions* translated with an Introduction and notes by Henry Chadwick (Oxford University Press, 1991) chapter xxvii.

St. Augustine was very effective in combating the errors of Donatism and Arianism. His involvement in the doctrinal controversies of the day led him to write on a number of important theological subjects including ecclesiology (the nature of the Church), the sacraments, the Trinity, grace, and relations with the state. Augustine's formulations on these subjects in many instances were subsequently confirmed by the Magisterium and became authoritative for the Church.

Augustine's other best known book is *Concerning the City of God Against the Pagans*. Augustine wrote this book to address the shock that had descended on the empire when Rome was sacked by Alaric in 410. It was Augustine's response to pagan critics who asserted that Christianity was sapping the strength of the empire and making it vulnerable to the barbarians. In the *City of God* Augustine refuted the notion that the empire, or any other "earthly city" can be truly sacred and therefore above reform or immune from chastisement. Indeed, for Augustine the existence of the state was itself a consequence of sin. Without the disobedience of original sin which disrupted all of creation there would be no need for men to rule over other men. St. Augustine's desacralization of government provided a theological basis for the elevation of spiritual authorities over the temporal powers. This understanding would aid the Church in the **West** against the "caesaro-papism" that would later prevail in the eastern half of the empire.

St. Augustine also contributed to shaping a more positive Christian attitude toward **Jews**. For Augustine, the law, the prophets and the people of the Old Testament were all essential to God's revelation of His Son, Jesus Christ. Additionally, Judaism, by spreading through the Mediterranean world before Christianity, facilitated the acceptance of the Gospel when at last the Messiah came. It was also part of the divine plan that the majority of Jews did not accept Jesus as the Christ. Their rejection of Jesus as the Messiah meant that in evangelizing the pagans, Christians could point to the Old Testament prophesies of the Messiah as independent, non-Christian testimonies to the truth of the Gospel. "By the evidence of their own scriptures they bear witness for us that we have not fabricated the prophecies about Christ…."

So, even though the Jews rejected Jesus, they had a special place in God's plan.

St. Augustine, *City of God*, 18, 46. Sermons 200, 201 in *Fathers of the Church, A New Translation* (1958). Fredriksen, *Augustine and the Jews: A Christian Defense of Jews and Judaism*, 290-352. Cohen, *Under Crescent & Cross*, 20-21.

St. Augustine possessed one of the greatest minds the Church has ever known and his influence on western civilization through his theology and other writings cannot be overestimated. St. Augustine died in 430. His feast day is August 28th.

St. Augustine, *Concerning the City of God Against the Pagans, trans.* Henry Bettenson Penguin Books, 1984). XIX, 15. Aumann, *Christian Spirituality in the Catholic Tradition*, 61-67. Kannengiesser, *"The Spiritual Message of the Great Fathers,"* in *Christian Spirituality: Origins to the Twelfth Century*, 84-86. Pope Benedict XVI, *"St. Augustine," The Fathers*. Pelikan, *Mary Through the Centuries: Her Place in the History of Culture*, 80-81.

A meeting of Catholic and **Donatist** bishops took place at Carthage in June **411**. After a century of tension and violence between the two groups, as well as years of effort by Augustine, it was hoped that through an open theological discussion an agreement could be reached to end the schism. St. Augustine argued that making the effectiveness of the sacraments as channels of grace dependent on the moral purity of the minister was to put one's hope in man not God. Instead, he argued that it is the Holy Spirit operating in the Church of Christ which bestows the grace of the sacraments. After days of debate, with the orthodox argument defended by Augustine, the imperial arbiter found in favor of the Catholic position. Six months later, in January 412, Emperor Honorius ordered that the Donatists unite themselves with the Catholic Church or they would be considered heretics.

St. Augustine, who had at first opposed such coercive measures, had by this time a change of heart. After years of witnessing violence on the part of Donatists against Catholics and especially against former Donatists who had returned to the Church, Augustine had reluctantly concluded that the state needed to intervene to force a resolution of the issue. Many of the Donatists complied but many did not. Although they gradually declined in number, their intransigence continued to weaken the Church in North Africa.

Danielou and Marrou, *The Christian Centuries Vol. I The First Six Hundred Years*, 246-248. Baus, *History of the Church Vol. II The Imperial Church from Constantine to the Middle Ages*, 148-161.

  The greatest opponent of the teaching of Pelagius was St. Augustine. It is sometimes erroneously said that Augustine "invented" the concept of "**original sin**." While he was the first to present a full exposition of original sin, Christian belief that the sin of Adam affected the whole human race is based on Scripture. This teaching is found in numerous places in the letters of St. Paul. He states it concisely in his letter to the Romans 5:12, "Therefore sin came into the world through one man and death through sin, and so death spread to all men because all men sinned." This teaching can in turn be traced to the Book of Wisdom 2:23-24 which states: "For God formed man to be imperishable; the image of his own nature he made him. But by the envy of the devil, death entered the world, and they who are in his possession experience it."

 In 411-412 the Council of Carthage condemned the **Pelagian heresy**. The heresy took its name from the British theologian Pelagius. Pelagius taught that man was in full control of his moral destiny and that God's help was limited to external means such as providing the Commandments, the example of Christ, etc. By insisting that we can earn our salvation Pelagius implicitly denied the effects of the sin of Adam on the human race and on our free will. Pelagius was excommunicated in 416 and disappeared from history shortly thereafter. However, the heresy of thinking we can save ourselves has never completely died.

   St. Augustine's argument for the reality of original sin and therefore the importance of infant baptism, worked "backward" from the truth of Jesus Christ. The proclamation of Jesus Christ as Savior makes no sense unless there was something to be saved from. However, the focus was always on Christ. Thus his treatise on the subject was titled **"On the Grace of Christ and Original Sin."** In this work St. Augustine, who is known as the "Doctor of Grace" because of his profound writings on the subject, explicitly stated that the Blessed Virgin Mary was without sin.

"We must except the holy Virgin Mary, concerning whom I wish to raise no question when it touches the subject of sins, out of honor to the Lord; for from Him we know what abundance of grace for overcoming sin in every particular was conferred upon her who had the merit to conceive and bear Him who undoubtedly had no sin."
St. Augustine, *"De Natura et Gratia,"* no 42. NewAdvent.org/

Third Ecumenical Council of Ephesus. *Vasily Surikov. 1876. Russian Museum, St. Petersburg.* Fathers. Pelikan, *Jesus Through the Centuries*, 79-80.

St. Patrick.

 In **428**, Nestorius, a monk from Antioch known for his preaching abilities, was chosen to be bishop of Constantinople by the Emperor Theodosius II. Nestorius soon aroused a controversy by his refusal to call the Blessed Virgin Mary the "Theotokus," the "God-bearer." Like other bishops educated in theology in Antioch, Nestorius was adamant in emphasizing both the humanity and the divinity of Christ. However, in doing so his writings suggested such a separation of Christ's divine and human natures as to imply a duality of persons within the Incarnate Word. Nestorius also used his position as patriarch to persecute those who did not adhere to his views in the matter.

Vasiliev, *History of the Byzantine Empire*, 98-99.

St. Cyril of Alexandria (+444) was probably born in the Egyptian capital around the year 375. He succeeded his uncle as bishop of Alexandria in 412 and over the next thirty-two years he jealously guarded the priority of his see *vis a vis* Constantinople. St. Cyril vigorously defended the propriety of the term "Theotokus." He also asserted that while the union of the divine and human is indescribable it "produced for us one Lord and Christ and Son."

In **427** the Vandal tribes, forced out of Spain by the Visigoths, crossed the sea into North Africa. As he lay dying in 430, St. Augustine heard their attack on his episcopal city of Hippo. By 442 the Vandals had captured much of Roman North Africa. Thus, imperial control in the West had been reduced to the Italian peninsula where it was exercised only tentatively.

Herrin, *The Formation of Christendom*, 33-34. Harl, *The World of Byzantium*, 123. Daileader, *The Early Middle Ages*, 27-29.

 **The Council of Ephesus** held in **431** was the third ecumenical council. It was called by Emperor Theodosius II to settle the controversy raised by "Nestorianism." At the Council the teachings of Nestorius were condemned, he was deposed as bishop of Constantinople and excommunicated. The Council of Ephesus also reaffirmed the Nicene Creed and formally approved the use of "Theotokus" as a title for Mary.

Baus, in *History of the Church Vol. II The Imperial Church from Constantine to the Early Middle Ages,* 93-107. Pope Benedict XVI, *The Fathers. The Oxford Dictionary of the Christian Church.* Hogan, *Dissent From the Creed,* 123-128.

Support for the position of Nestorius continued in the East and led to the formation of a Nestorian church in Persian territory outside the boundaries of imperial control. This church, based in Babylon, eventually spread into India, China and Mongolia.

Jenkins, *The Lost History of Christianity: The Thousand Year Golden Age of the Church in the Middle East, Africa, and Asia,* 57-70, 138-140, 159. Hans-Georg Beck, *History of the Church Vol. II The Imperial Church from Constantine to the Early Middle Ages,* 463-468.

St. Leo the Great. *Francisco Herrera the Younger. 1600.*

About the year **431 St. Patrick** (c. 390-460) began his mission to Ireland. A Christian born in Britain, Patrick was captured by pirates at age sixteen and taken to Ireland where he was enslaved. Six years later he escaped. After being trained and ordained a priest Patrick began his mission to evangelize the Irish. Patrick spent the rest of his life in Ireland and established his episcopal see at Armagh. Near the end of his life Patrick wrote a short autobiography called Confessions. St. Patrick, whose feast day is March 17th, is rightfully called the Apostle to the Irish.

Sometime between 435 and 450, St. Vincent, a monk of the monastery of Lerins in Gaul, wrote a work against heresies which established a formula for evaluating whether teachings were orthodox doctrine or not. According to his formula, which became known as the "Vincentian Canon," orthodox teaching or doctrine is that which has been held everywhere, always and by all. Thus orthodoxy is determined by its universality, antiquity and acceptance. While a useful measure, when rigidly held the Vincentian canon could obscure the fact that Christian doctrine has developed and deepened down through the centuries.

Phillip Cary, *The History of Christian Theology Course Guidebook* (The Teaching Company, 2008), 2. H.G. J. Beck, *St. Vincent of Lerins in the New Catholic Encyclopedia.*

 **Attila the Hun** and his brother, Bleda, succeeded their uncle as ruler of the Huns in **434**. The Huns were a nomadic people who arrived in southeastern Europe in the middle of the fourth century. Skilled horsemen, the Huns were also fierce warriors who terrified the other nomadic tribes and eventually the Romans as well. Beginning in 435 Attila launched a number of attacks on the eastern empire. Imperial forces tried to ward of these attacks but when these efforts failed they negotiated humiliating treaties with Attila which required them to pay him financial tributes. Attila murdered his brother in 445 and his apparent invincibility earned him, from his victims, the title "Scourge of God."

Harl, *The World of Byzantium*, 123-125. E.A. Thompson, *"Attila,"* Britannica Online Encyclopedia.

St. Leo the Great (c.400-461) was elected pope in 440. A deacon prior to his election, Leo had served the two previous popes as an advisor and had been involved in the controversy over Nestorianism. He was also enlisted by the emperor of the West, who was then headquartered in Ravenna, to mediate a political dispute in Gaul. It was while he was on this mission in 440 that Leo was elected pope.

 As with Popes Siricius and Innocent before him, Leo sincerely believed that St. Peter himself spoke and acted through his successors. Thus convinced, Leo asserted that the pope was the supreme ruler, teacher and judge of the Church. The other bishops shared in his authority but the pope was the "primate of all the bishops." During his papacy the Holy See dramatically asserted its supreme and universal authority as evidenced by Leo's involvement in the Council of Chalcedon.

The fourth ecumenical council, the **Council of Chalcedon**, was held in 451. The council was necessitated by developments following the Council of Ephesus which led some theologians, particularly in Egypt, to teach **monophysitism**. Monophysitism is the theory that in the Incarnate Christ there was only one, single divine nature. The council was attended by some 500 bishops. However, apart from two bishops from Africa and two delegates sent by Pope Leo, all the rest were from the East. The Council of Chalcedon reaffirmed the decrees of the previous ecumenical councils. It also accepted as an authoritative statement Pope Leo's "**Tome**", a doctrinal letter he wrote in 449. Leo maintained that Jesus Christ is One Person in whom there are two natures, the Divine and human. These natures are permanently united but each exercise its own particular faculties. Leo's Tome became the standard of Christological orthodoxy. The Council also condemned monophysitism. While the Council accepted his Tome, Leo refused to accept canon 28 of the Council which gave Constantinople second place among patriarchates and authority over local churches. His feast day is November 10.

Baus, *History of the Church Vol. II The Imperial Church from Constantine to the Middle Ages,* 114-121, 264-266. Pope Benedict XIII *"St Leo the Great,"* Church Fathers and Teachers: From Saint Leo the Great to Peter Lombard (Ignatius Press, 2010).

However, monophysitism remained strong in the East particularly in Armenia, Syria, Egypt and Ethiopia. In fact, monophysitism would continue to divide the Church in the East for centuries. There were also monophysite Christians who fled government persecution to Persian-held lands and Ethiopia so that they could operate their churches free from imperial oversight.

Jenkins, *The Lost History of Christianity: The Thousand Year Golden Age of the Church in the Middle East, Africa, and Asia*, 57-59. K. O'Mahoney, *"Ethiopian (Ge-ez) Catholic Church," New Catholic Encyclopedia.*

Meanwhile, following a series of sporadic wars in the East, Attila had turned his attacks to the West and invaded Gaul in 450. There he experienced his first and only defeat at the hands of a combined imperial and Visigoth army. Following this setback, Attila invaded Italy and sacked many cities as his forces drove south.

Like some of his predecessors, St. Leo had to address the issue of the continence of clergy who were married. Writing to a bishop in Thessalonika (Greece) around the year 446, Pope Leo stated the following. "Indeed, if those who do not belong to the Order of clerics are free to enjoy conjugal relations and to beget children, we must, in order to manifest [what is] the purity of perfect continence, not permit carnal relations even to subdeacons." A decade later Leo insisted, in response to a question from the bishop of Narbonne in southern France, that while married men who became clerics must cease having relations, they must not send their wives away as it would be contrary to love. Leo was an adherent to the notion of "cultic purity" for the clergy. However, it is worth noting that the pope believed that non-

clerics "are free to enjoy conjugal relations and to beget children...." In other words, Leo believed that for the laity sexual relations had both a pleasurable as well as a procreative purpose.

Quotation cited in Cochini, *The Apostolic Origins of Priestly Celibacy*, 396-406.

By the time of Leo the Great's pontificate (440-461), Roman civil authority in the western empire was collapsing. Thus, when the barbarians threatened again in **452**, it was left to him to negotiate with Attila the Hun on behalf of the city of Rome. Some credit Leo's negotiations as saving Rome from Attila's attack. Others suggest that the Huns were forced to end their campaign because of famine and plague. Whatever the case, after meeting with Pope Leo, Attila's forces withdrew from Italy. After Attila's death in 453 the Huns quickly declined as a fighting force capable of terrorizing other peoples. Two years later, in 455, Leo had similar successful negotiations with the Vandal leader, King Gaiseric, who also had designs on Rome. After **457** the emperors in Constantinople focused their attention and resources on the eastern empire. As a consequence the pope had become the de facto authority in Italy.

Baus, *History of the Church Vol. II The Imperial Church from Constantine to the Middle Ages*, 264-266. Harl, *The World of Byzantium*, 123-127.

In **476** the barbarian leader Odoacer deposed the **last emperor in the West**, Romulus Augustus, who was the eleven year old son of another barbarian general. While this event marked the "fall" of the empire in the West, contemporaries noticed little change in their lives as Germanic military leaders had been installing and deposing the western emperors for some time. There were nine puppet emperors from 455 until 476 and six of them were killed in office. From this time forward, the emperors in

Constantinople claimed authority over the empire in the West although rarely did they have the power to exercise it. **Odoacer**, with recognition from the Roman Senate and the eastern emperor, ruled as king of Italy from 476-493 while other barbarian leaders ruled over the other western provinces. In 493, with the blessing of the eastern emperor, the Arian king of the Ostrogoths, **Theodoric**, deposed Odoacer. Theodoric then ruled in northern Italy until 526.
Brown, *The Rise of Western Christendom*, 124, 194. Herrin, *The Formation of Christendom*, 19-20, 34-35. Harl, *The World of Byzantium*, 125-126.

The **Acacian Schism** between Rome and Constantinople occurred in **482** as a result of continued agitation in the East over the monophysite heresy. Emperor Zeno had sought to placate the monophysite faction by promoting a theological formula, known as the "henoticon," written by the patriarch of Constantinople, Acacius. This formula made concessions to the monophysites and was rejected by the popes as a deviation from the decrees of the Council of Chalcedon.
The Oxford Dictionary of the Christian Church.

Clovis, King of the Franks. *Francois-Louis Dejuinne. 1835.*

The Gelasian Letter was written by Pope Gelasius to the Emperor Anastasius in **494** in an attempt to end the Acacian Schism. In his letter Pope Gelasius articulated what became known as the theory of the two powers: "There are, most August Emperor, two powers by which this world is chiefly ruled: the sacred authority of bishops and the royal power. Of these the priestly power is much more important, because it has to render account for the kings of men themselves at the judgment seat of God. For you know most gracious son, that although you hold the chief place of dignity over the human race, yet you must submit yourself in faith to those who have charge of divine things, and look to them for the means of your salvation."

Pope Gelasius was asserting the authority of the Church to determine spiritual matters without interference from the imperial power. Gelasius maintained that the Church's authority is superior to royal power. This statement remained the position of all subsequent popes. A document from a synod held the following year by Gelasius has the earliest reference to the pope as the "Vicar of Christ." Pope Gelasius' position notwithstanding, the schism continued until a new emperor, Justin I, compelled the eastern bishops to accept a formula written by Pope Hormisdas which upheld the teaching of Chalcedon.
J. Chapin, *"Pope St. Gelasius" New Catholic Encyclopedia.*

 **Clovis (466-511),** King of the Franks in northen Gaul (France) from 481, was baptized into the Catholic Church in **496** and brought his people with him. After the conversion of Constantine, perhaps the conversion of no other ruler had greater historical importance than that of Clovis. Clovis and his Franks were fierce warriors. After eliminating the last imperial forces in Gaul, they then pushed out the Arian Visogoths. Because he vanquished the Arian tribes, the often brutal Clovis was heralded as a great servant of the Catholic Church. Further, the conversion of the Franks to Catholicism meant that now both the barbarian conquerors and the conquered Gallic-Romans shared the same faith. This facilitated the integration of these peoples. Clovis' rule also marks the beginning of the Merovingian dynasty as rulers of the Franks. This dynasty would last almost two-hundred and fifty years. As the Franks went on to conquer other Germanic peoples, like the Visigoths, Burgundians and Suevi, they were also assimilated into the Catholic Church.

Brown, *The Rise of Western Christendom*, 133-139. H. Thchle, *"The Catholic Church in Germany," New Catholic Encyclopedia.*

Around the year **500** Constantinople's population reached a half-million people. By contrast, with imperial institutions tottering in the west, the population of Rome had fallen below one-hundred thousand.

Brown, *The Rise of Western Christendom*, 57.

SUMMARY OF CHAPTER THREE

Authority

During the course of the fourth and fifth centuries, the **papacy** found it necessary to define its responsibilities in leading the Church against encroachments from imperial powers. Various popes also asserted their prerogatives in leading their fellow bishops, including the patriarch of Constantinople. The most important statements regarding papal primacy were issued by Popes Sircius, Damasus, Innocent I, Leo the Great and Gelasius.

The authority of **bishops** over their local churches also grew in these centuries particularly as they were given both honors and responsibilities from the imperial state. Additionally, their collective authority grew and was exercised through regional synods and the four ecumenical councils which occurred in this time period.

The growth of the Church accentuated the need for local **presbyters** (priests) who acted as delegates of bishops in local parishes, presiding at Mass, preaching and reconciling penitents. The increased importance of priests diminished the role of **deacons**. The diaconate, along with the minor orders that cropped up with the growth of the Church, became simply a step to the priesthood.

Doctrine

There were two major doctrinal controversies in the fourth century. First was the **Donatist Schism** in North Africa where a faction rejected the bishop of Carthage in 311 who had been consecrated by a "traditor," one who surrendered church books, under the persecution of Diocletian. These extreme rigorists held that the Church of the saints must remain holy and that sacraments administered by "traditores" were invalid. Their position made all sacraments dependent on the moral purity of the Church's ministers. They eventually set up their own church. While supposedly suppressed in 412 by imperial decree, the schism persisted, undermining the strength of Christianity in North Africa.

The second major doctrinal controversy of the fourth century was caused by the **Arian heresy**.

Arius taught that the Second Person of the Trinity was created by the Father. According to Arius, although the Son was more than a man, he was not equal to God. The first ecumenical council, the **Council of Nicaea**, was called in **325** in response to the Arian heresy. The Council formulated what became known as the **Nicene Creed** as a statement of orthodox belief. It also condemned Arianism. However, Arianism continued to have influential supporters among many bishops in the East and among some of the emperors. It was not until the Council of Constantinople in 381 that Arianism was finally crushed. In response to another, smaller heretical group, the Council of Constantinople also stated that the Holy Spirit was of the same essence and therefore equal to the Father and the Son.

The Church also faced a number of doctrinal controversies in the fifth century. The first of these was **Pelagianism**, named for its champion, Pelagius, who denied the transmission of Adam's original sin and therefore the fallen nature of the human race. As a consequence, Pelagians also denied the necessity of infant baptism. They believed the human person was in full control of his moral destiny. God's role was simply to provide guidance in the Ten Commandments and in the example of Christ. Pelagianism was vigorously opposed by St. Augustine and condemned at the Council of Carthage in 411.

Other fifth century doctrinal controversies concerned the nature of Jesus Christ. **Nestorianism** taught that there were two separate persons in the Incarnate Christ, one divine and one human as opposed to the orthodox teaching that Christ is a single person, at once both God and man. Therefore, it is improper to speak of Mary as the "**Theotokus**," the God-bearer or "Mother of God." Nestorianism was condemned at the **Council of Ephesus** in 431 which also gave formal approval to the title "Theotokos" for the Blessed Virgin Mary. Despite imperial persecution, Nestorianism remained strong in the eastern half of the empire and was carried all the way to China.

The **Monophysite heresy** said Christ has only one, divine nature instead of two natures, divine and human. This position was condemned at the **Council of Chalcedon in 451**. Like Nestorianism, it endured in those regions in the East where imperial authority was weak or non-existent. An attempt by the eastern emperors to placate the Monophysites led to the Acacian Schism between Rome and Constantinople at the end of the fifth century.

Pastoral Practice

With **religious toleration** and a huge influx of new members, larger public churches were built following the basilica style. Now that the **liturgy** could be celebrated publicly, it was enhanced with grander rituals. Gradually, five main liturgical traditions, developed along linguistic lines, emerged: Romano-African (Rome-North Africa), Gallican (Western Europe), West-Syrian (Antioch), Coptic (Alexandria), and Byzantine (Constantinople).

Easter was the principal holy day, although the date was calculated differently in different parts of the empire. Pentecost was observed and Lent soon developed as a time of preparation for Easter. The feast of the Epiphany began in the East while Christmas was established first in the West to replace a pagan feast in honor of the sun.

Given an honored status in society, the **clergy** gradually dedicated themselves solely to the care of the Church and gave up secular occupations. The increased theological emphasis on the sacrifice of the Mass led to the sacralization of clergy. While many bishops and priests were married, they were expected to abstain from sexual relations once they were ordained. Eventually Pope Siricius (+399) made **celibacy** a requirement for the clergy in the West although it was not universally observed.

Unfortunately, the honors given to the clergy set them apart from the laity. Further, the increasing wealth of the Church led some to seek ordination for material motives. On the other hand, the dilution of fervor that came with the legalization of Christianity led more men and women to embrace asceticism and **monasticism**.

Aided by imperial support, the Church's system of charity, hospitals and orphanages expanded.

Saints

St. Athanasius (+373) was the bishop of Alexandria and a great defender of orthodox teaching on the divinity of Christ against the Arians. Banished from his diocese five times, Athanasius spent seventeen years in exile for upholding orthodox belief. His *Life of St. Anthony* popularized the life and example of the founder of Christian monasticism.

Influenced by the example of his sister, **St. Marcina** (+379), **St. Basil the Great** (+379) was a monk and bishop. He wrote a monastic rule and liturgical prayers that are very influential in the East. He was a great defender of orthodoxy against Arians and stands out as a doctor of the Church for his writings on the Holy Spirit. His brother, **St. Gregory of Nyssa**, and his friend, **St. Gregory Nazianzen**, collaborated in his work.

St Ambrose (+397) was the bishop of Milan who moved to root out Arianism there. He was also a great preacher and baptized St. Augustine. Ambrose was noted for his simplicity of life and accessibility to all his people. He wrote important works on consecrated virginity and the Bible.

St. Augustine (354-430) is a Doctor of the Church. Trained as a teacher of rhetoric, Augustine abandoned Christianity for Manichaeanism as a young man. After much study, and in answer to the prayers of his mother Monica, Augustine was baptized in Milan in 387. When he returned to his home town in North Africa he established a monastic community. Augustine was ordained a priest by popular demand in 391 and bishop of Hippo in 396. St. Augustine possessed one of the greatest minds the Church has ever known, and his influence on western civilization through his theology and other writings, especially *Confessions* and *The City of God*, cannot be overestimated.

St. Monica (332-387), mother of St. Augustine, never gave up hoping for her son's conversion which she witnessed shortly before her death.

Evangelization

The establishment of Christianity as the favored religion of the empire in the fourth century led to many conversions. Prior to the reign of Constantine much of the aristocracy looked down on Christianity as not only contrary to their tradition, but simplistic and barbarian. However, through promotion by Constantine and his successors, Christians began to be numbered in the senate and among the aristocracy.

The Church's strong organization, charitable works and ethical ideals aided its efforts to convert pagans. However, many new converts were only half-hearted about the practice of the faith. Some intrepid missionaries did venture beyond the borders of the empire to evangelize various barbaric tribes. However, many of these missionaries taught Arianism. The conversion of Clovis and the Franks to Catholicism established the foundation of western Christendom. Despite repressive laws, paganism continued to be practiced especially in rural and remote areas of the empire.

State

Constantine began the union of church and state which had both good and bad consequences. Constantine favored Christianity and was very generous to the Church. He granted social privileges to clergy; invested bishops with civil authority; mandated Sunday rest and enforced Christian moral teaching against offenders. He also built churches and donated property to the Church. Additionally, Constantine intervened in Church controversies, most importantly the Donatist schism in Africa in 316 and the Council of Nicaea debate on Arianism in 325.

Constantine's successors continued to favor Christianity. However, they also manipulated the Church in order to advance the interests of the empire. This occurred when some of the emperors favored Arianism and monophysitism. Also troubling, there were violent persecutions of religious dissenters to preserve the unity of the empire.

In 390 St. Ambrose required Theodosius to do public penance in Milan for perpetrating a massacre. This action illustrated the Church's authority over rulers in the moral realm. It also set the foundation of medieval papacy's authority over kings.

In 392 Theodosius made Christianity the official religion of the empire and outlawed paganism.

St. Basil the Great.

Our Lord made a covenant with us through baptism in order to give us eternal life. There is in baptism an image both of death and of life, the water being the symbol of death, the Spirit giving the pledge of life....This then is what it means to be born again of water and the Spirit: we die in the water, and we come to life again through the Spirit...Through the Holy Spirit we are restored to paradise, we ascend to the kingdom of heaven, and are reinstated as adopted sons. Thanks to the Spirit we obtain the right to call God our Father, we become sharers in the grace of Christ, we are called children of light, and we share in everlasting glory.

From *On the Holy Spirit* by St. Basil the Great, Bishop

CHAPTER FOUR

"ORA ET LABORA"
NEW FOUNDATIONS C. 515 TO 750 A.D.

"Hear and heed my son, the master's teaching and bow the ear of your heart. Willingly take to yourself the loving Father's advice and fulfill it in what you do. Thus, by laborious obedience will you return to him, from whom you have withdrawn by idle disobedience. To you my word is now directed, whoever you are, if you renounce self-will and grasp the tough, shining weapons of obedience, in order to serve the true king, Christ the Lord." - The Rule of St. Benedict

Following the deposition of the western emperor in 476, imperial social institutions continued to function in most Roman provinces of the West. In these provinces surprisingly small minorities of barbarians ruled over the Latinized populations of Spain, Italy and Gaul. In these lands the Visigoths, Ostrogoths and the Franks, respectively, gradually developed from loose tribal federations to kingdoms dominated by dynastic families that were strong enough to take on the trappings of royalty. While the rulers were new, daily life went on much as before, just not as efficiently as under Roman rule.

The borderlands of the western empire, where Roman rule had only a shallow foundation, were a different matter. In these lands, particularly Britain, the imperial inheritance was largely effaced.

In the East, the imperial bureaucracy continued to keep the wheels of government turning. The biggest threats to the empire there were continued internal dissension over doctrinal matters and rival external powers, first the Persians and then the Muslims.

Early in the sixth century **Dionysius Exiguus (c. 500-550)**, a monk living in Rome, devised a new calendar of years which centered on the coming of Jesus Christ. History in the Christian world was now divided between the time before the coming of Christ ("B.C.") and the years that followed, "Anno Domini," or "the year of our Lord." The fact that the Son of God had become incarnate as man in this world had made both time and place sacred to Christians. The new calendar system was an affirmation of this understanding of history. Unfortunately, in correlating the previous Roman calendar to the new Christian one, Dionysius miscalculated. This is why it is sometimes written that Jesus was born in 4 B.C. Prior to this timeline most dating was related to the founding of Rome or the years of a particular emperor's rule. This new method of dating was popularized later by the English monk and historian, the Venerable Bede.

Jaroslav Pelikan, *Jesus Through the Centuries: His Place in the* History of Culture, 32-33. Eugen Ewig in *History of the Church Vol. III The Church in the Age of Feudalism*, 600.

 The Christian understanding of the sacred also brought about a change in burial practices. For pagans, cadavers were spiritually contaminating. Thus, under paganism cemeteries were always outside the city and away from where people lived. For Christians, again because of His incarnation, Jesus Christ had made the human body holy, the bodies of the saints especially so. From the earliest times of the Church, the faithful had reverenced the relics of the martyrs and built shrines around them. With religious toleration, these shrines began to be built within cities. Gradually, burial alongside the saints was seen as desirable. First the social elites and then commoners were being buried in church cemeteries near the saints, hoping perhaps for salvation by association.

Chris Wickham, *The Inheritance of Rome: Illuminating the Dark Ages 400-1000*, 55.

St. Benedict (c.500-575) of Nursia was a student in Rome when the depravity of the faded capital prompted him to become a hermit at Subiaco. Italy at that time was enveloped in political and social chaos. For the entire sixth century imperial armies contended with Arian Goths and pagan Lombards for control of the peninsula. At Subiaco Benedict's reputation for holiness soon attracted followers so he established several monasteries. However, local hostility caused him to move to Monte Cassino in 529 where he remained until his death. It was there that he composed the rule of monastic life which bears his name.

The Rule of St. Benedict is meant to form monks into the image of Christ by helping them to live out the Beatitudes. Benedict utilized his knowledge of earlier eastern monastic rules to compose his Rule. Thus, the Rule of St. Benedict is a synthesis which combines the spirituality of both the East and West. Benedict's Rule is more systematic and less austere than the Celtic monastic rules which were practiced in the West. It drew many men and women to monastic life. The moderate approach of the Benedictine rule to work and prayer, "ora et labora," facilitated the emergence of monasteries as the religious, economic and educational centers of western Europe.

St. Benedict was buried at Monte Cassino in the same grave as his sister, St. Scholastica. St. Benedict is considered the father of western monasticism and is one of the patron saints of Europe. His feast day is July 11.

The Rule of St. Benedict: A Guide to Christian Living, Commentary by Georg Holzherr, Abbot of Einsiedeln, Translated by the Monks of Glenstal Abbey (Four Courts press, 1994), 1-15. Prologue 1-3. Aumann, *Christian Spirituality in the Catholic Tradition*, 68-72.

For much of the sixth century the leading figure in the Christian world was the eastern emperor **Justinian I (483-565)**. Sometimes honored as the last great Roman emperor, Justinian came from the province of Illyria in the Balkans and was the last Latin-speaker to wear the imperial crown. Justinian came to power as the "co-Augustus" under his uncle and adoptive father, Justin I, in 518. Upon the latter's death in 527, Justinian became emperor in his own right. Seeing himself as a new Constantine, it was Justinian's goal to restore the glory of the Roman Empire. In 524 Justinian married a former courtesan, Theodora (c.505-548). Until her death, Theodora ably advised Justinian and she is credited with helping him attain many of his accomplishments.

Vasiliev, *History of the Byzantine Empire Vol. 1*, 132-135. Harl, *The World of Byzantium*, 133-134.

Justinian I. The Last Latin Emperor and his wife, Theodora.

In order to restore the glory of the empire Justinian needed to establish unity of belief among his Christian subjects. To this end Justinian and his uncle repaired the Acacian schism in **519**. They did so by compelling the eastern bishops to sign a statement drawn up by Pope Hormisdas denouncing Nestorianism and the teachings of Acacius. Known as the "Formula of Hormisdas," the statement addressed to Hormisdas affirmed the unique role of the pope as successor to St. Peter to be the final arbiter of orthodox teaching.

"The first condition of salvation is to keep the norm of the true faith and in no way to deviate from the established doctrine of the Fathers. For it is impossible that the words of our Lord Jesus Christ, who said, "Thou art Peter, and upon this rock I will build my Church," [Matthew 16:18], should not be verified. And their truth has been proved by the course of history, for in the Apostolic See the Catholic religion has always been kept unsullied.

From this hope and faith we by no means desire to be separated and, following the doctrine of the Fathers, we declare anathema all heresies. ... Following, as we have said before, the Apostolic See in all things and proclaiming all its decisions, we endorse and approve all the letters which Pope St. Leo wrote concerning the Christian religion. And so I hope I may deserve to be associated with you in the one communion which the Apostolic See proclaims, in which the whole, true, and perfect security of the Christian religion resides. I promise that from now on those who are separated from the communion of the Catholic Church, that is, who are not in agreement with the Apostolic See, will not have their names read during the sacred mysteries. But if I attempt even the least deviation from my profession, I admit that, according to my own declaration, I am an accomplice to those whom I have condemned. I have signed this, my profession, with my own hand, and I have directed it to you, Hormisdas, the holy and venerable pope of Rome."

"The Formula of Pope St. Hormisdas," www.byzantineforum..org. Duffy, *Saints and Sinners: A History of the Popes*, 41-42. Beck, *History of the Church Vol. II The Imperial Church from Constantine to the Early Middle Ages*, 438-443. Walsh, *Lives of the Popes*, 50-51.

Over the course of the sixth century the nobility in Ireland converted to Christianity which had been brought to them by St. Patrick and other captured Britons. Around the year **520** an Irish monk named **Finnian** (c. 495-549) founded the monastery of Clonard in Ireland. It was among the first great Celtic monasteries and numbered among its famous saints Columba, Brendan and Kieran. Supported by the Irish nobility, these monks established a number of other important monasteries. Combining elements of traditional Celtic spirituality with monastic practices from the East, Irish monasticism had a profound impact on the Church not only in its native land but also in Britain and in continental Europe. Their Celtic love of nature fostered an incarnational appreciation of creation. From eastern monasticism they adopted devotion to the reading of Scripture. This required that they read the Latin books that were available to them. Since Ireland had never been part of the Roman Empire, Latin was totally foreign to the Celtic speaking Irish. It had to be taught and studied. Thus their desire to read Scripture and other spiritual works coupled with the need to learn Latin gave Irish monks a scholarly orientation that they would eventually impart to the monks of the continent. Irish monks were also noted for their rigorous ascetical practices such as fasting and praying for hours while kneeling with their arms extended as if on the cross.

The missionary zeal of the Irish monks made them an important influence on the development of the Church in other lands. Their travels beyond Ireland combined a response to Christ's mandate to "go out to all the nations" with their own peculiarly Celtic understanding of being pilgrims for Christ. As members of a clan-based society, they saw separation from home and family as one of the severest forms of penance. Thus, for them voluntary exile as pilgrims was almost a form of martyrdom. Such a vision propelled hundreds of Irish monks on their missionary journeys abroad.

Pierre Riche, "Spirituality in Celtic and Germanic Society," in Christian Spirituality: Origins to the Twelfth Century, 165-171. Brown, The Rise of Western Christendom: Triumph and Diversity, A.D. 200-1000, 239-241.

Another penitential practice of the Irish monks would transform how the Church celebrated the Sacrament of Penance. Documentation on how the Sacrament of Penance was celebrated in the first four centuries of the Church is minimal. There are many references in the writings of the Fathers and

in various council decrees concerning the authority of the Church to "bind and loose" sins (Mt 16:19). What lack are detailed descriptions of how this was done. From the sources that do exist it seems that a person conscious of grave sin would make their condition known to the bishop or priest. They would then be expected to practice public penance for a period of time corresponding to the gravity of their sin. This public penance could include fasting, the wearing of sackcloth and ashes and the performance of charitable works. Often the practice of celibacy during the penitential period was also required. Depending on the gravity of the sin, the penitential period could last years. Then, after penitents had completed the period of penance they would participate in a liturgical rite during which the bishop or priest would impose hands on them signifying their readmission to full communion. This usually occurred right before Easter.

However, although Church leaders affirmed her authority to forgive sin in the name of Jesus Christ, paradoxically, they held that the Church was limited to only doing this once for a serious sinner. Coupled with the public nature of the process and the severity of the penances involved, reconciliation for many penitents only occurred when they were on their deathbeds. Another approach to the problem was for the penitent to go through the process of conversion privately under the guidance of a spiritual advisor or "soul friend." Often these advisors were non-ordained monks or nuns.

Martos, Doors to the Sacred: A Historical Introduction to Sacraments in the Catholic Church, 323-328. James Dallen, "The Sacrament of Penance," New Catholic Encyclopedia.

Within the Irish monasteries the abbots acted as spiritual directors for each monk and they imposed penances when their charges confessed their sins. To assist them in finding appropriate penances for the sins confessed, books called "penitentials" were developed. One of the oldest of these surviving penitentials is attributed to the aforementioned St. Finnian, the founding abbot of the monastery at Clonard:

"If someone sins by abusive speech and forthwith repents, he will undertake a prolonged fast. If someone argues with a cleric and minister of God, he will fast for a week on bread and water. If a cleric has once or twice committed the sin of theft by stealing a sheep, a pig, or another animal, he will fast for one year on bread and water and pay back what he has stolen fourfold. If a religious has given birth to a child and if her sin is known to all, she will fast on bread and water for six years. If a cleric desires carnally a virgin or any other woman without having at once confessed it, he will fast for seven days on bread and water...."

Cited in Pierre Riche, *"Spirituality in Celtic and Germanic Society,"* in *Christian Spirituality: Origins to the Twelfth Century,* 168.

St. Brigid of Ireland.

Before long, these penitential "tariffs" were being prescribed for lay people who sought reconciliation for their sins. If a penitent could not perform the prescribed penance the penitential books had a system through which another penance could be assigned. The penitentials also allowed that another person, a monk perhaps, could do the penance on the penitent's behalf. Penances could also be substituted for by giving alms to churches or monasteries. These last two developments, which began innocently enough, would, over time, be the cause of corruption and scandal in the Church.

While the use of the "penitentials" eventually caused problems, the development of the Sacrament of Penance in this period was, overall, a blessing. Instead of a one-time reception of the forgiveness of serious sin, and only after long, public penances, the repentant now had recourse to this sacrament of healing as often as it was necessary to help them along the way of holiness. The Irish practice of "private" auricular confession was taught by the monks wherever they went. Similar developments had taken place in Spain and, by the eighth century, auricular confession from penitent to priest, accompanied by the prescription of a penance and a prayer of absolution, was the accepted form of sacramental reconciliation in the West.

Eugen Ewig and Hermann Josef Vogt, *History of the Church Vol. II The Imperial Church from Constantine to the Early Middle Ages,* 438-443, 523, 596, 600, 667-676.

An important contemporary of St. Finnian is one of the most popular saints of Ireland, **St. Brigid (c.460-c.528)**. There is not much of a genuine historical record for the life of Brigid and because of her enormous popularity in the early Middle Ages the facts of her life are submerged in legends. What seems plain is that Brigid was educated to read and write, which in itself is remarkable for the time. Against her parents' wishes she renounced the prospect of marriage and chose a life of consecrated virginity. Near the Liffey River she founded a church, "Kill-dara," the church of the oak. Nearby lived a hermit named Conleth. Together they founded a double monastery with a house for women and one for men, with both groups sharing the church. St. Brigid was known for her charitable works and for her powerful intercession manifested in many healing miracles. St. Brigid's example has inspired countless Irish sisters and the Irish gave her the magnificent title "Mary of the Gael." Along with St. Patrick and St. Colmcille, St. Brigid is a patron saint of Ireland. Her cult spread to Scotland and England and in the latter nation she is called "St. Bride." Her feast day is February 1st.

John Ryan, *"St. Brigid of Ireland," New Catholic Encyclopedia. "St. Brigid,"* Thurston, and Attwater, eds. *Butler's Lives of the Saints.*

As the practice of baptizing infants eclipsed adult baptism, the preparations for the sacrament and it celebration also changed. **St. Caesarius (c.470-542)**, the Archbishop of Arles provides some information on baptismal practices in Gaul during his time. While having baptisms at the Easter Vigil was still the ideal, in effect they were taking place all the time. Parents and godparents received some instruction and the latter pledged to teach the child the Creed and the Lord's Prayer when they were older.

Before the day of baptism the parents were expected to fast. Because of the number of children to be baptized, most received the sacrament from a priest not their local bishop.

In the East the principle of baptism by immersion was retained while in practice the rite was modified. In the eastern church when a child was baptized, if they could not be fully immersed in the font, then water was poured over their whole body. Children baptized in the eastern church received the other sacraments of initiation, Confirmation and Holy Eucharist, at that time as well. In the West it gradually became customary to administer these sacraments later. Practices varied depending on local traditions.

Vogt, *History of the Church Vol. II The Imperial Church from Constantine to the Early Middle Ages,* 676-677.
Paul Turner, *"Confirmation," New Catholic Encyclopedia* (2003). Johnson, *The Rites of Christian Initiation: Their Evolution and Interpretation,* 219-267. Timothy Ware, *The Orthodox Church, (Oxford, 1997),* 277-278.

In his quest for religious uniformity, **Emperor Justinian** ordered that all pagans convert to Christianity or they would have their property confiscated. Christians who relapsed into paganism would be executed. Arians living under imperial rule were forced to convert to the Catholic faith and their churches were confiscated. Those adhering to nonorthodox forms of Christianity were barred from government office, practicing law or teaching. Jews were allowed to continue to practice their religion but Justinian placed numerous legal restrictions on them. He also forbade the reading of the Torah in Hebrew in synagogue services and compelled the Jews to read from Greek or Latin texts instead. Justinian believed that the Jews would be able to see the coming of Christ as the fulfillment of Old Testament prophecies if their reading of these texts was uncorrupted by the commentaries of rabbis. So, Justinian forbade the reading of the commentary known as the "Mish-

121

na." The Samaritans in Palestine were considered pagans and treated as such. Both Jews and Samaritans rebelled against Justinian's decrees in 529 and some 20,000 were killed during the revolt.

Duffy, *Saints and Sinners: A History of the Popes*, 41. Beck, *History of the Church Vol. II The Imperial Church from Constantine to the Early Middle Ages*, 438-443. Vasiliev, *History of the Byzantine Empire Vol. 1*, 148-150. Cyril Mango, *Byzantium: The Empire of New Rome* (Scribners, 1980), 88-92.

Basilica of Hagia Sophia.

 The Arian king of Italy, Theodoric, was incensed when he learned of the forced conversions of his co-religionists living in imperial lands and the confiscation of their churches. In **526** he demanded that Pope John I go to Constantinople and get the emperor to end these policies and allow the "converts' to return to Arianism. The reluctant pope made the journey to Constantinople. He was the first pope to do so. Once there, Pope John was welcomed as a hero and his precedence over the patriarch was acknowledged. However, when he returned to Theodoric's court at Ravenna the suspicious king had John imprisoned. He died days later and was quickly revered as a martyr by the Roman church. As such, he was the first pope to be martyred following the Constantinian settlement.

Duffy, *Saints and Sinners: A History of the Popes*, 41-42. Ewig, *History of the Church Vol. II The Imperial Church from Constantine to the Early Middle Ages*, 625.

 **Seven years later** a priest in Rome named "Mercury" was elected pope. Judging his rather pagan sounding name inappropriate for the successor of St. Peter, he changed it, and was called Pope John II. He was the first man to change his name upon being elected pope. Later this became the standard practice. Walsh, *Lives of the Popes*, 50-51.

Justinian's aim to restore imperial control of the West had as an immediate goal the reconquest of Italy, North Africa and coastal Spain. Before launching his campaign in the West, Justinian concluded a peace treaty with the Persian empire. Agreed to in 532, the treaty obliged Constantinople to pay a large annual "tribute" to the Persian emperor. Despite the misgivings of Justinian's advisors regarding the venture's success, in the years **533 and 534** imperial forces took back large portions of North Africa from the Vandals.

Harl, *The World of Byzantium*, 151-153. Vasiliev, *History of the Byzantine Empire Vol. 1*, 148-150.

The initial successes in Africa inspired imperial efforts to retake Italy from the Ostrogoths. By **536** the imperial general in the West, Belisarius, drove the Ostrogothic forces out of Rome. After this victory, one of his first acts on behalf of the Emperor was to depose the Pope, St. Silverius, because of his perceived support for the Goths. He was succeeded by Pope Vigilius, the favored candidate of the emperor. Vigilius had previously served as the papal ambassador to Constantinople. While there he had secured the favor of the

Empress Theodora. The empress, an ex-actress with a questionable reputation, greatly influenced Justinian with her strong monophysite views. Pope Vigilius' subservience to the imperial couple would lead him to vacillate between upholding the orthodox teachings of the Council of Chalcedon on the two natures of Christ and placating his sponsors.

Walsh, *Lives of the Popes*, 58-59. Duffy, *Saints and Sinners: A History of the Popes*, 43-44.

In 537 the **Hagia Sophia**, the church of "Holy Wisdom," was dedicated in honor of the Holy Spirit by Justinian in Constantinople. An architectural marvel that still stands, the Hagia Sophia was erected on the site of a previous church built by Constantine. The Hagia Sophia was the cathedral of the eastern patriarch and the most impressive church in the East. For several centuries it was a mosque. Currently it is a museum.

Beginning in **541**, a **plague** which began in Egypt quickly ravaged the Near East and over the next fifty years traveled west to Europe. This was the first known pandemic. It is estimated that the eastern empire lost one-third of its population. As much as half of Constantinople's population died from the plague. The plague remained endemic, precipitating a demographic collapse in the Mediterranean world between 542 and 750.

Harl, *The World of Byzantium*, 155-156. David MacGillivray, "Byzantine Empire," *Britannica Online Encyclopedia*.

 Around the year **543,** Justinian launched another effort to reconcile the monophysite faction which remained strong in the East, especially in Egypt and Syria. The monophysites continued to reject the teaching of the Council of Chalcedon that Jesus Christ has a human as well as a divine nature. Justinian's gambit was to issue a decree condemning as "Nestorian" certain writings written by three deceased opponents of monophysitism. These writings are known as "The Three Chapters." To many bishops in the West, particularly in North Africa, the condemnation of The Three Chapters was perceived as an attempt to undermine the decrees of Chalcedon on the divine and human natures of Christ. They also objected to Justinian's effort to overrule a council by issuing an imperial mandate. As a consequence, numerous bishops in the West publicly opposed the emperor's decree.

Beck, *History of the Church Vol. II The Imperial Church from Constantine to the Early Middle Ages*, 450-457, 469-474.

In **545** Justinian had Pope Vigilius brought to Constantinople where he was under house arrest. The emperor hoped that he could pressure Vigilius into approving the condemnation of the Three Chapters. Vigilius shared his imprisonment with two bishops from North Africa for several years.

The wars to retake Italy from Gothic rule lasted until 552. The eighteen years of strife were devastating to the population and social institutions. Under their impact and coupled with the plague, the late Roman urban culture of Italy almost completely disappeared. Italy now entered into the agrarian life of the Middle Ages.

Brown, *The Rise of Western Christendom*, 176-182. Harl, *The World of Byzantium*, 148-158.
Vasiliev, *History of the Byzantine Empire Vol. 1*, 134-138.

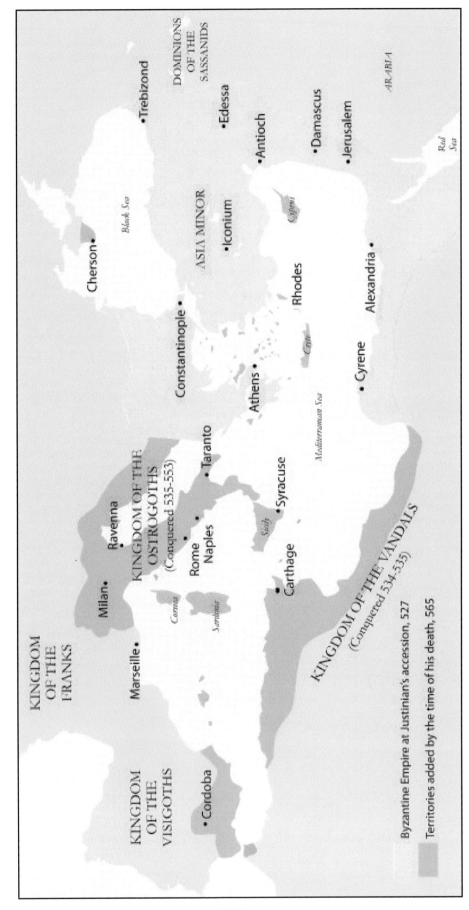

Roman Empire in 565.

KINGDOM
OF THE
FRANKS

KINGDOM
OF THE
VISIGOTHS

• Cordoba

• Marseille

Milan •

Corsica

Sardinia

• Ravenna

KINGDOM OF THE OSTROGOTHS
(Conquered 535–553)

Rome •
Naples •

• Taranto

Sicily

• Syracuse

• Carthage

KINGDOM OF THE VANDALS
(Conquered 534–535)

Athens •

Crete

Mediterranean Sea

• Cyrene

Constantinople •

Cherson •

Black Sea

• Trebizond

**DOMINIONS
OF THE
SASSANIDS**

• Edessa

• Antioch

• Damascus

• Jerusalem

ARABIA

Red
Sea

ASIA MINOR

• Iconium

Cyprus

Rhodes

Alexandria •

Byzantine Empire at Justinian's accession, 527

Territories added by the time of his death, 565

124

Justinian convened the **Second Council of Constantinople in 553**. There were 168 bishops in attendance in the church of Hagia Sophia but only eleven of them were from the West. Pope Vigilius refused to attend the council sessions. In his absence and at Justinian's direction the council was presided over by the patriarchs of Constantinople, Antioch and Alexandria. The specific purpose of the council was to condemn the Three Chapters as "Nestorian." After some discussion the council voted to condemn the targeted writings. Initially, Vigilius refused to endorse the condemnation. However, after years of imprisonment, physical abuse and the death of one of his fellow prisoners, Vigilius finally acquiesced in February 554. Justinian then discredited Vigilius by publicizing the latter's written vacillations on the matter. Vigilius was finally released from confinement but he died while making his return to Rome.

Herrin, *The Formation of Christendom*, 121-122. Duffy, *Saints and Sinners; A History of the Popes*, 43-45.

Vigilius was denounced in the West for his capitulation. Some bishops in northern Italy broke relations with the papacy over this matter and remained in schism for many years. The monophysites for their part refused to be reconciled. The episode increased opposition in the West to imperial involvement in theological matters. It also increased western disdain for the perceived eastern tendency to deviate into unorthodox teachings. In the end, Justinian's effort to unite eastern Christians by ending the monophysite schism had succeeded only in humiliating the papacy and creating greater divisions between East and West.

Harl, *The World of Byzantium*, 163-173. Herrin, *The Formation of Christendom*, 123-125.

Even as Justinian was endeavoring to reconcile the monophysites to orthodoxy, some among them were laying the foundation for a new, separate church. Between 542 and 578, **Jacob Baradaeus**, the monophysite bishop of Edessa, ordained thousands of bishops and priests. This monophysite church was strong among the Syriac-speaking peoples of northern Mesopotamia and is often referred to as the "Jacobite Church" in honor of its great missionary bishop. Missionaries would eventually carry monophysite Christianity to India and China.

Jenkins, *The Lost History of Christianity*, 60-64. Beck, *History of the Church Vol. II The Imperial Church from Constantine to the Early Middle Ages*, 475-479. Mango, *Byzantium: The Empire of New Rome*, 95-96.

Around **563** the Irish missionary monk, **St. Columba (521-597)** and twelve companions established a monastery on the island of **Iona**. Located off the western coast of Scotland, Iona became the center of Celtic Christianity. From there the monks embarked on missionary journeys to Scotland and England. St. Columba succeeded in converting Brude, the king of the Picts and his people in 574.

Brown, *The Rise of Western Christendom*, 325-329.

At the time of Justinian's death in **565**, the **Roman Empire** once again included the western provinces of North Africa, Italy and Sicily. Parts of coastal Spain were also in imperial hands. However, the empire was exhausted and impoverished from Justinian's wars. Additionally, the theological divisions in the Church had been exacerbated by his attempts to force religious unity.

Having finally vanquished the Goths, the imperial army faced a new foe. In **568** the **Lombards**, "a wild barbarian horde," invaded northern Italy. Having only recently converted from paganism to Arianism, the Lombards' conquest of northern Italy led to the region being known as "Lombardy." The invaders then moved south encircling both the administrative capital at Ravenna and the ancient capital of Rome. While the Lombards were conquering Italy, the Avars and Slavs swept in to the Balkans.

Meanwhile, after Justinian's successor, Justin II (565-578), refused in 572 to continue paying the Shah of Persia a "tribute" in exchange for peace, the Persians once again made war on the empire in the East. The wars with Persia continued intermittently for a period of almost sixty years. These conflicts made it very difficult for the emperors in Constantinople to exercise authority in the West.

Harl, *The World of Byzantium*, 192-199. Vasiliev, *History of the Byzantine Empire*, 170-173.

St. Columban.

The tradition of **monks** producing **books** by painstakingly copying existing works was the result of monks needing to reproduce prayer texts for their own use. The Abbott **Cassiodorus (d.580)** furthered this development by putting his monks to work copying ancient texts of all types as an exercise in cultural preservation. In another advance in the use of the written word, Irish monks are credited with having started writing individual words with spaces between them. Prior to this time all words in a text ran together and had to be "separated" by the discerning eye of the reader.

Foley, *From Age to Age: How Christians Have Celebrated the Eucharist*, 159-160. Brown, *The Rise of Western Christendom*, 23.

In **580** the **exarchates** of Italy, based in **Ravenna**, and of Africa, based in **Carthage**, were established to exercise imperial authority in the West. They were governed by military rulers called "exarchs" who were appointed by the emperor in Constantinople. By the creation of what were in effect military dictators in these provinces, the imperial government believed it could offer a more rapid and effective response to barbarian attacks.

Vasiliev, *History of the Byzantine Empire*, 174-176.

 In **587 Recared**, the king of the Visogoths in Spain (586-601) renounced Arianism and was received into the Catholic Church by his uncle, St. Leander of Seville. The conversion of the Visogothic nation was proclaimed at the **Third Council of Toledo in 589**. Arianism soon waned in Spain.

Ewig, *History of the Church Vol. II The Imperial Church from Constantine to the Early Middle Ages*, 564-565.

 About **590 St. Columban** (c.543-615) and twelve fellow monks made themselves pilgrims for the sake of Jesus Christ and traveled to Bretton in Gaul. There they were welcomed by the local Frankish leader who gave them some uncultivated land. While farming their land they evangelized the inhabitants. They were soon joined by other would-be monks and this led to the founding of another monastery at Luxeuil. The monastery became the center of Irish monasticism on the continent. From here Columban and his monks spread the Irish practices of asceticism and scholarship. They also introduced the Irish practice of individual, "private" confession and penitential tariffs. This form of reconciling penitents then spread through the Church in western Europe.

Pope Benedict XVI, *"St. Columban," Church Fathers and Teachers*, 49-52.

Gregory the Great (540-604) served the Church as pope from **590-604**. The son of a senator and grandson of Pope Felix III, Gregory entered the civil service and became prefect of Rome, the civil ruler of Rome, in 573. However, shortly after taking office Gregory felt called to become a monk. Desiring nothing more than to devote himself to contemplation and penance, Gregory was prevailed upon by the pope to become one of the seven deacons of Rome.

In 579 Gregory was sent as the papal legate to the imperial court at Constantinople where he served until about 585. While there he unsuccessfully sought the emperor's assistance against the Lombards. This experience persuaded him that the eastern empire was unable to help the West against the barbarians. After returning to Rome, Gregory reluctantly accepted election as pope in 590. He immediately became the leading civil as well as religious figure in Italy. Twice, in 592 and 593, Pope Gregory negotiated with the Lombards to prevent the sack of Rome when the imperial exarch at Ravenna was unable to protect the city. From this point on, the popes were de facto rulers of central Italy, even though the eastern emperors continued to claim to rule in Italy through their exarchs at Ravenna.

St. Gregory the Great strengthened papal authority within the Church in the West by asserting his authority over local churches and contributing resources to help them. Gregory wrote the first biography of St. Benedict and was a great promoter of Benedictine monasticism. He also gave monasteries papal privileges which partially exempted them from local episcopal authority. This established a pattern of papal direction of religious reform and evangelization. Thus, after Gregory sent **St. Augustine of Canterbury** (+604) in **596** to evangelize the Anglo-Saxons, a close link was forged between the papacy and the church in England.

Gregory also wrote important spiritual and theological treatises which remained influential throughout the Middle Ages, including his Rule for Pastors which was a book of pastoral advice for clergy. Because of his writings Gregory is regarded as one of the four great doctors of the Latin Church along with Jerome, Ambrose and Augustine. St. Gregory also fostered liturgical singing and his name became associated with plainsong, i.e. "Gregorian Chant." Although St. Gregory did much to strengthen the role of the papacy as the supreme authority in the Church, he was known for his personal humility, exemplified by his frequent use of the title "servant of the servants of God." His feast day is September 3.

Pope Benedict XVI, *"St. Gregory the Great," Church Fathers and Teachers,* 37-48. Brown, *The Rise of Western Christendom,* 198-215. Duffy, *Saints and Sinners: A History of the Popes,* 46-56. Westermeyer, *Te Deum: The Church and Music,* 102-103.

An important friend and contemporary of Pope Gregory's was **St. Isidore of Seville** (560-636). Isidore, not to be confused with St. Isidore the Farmer, was the younger brother of Archbishop Leander and succeeded him as archbishop of Seville around the year **600**. As a theologian and historian, Isidore possessed an impressive knowledge of both pagan classical works and those of the Church Fathers. Declared a Doctor of the Church in 1722, Isidore is considered the last of the Latin Church Fathers. St. Isidore wrote one of the first manuals of patristic theology which he called "Sententiae." This work would be a model for theological writing throughout the Middle Ages. Isidore also influenced the Middle Ages with his twenty volume encyclopedia called the "Etymologiae." As a bishop and pastor, Isidore is remembered as a leading member of the hierarchy in Spain, an advisor to the Visogothic kings who ruled there and a polemicist against various heresies. He also conducted a writing campaign against rabbinical attacks on Christianity while opposing the forced conversion of Jews.

J.T. Crouch, *"St. Isidore of Seville," New Catholic Encyclopedia. Oxford Dictionary of the Christian Church.*

Hodegetria.

By the beginning of the seventh century knowledge of the Greek language had become rare in the West. During the middle of the century Latin ceased to be used as an official language of the eastern imperial government. Thus language differences became another obstacle to Christian unity.

Daileader, *The Early Middle Ages,* 38-40.

From **603** on, the eastern empire was locked into a perpetual and exhausting twenty-five year war with the Persian empire. It would be the last war between these ancient foes.

In **610 St. Columban** and his monks were expelled from Luxeuil in Gaul after years of controversies with the local rulers and clergy. They had battled over the monks' moral rigorism and the date for celebrating Easter. Columban and his monks followed the calendar of the East. The last straw seems to have been Columban's condemnation of the king for living in adultery. Although they intended to return to Ireland, providential circumstances led them to evangelize the Alemanni tribes in what is now Switzerland. After further controversy, Columban and all but one of his monks traveled south to Italy. The one who stayed behind was **St. Gall** and eventually an important monastery would be established at the site of his hermitage. Meanwhile, Columban and the rest of his monks established an equally important monastery at **Bobbio** in Italy where Columban died on November 23, 615.

Jean Leclerq, *"Monasticism and Asceticism,"* in *Christian Spirituality: Origins to the Twelfth Century*, 121-122. Pope Benedict XVI, *"St. Columban,"* *Church Fathers and Teachers*, 52-54.

The Persians captured Antioch in 613. After a twenty day siege, Jerusalem fell in 614. Christians were slaughtered and their churches burned. The Church of the Holy Sepulcher was looted and the relic of the True Cross taken. By 619 the Persians had also conquered Egypt. Most of the population of Syria and Egypt did not hold to the official, orthodox faith of the empire. The imperial persecution of monophysites and religious minorities like the Samaritans and Jews led many among these groups to welcome the Persians. At times they also aided them. In another sad chapter in Jewish and Christian relations, after Jerusalem was captured by the Persians some Jews purchased Christian prisoners and then executed them. Jews also joined the invaders in attacking monasteries, killing monks and burning churches.

Mark Whittow, *The Making of Byzantium*, 600-1025 (University of California Press, 1996), 74-76. Mango, *Byzantium: The Empire of New Rome*, 92, 96. Vasiliev, *History of the Byzantine Empire*, 194-196.

In **626**, along with the Avars, the Persians besieged Constantinople. However, the defenders held off the attack. It was said that after an icon of the Blessed Mother known as the "Hodegetria," was carried around the walls of the city the besiegers withdrew. Soon after, in a dramatic reversal, **Emperor Heraclius** decisively defeated the Persians at a battle near the city of Nineveh. Heraclius won back the territory lost in the previous decades, forced the Persians to pay for the cost of the war and recovered the True Cross.

Whittow, *The Making of Byzantium*, 78-79. Vasiliev, *History of the Byzantine Empire*, 197-199. Harl, *The World of Byzantium*, 192-200.

The apparently effective recourse to an icon of the Blessed Virgin Mary during the siege of Constantinople both signified and stimulated the popularity of icons at all levels of eastern society. **Icons** were believed to mediate the presence of Christ, or the saint depicted, in much the same way that relics did. Believers seeking healing and cures for infertility prayed before icons of various saints. Soldiers utilized icons for protection in battle and the oil burned in lamps before icons was thought to have curative powers. The veneration of icons provided opportunities for personal and private devotions seeking the intercession of the saints. Icons also were employed to bolster the authority of the imperial government. A very large icon of Christ graced the gate of the imperial palace in Constantinople.

Herrin, *The Formation of Western Christendom*, 306-311.

During the sixth and seventh centuries the "Jesus Prayer" became more widely known although it is believed that it was in use in the East in the fourth

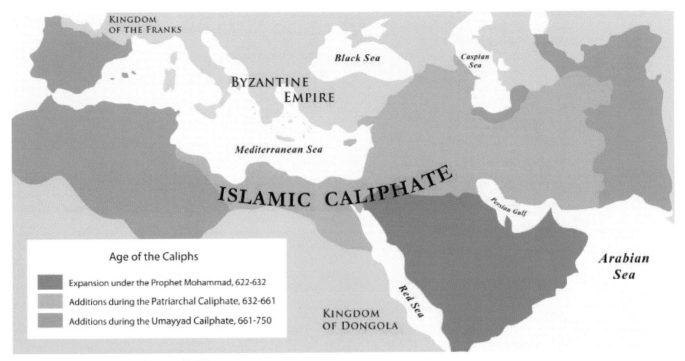

Map of Islamic Expansion until 732.

Within the map:

KINGDOM OF THE FRANKS

Black Sea

Caspian Sea

BYZANTINE EMPIRE

Mediterranean Sea

ISLAMIC CALIPHATE

Persian Gulf

Arabian Sea

Red Sea

KINGDOM OF DONGOLA

Age of the Caliphs

Expansion under the Prophet Mohammad, 622-632

Additions during the Patriarchal Caliphate, 632-661

Additions during the Umayyad Cailphate, 661-750

or fifth centuries. This simple but profound prayer centers on the invocation of the Holy Name of Jesus and appeals to Him as God for mercy. "Lord Jesus, Son of God, have mercy on me."

Kallistos Ware, *"Ways of Prayer and Contemplation," Christian Spirituality: Origins to the Twelfth Century,* 402-408.

In **630 Mohammed** (c.570-632) and his followers captured Mecca in Arabia. Ten years earlier, around 620, Mohammed claimed to have had revelations from the one God. According to these revelations, which he had written down in the Qur'an, Mohammed had been called by the God of Abraham to proclaim the true religion which had been corrupted by Jewish and Christian adulterations. His revelations became the basis of the religion of Islam which quickly swept over the previously polytheistic Arab world. Islam unified Arab tribes and gave them confidence and pride. Armies soon rode out of Arabia to take Islam to the world. They first defeated the staggering Persian empire, which was exhausted after decades of war with the Byzantines. Then the Arab soldiers, many of whom had served in both the imperial and Persian armies, began conquering the Middle East in the name of Allah. In 637 Antioch fell and in 642 the city of Alexandria was captured.

Wickham, *The Inheritance of Rome,* 282-285. Harl, *The World of Byzantium,* 201-202. Whittow, *The Making of Byzantium,* 86-89.

Once again, dissatisfaction with imperial authority in Constantinople undermined the defense of Syria, Palestine and Egypt when they were attacked this time by the Muslim armies. Additionally, there were racial and linguistic affinities between the conquering Arabs and the peoples of Syria and Palestine. The poor condition of the imperial army in these areas and their general weakness after the long Persian wars also undermined their defenses against the Arabs. Christians in the captured lands were allowed to practice their faith and to keep their churches. However, they had to pay a special tax for being dissenters from the official religion, Islam.

Vasiliev, *History of the Byzantine Empire,* 208-210, 217.

Pope St. Martin I.

The loss of Egypt, Palestine and Syria in the first half of the seventh century greatly reduced the size and strength of the eastern empire. With their capture, the empire no longer included its formerly large Coptic and Syriac-speaking populations and was now predominantly Greek in culture. The change was so dramatic that many historians refer to the surviving state as the "Byzantine Empire." However, the people of the empire continued to consider themselves "Romans" and so did their neighbors. Whittow, *The Making of Byzantium*, 90-104. Wickham, *The Inheritance of Rome*, 256-257.

In **635** Persian Christians of the East Syrian Church established a mission at the imperial capital of **China**, Chang'an. Located in northwestern China, Chang'an (modern day "Xi'an") was a city of over a million people. The emperors at that time, Taizong (r. 626-649) and Gaozon (649-683) were open to these wise men who brought "the Luminous Religion" of the West and gave their approval to their mission. Jean-Piere Charbonnier, *Christians in China A.D. 600 to 2000*, (Ignatius Press, 2007), 20-51.

In another attempt to strengthen the empire in the East by ending divisions in the Church over monophysism, **Emperor Heraclius** and the Patriarch of Constantinople, proposed a compromise in **638**. While agreeing with Chalcedon that Jesus Christ has a divine and a human nature, the compromise proposed that He had only one will. This teaching is called **monothelitism**. The compromise was initially well received as a solution to the conflict. Even **Pope Honorius** apparently accepted it. However, it was soon realized especially in the West that to deny that Christ had a human will was also to deny His humanity. Subsequent popes refused to agree to the compromise and were punished for their opposition by various emperors.

Following the Muslim conquest of Egypt, financial and social restrictions were placed on orthodox Christians because of their loyalty to the emperor in Constantinople. The patriarchate of Alexandria remained vacant from 652 to 737. Coptic Christians, even though they did not support the emperor in Constantinople, were also oppressed under Muslim rule. The orthodox patriarch of **Antioch** lived in exile in Constantinople after Syria fell to the Muslims. G.A. Maloney, *"Patriarchate of Alexandria,"* and *"Patriarchate of Antioch,"* New Catholic Encyclopedia.

In **653** the emperor Constans II had **Pope St. Martin I** brought to Constantinople and tried for treason for allegedly conspiring with Muslims and other enemies of the emperor. Pope Martin had incurred imperial wrath by ascending the papal throne without first seeking the emperor's approval of his election. The emperor was further incensed when Martin presided at a synod in Rome in 649 at which monothelitism and its advocates were condemned. The decrees of this synod were widely spread in both the East and the West. Soon after, imperial troops arrested the pope and took him to Constantinople. After being convicted in a show trial, Martin was dragged through the streets of the eastern capital, publicly flogged and condemned to death. His sentence was commuted to exile in Crimea where he died in 655. Before his death Martin endured the additional cross of learning that under imperial pressure a new pope had been elected in Rome. St. Martin was the second pope to receive a martyr's crown following the legalization of Christianity in the Roman empire.

Duffy, *Saints and Sinners: A History of the Popes*, 58-61. *The Oxford Dictionary of the Christian Church*. Hogan, *Dissent From the Creed*, 143-146. R.E. Sullivan, *"Pope St. Martin I," New Catholic Encyclopedia*.

 Another important victim of the imperial persecution was St. **Maximus the Confessor** (c.580-662) a Greek monk and theologian. Before becoming a monk, Maximus had been a secretary to the Emperor Heraclius I. Forced by Persian attacks to flee from his monastery in 626, Maximus went to North Africa.

A prolific theologian, Maximus proposed that Jesus Christ is the center of creation. History before His incarnation was to prepare the world for God to become man. After the incarnation history is the story of man becoming divine through the grace of Jesus Christ, mediated by the Holy Spir-

Dome of the Rock, mosque erected in Jerusalem on site of ancient Jewish Temple.

it. It is in the communion of love between God and man that the human person experiences ultimate fulfillment.

While Maximus was in North Africa he fought against monothelitism which was being imposed by the emperor. Maximus was present at the Synod in Rome in 649 which condemned monothelitism. Maximus was arrested with Pope Martin on the charge of treason and suffered a similar fate. Sent into exile in 655, his tongue was cut out and his right arm cut off when he refused to end his opposition to monothelitism. Maximus died soon afterwards in **662**.

John Meyendorff, *"Christ as Savior in the East,"* in *Christian Spirituality: Origins to the Twelfth Century*, 240-242. H. Hermaniuk, *"Maximus the Confessor," New Catholic Encyclopedia*.

Meanwhile, Pope Martin's successors, Popes Eugene and then Vitalian, seeking to quell imperial persecution, worked at reconciling differences with the patriarch and Emperor Constans II. The latter was welcomed to Rome with great fanfare in **663**. He was the first and last eastern emperor to visit the ancient imperial capital.

Pope Benedict XVI, *"St. Maximus the Confessor," Church Fathers and Teachers*, 60-65. *The Oxford Dictionary of the Christian Church*.

In England, at the **Synod of Whitby in 664**, King Oswy of Northumbria decided in favor of Roman practices over Celtic ones especially in regard to the observance of Easter. This decision united the English church under Roman influence and effectively ended the Easter controversy in the West. Subsequently, English monks would promote loyalty to the See of Peter on their missionary journeys in northern Europe.

Herrin, *The Formation of Christendom*, 269-272.

Islamic expansionism into the eastern empire continued through the last decades of the seventh century. In **674** Muslim forces besieged Constantinople itself. However, after three years they were forced to withdraw when their fleets were destroyed by "Greek fire." This "Greek fire" was a mixture of petroleum, sulfur and lime which ignited on contact with water.

Vasiliev, *History of the Byzantine Empire*, 214-216. Harl, *The World of Byzantium*, 209.

Around **680** a Turkic nomadic people known as the **Bulgars** established an independent state in the Balkans along the Danube. Not only did this cost the eastern empire territory, it presented a new threat from the north.

Harl, *The World of Byzantium*, 209-210.

The Muslim conquest of the eastern territories of Syria, Palestine and Egypt meant that those areas where monophysitism was the strongest were no longer under imperial control. The heresy had become a moot issue for the emperor, **Constantine IV** (668-685). At the same time, having lost its eastern territories, the empire sought to reassert itself in Italy. Needing papal support for this effort, the emperor made amends with the pope.

Constantine IV presided at the sixth ecumenical council, the third **Council of Constantinople, 680-681**. Assenting to a decree sent by Pope Agatho, the two natures and the two wills of Christ were both reaffirmed by the Council fathers. The supporters of monotheletism, including Pope Honorius, were condemned. The teaching of the Council of Chalcedon had once again prevailed and with the sixth ecumenical council the Church's Christological teaching was definitively settled.

Beck, *History of the Church Vol. II The Imperial Church from Constantine to the Early Middle Ages*, 460-463. Herrin, *The Formation of Christendom*, 277-280.

 Between the years 687-752 eleven of the thirteen men elected pope were Greek-speaking. During this time there were many Greek-speaking clergy in Rome. Some were refugees from lands overrun by the Muslims; others fled imperial persecution during the iconoclast controversy. Under eastern influence, the four great Marian feasts, the Purification, Annunciation, Assumption and Birthday of Mary, as well as the Exaltation of the Cross, were added to the Roman liturgical calendar. Also, imperial court rituals were adopted by the papal household.

Duffy, *Saints and Sinners: A History of the Popes*, 64-68. Ewig, *History of the Church Vol. III The Church in the Age of Feudalism*, 4-5.

By **687** Pepin II (635-714), who served the king as "Mayor of the Palace," established himself as the true ruler of the **Franks**. From this time on, the Merovingian kings descended from Clovis were mere figureheads while Pepin's descendants ruled in Francia.

St. Bede the Venerable. *James Doyle Penrose. 1902.*

From **689-691** the **Dome of the Rock** was constructed in Jerusalem at the direction of the Caliph, Abd al-Malik, on the site of the second Temple of Israel which had been destroyed by the Romans in 70 A.D. The erection of this Muslim shrine on the holiest ground of the Jews continues to exacerbate relations between the two religions.

Wickham, *The Inheritance of Rome*, 283.

The **Quinsext Council** of **691-692** also known as the **Synod of Trullo**, was a gathering of approximately 215 eastern bishops for the purpose of drawing up disciplinary canons to complete the work of the fifth and sixth ecumenical councils. (Thus the name 'quin-sext" was given to this council.) Among its 102 canons the council concerned itself with clerical marriage, matrimony in general, clerical attire, the age of ordination and fasting practices. The council approached these issues from a narrowly eastern viewpoint while ignoring previous papal legislation on the same matters. Some of this synod's decrees even had an anti-Latin tenor. This was particularly true of its decrees banning the depiction of Christ as a lamb and on fasting practices. Then too, the council asserted that the patriarch of Constantinople shared equality with the pope and took precedence over the patriarchs of Jerusalem, Antioch and Alexandra.

ian members of the imperial army in Italy came to Pope's Sergius' defense and expelled the imperial officials from Rome. Not long after, the emperor was deposed. Embracing the witness of Scripture to Jesus as the "Lamb of God," Pope Sergius had the "Agnus Dei" prayer added to the Mass during the fraction rite.

While the decrees of the Quinsext Council were canon law in the eastern churches, they were not accepted in the West and the council was resented as one more instance of imperial overreaching into the affairs of the Church.

Thomas F. X. Noble, *The Republic of St. Peter: The Birth of the Papal State*, 680-825, (University of Pennsylvania Press, 1984), 15-17. Walsh, *Lives of the Popes*, 74-75. Herrin, *The Formation of Christendom*, 284-287.

Foley, *From Age to Age: How Christians Have Celebrated the Eucharist*, 97.

Because of its eastern bias Pope Sergius I refused to ratify the decrees of the council. Emperor Justinian II then sent word to imperial officials in Italy to compel the pope to accept the decrees. However, in this instance the Ital-

The Quinsext Council's decrees concerning clerical celibacy illustrate the increasing divergence between East and West on this matter. Canon twelve enjoined celibacy on bishops and canon forty-eight required their wives to enter monasteries. Canon thirteen permitted married men to become priests and deacons. However, once ordained, a cleric could not marry. Additionally, priests and deacons were not to have relations with their wives during their time of service; "knowing that there is a time for all things and especially for fasting and prayer. For it is meet that they who assist at the divine altar should be absolutely continent when they are handling holy things, in order that they may be able to obtain from God what they ask in sincerity."

The synod explicitly condemned the Latin practice which required married priests and deacons to permanently cease having relations with their wives after they had been ordained. In the East, priests and deacons were only required to abstain during the periods that they were assigned to perform liturgical services. In effect, married clerics were expected to follow the norms for married lay people who were to abstain from relations for one to three days before receiving the Eucharist as well as on fast days. Thus, both in the East and the West, Christians had come to accept Old Testament notions of cultic purity regarding sexual activity as found in the Book of Leviticus, Chapter 15. This was reinforced by the Pauline teaching that abstention was good for prayer.

However, the eastern church allowed its priests and deacons to be married while somewhat inconsistently requiring bishops to separate from their wives upon elevation to the episcopate. The rules on clerical marriage and celibacy established by the Quinsext Council remain in effect in the Eastern Orthodox Church. The eastern practice of abstention days before receiving the Eucharist discouraged both frequent communion by the laity and the daily offering of the Eucharist by the parish clergy. Contrary to church legislation in the West, parish priests in the East were expected to be married. Monks are universally required to be celibate.

Cochini, *The Apostolic Origins of Priestly Celibacy,* 396-406. Roman Cholij, *"Priestly Celibacy in Patristics and in the history of the Church,"* www.vatican.va/roman_curia/nongregations/clergy/documents. P. Delahaye, *"Celibacy," New Catholic Encyclopedia.*

Muslim siege of Constantinople.

 **St. Bede the Venerable** (c.673-735) was an English monk, Scripture scholar and historian. Although he spent his entire life within the Benedictine monastery at Jarrow in northern England, Bede was one of the most influential scholars of his time. Relying on his extensive knowledge of the western Church Fathers, Bede composed numerous scriptural commentaries that were utilized by his contemporaries. Pope Sergius even sought unsuccessfully to have Bede come to Rome to be his advisor. It is said that Sergius was the first to honor Bede with the title, "venerable." It was largely through his historical works, that the practice of dating all events in relation to the Incarnation of Christ became widely accepted in the West. Bede's best known work is his Ecclesiastical History of the English People. For an eighth century work it is meticulously documented and remains a primary source for early English history. St. Bede was declared a "Doctor of the Church" in 1899. His feast day is May 25.

Benedict XVI, *"St. Bede the Venerable," Church Fathers and Teachers,* 73-78. *Oxford Dictionary of the Church.*

In **698** Muslim armies completed their conquest of **North Africa** by capturing Carthage. After Byzantine forces briefly retook Carthage, a Muslim fleet burned the city and most of the inhabitants were killed. Italy and Sicily were the only imperial territories in the West that remained under the control of Constantinople.

Brown, *The Rise of Western Christendom*, 295-297. Rodney Stark, *God's Battalions: The Case for the Crusades* (Harper One, 2009), 21.

Pope Constantine, who was elected in 708, made a visit to the eastern emperor in Constantinople in **710** as part of a mutual effort at rapprochement following the division over the decrees of the Quinsext Council. He was the last pope to make the journey to Constantinople voluntarily or otherwise.

Walsh, *Lives of the Popes*, 76-77.

In **711** an army of seven to ten thousand Muslims from Morocco crossed the narrow straight to **Spain**. This surprise attack was followed by a seven-year campaign which led to the Muslim conquest of most of Spain, which they called Al-Andulus. Only the northwestern region of Asturias remained in Christian hands. The Muslims established their capital at Cordoba and were ruled by an emir (governor) sent from the caliph ("successor to the prophet") in Damascus. They also erected a mosque on the site of the cathedral.

Stark, *God's Battalions: The Case for the Crusades*, 21-22.

The second Muslim **siege of Constantinople** took place in **717-718**. Leo III, a general who had recently seized the imperial throne, successfully broke the siege. His forces' use of "Greek fire" drove back the invaders. Although the Muslims would continue to attack Constantinople over the next twenty years in the hope of making it their own capital, the

St. Boniface.

failure of the Islamic armies to overcome the "queen city" blocked their further movement north into Europe.

Vasiliev, *History of the Byzantine Empire*, 235-237. Harl, *The World of Byzantium*, 210-211. Herrin, *The Formation of Christendom*, 139-140.

 **St. Boniface** (680-754) the "Apostle of the Germans" was born in England and baptized as "Winfrid." After entering monastic life, Winfrid was inspired to become a missionary. His first mission to the Frisia (Holland) in **716** was unsuccessful. Winfrid then traveled to Rome where he was given official approval and the name "Boniface" by Pope Gregory II (715-731). With papal encouragement Boniface returned to his missionary efforts, this time among the Germans, and was quite successful in organizing new church communities and reforming existing ones. In **723** he was ordained a bishop by Pope Saint Gregory II. Boniface's devotion to the papacy, coupled with his success, greatly

St. John Damascene

assisted the spread of papal influence north of the Alps. With the assistance of Benedictine monks and nuns from England, Boniface established many monasteries which also became educational and cultural centers in German-speaking lands. The most famous of these was the monastery at Fulda. As archbishop and papal legate for Germany, Boniface erected several dioceses to serve the Germans. When he was almost eighty, Boniface returned to Frisia. While beginning to offer Mass he was martyred on June 5th which became his feast day.

Pope Benedict XVI, *"St. Maximus the Confessor," Church Fathers and Teachers,* 79-85.

Needing more funds to support imperial armies, Emperor Leo III dramatically increased the tax assessments for estates in Italy. Pope Gregory along with other Italian rulers rejected the emperor's demands for more revenue as the empire was doing little to defend them. When the emperor sent officials to punish the Pope in 725 the imperial army was once again turned back by local forces.

Noble, *The Republic of St. Peter: The Birth of the Papal State,* 680-825, 28-29.

In the **720s** some bishops in Asia Minor began to remove icons from churches and to ban their veneration as they believed the use of icons violated the Bible's prohibition of idols. The **"iconoclasts"** as they came to be known argued that depictions of Christ were illicit because an artist was incapable of rendering the immortality of the Risen Lord. After failing to enlist the support of Patriarch Germanus of Constantinople, they were more successful with the emperor, **Leo III**. Some apparently thought that the civil disturbances, wars and natural calamities the eastern empire had experienced were punishments from God because devotion to icons was widely practiced. In 726 Leo urged the people to get rid of icons and removed a popular icon of Christ which hung in front of the Hagia Sophia. Riots followed in the streets of Constantinople.

Beck, *History of the Church Vol. III The Church in the Age of Feudalism,* 28-29. Pelikan, *Jesus Through the Centuries,* 87-88.

When he failed to persuade Patriarch Germanus to join the effort against icons, Emperor Leo issued a decree himself in **730** banning their use. Germanus was forced aside and replaced by Anastatius who supported the emperor's policy.

Charles Martel.

The ban on **icons** was widely opposed, especially by the monastic communities. The conflict over icons divided the Church in the East for over a century. Widespread opposition was met with government persecution especially of monks and many were martyred. Those who championed the use of icons were called "iconodules."

Vasiliev, *History of the Byzantine Empire*, 251-257. Harl, *The World of Byzantium*, 242-243.

 After he was deposed by the emperor, Patriarch Germanus, appealed to Pope Gregory for support. The pope denounced iconoclasm as a heresy and refused to recognize the replacement for Germanus as patriarch of Constantinople. Pope Gregory also refused the emperor's order to remove icons from Roman churches and appealed for support against the heresy. The aristocracy in Italy, which for some time had been growing restive under the empire's control, rose up in defense of the pope. As a result, the central prov-

inces of Italy effectively removed themselves from imperial control.

Noble, *The Republic of St. Peter: The Birth of the Papal State*, 30-34, 57-58. Herrin, *The Formation of Christendom*, 346-352. R.E. Sullivan, *"St Gregory II,"* The New Catholic Encyclopedia. Brown, *The Rise of Western Christendom*, 383-395. Duffy, *Saints and Sinners; A History of the Popes*, 62-63.

A great defender of the use of sacred images emerged at this time, **St. John Damascene** (c.675-754). An Arab Christian from Damascus, thus "Damascene," John like his father had served the Muslim caliphate of Syria before entering a monastery near Jerusalem. John was ordained a priest in 726 and dedicated himself to theological study and writing. John Damascene asserted against the iconoclasts that, since the Son of God had become man in Jesus Christ, it was permissible to venerate icons of Christ. In his work "On Holy Images," St. John wrote the following:

"In former times God, who is without form or body, could never be depicted. But now when God is seen in the flesh conversing with men, I make an image of the God whom I see. I do not worship matter; I worship the Creator of matter who became matter for my sake, who willed to take His abode in matter; who through matter, worked out my salvation."

Cited in John Meyendorff, *"Christ as Savior in the East,"* Christian Spirituality: Origins to the Twelfth Century, 243.

Following St. Augustine, John Damascene was among the first theologians to make the distinction between worship (Greek-"latreia"), which can be rendered to God alone, and veneration (proskynesis), which can be given to the saints. St. John Damascene was declared a Doctor of the

Church in 1890 for his theological writings. His feast day is December 4th.

Enzo Lodi, *Saints of the Roman Calendar* translated and adapted by Jordan Aumann, O.P. (Alba House, 1992), 379-380. Pope Benedict XVI, *"John Damascene," Church Fathers and Teacher*, 99-104. Pelikan, *Jesus Through the Centuries*, 92-94 *and Mary Through the Centuries*, 99-102.

 Elected as pope in **731, St. Gregory III**, was of Syrian origin. He was also the last pope to follow the custom of notifying the eastern emperor of his election. Gregory III continued his predecessor's resistance to Leo's iconoclasm. After his efforts at dialogue with the emperor were ignored, Pope Gregory III called a synod in Rome which condemned iconoclasm and anyone who destroyed sacred images.

In retaliation, the emperor confiscated the territories of Sicily and Calabria, which were the main sources of papal revenue. Leo also declared that the patriarch of Constantinople would have ecclesiastical jurisdiction over these territories. These decrees coupled with the iconoclastic heresy hastened papal alienation from the empire and succeeding popes were less inclined to look to Constantinople for protection against the Arab raiders or the Lombards.

Noble, *The Republic of St. Peter: The Birth of the Papal State*, 680-825, 28-29, 59.
Herrin, *The Formation of Christendom*, 347-352. R.E. Sullivan, *"St Gregory III," New Catholic Encyclopedia*.
Harl, *The World of Byzantium*, 243-244.

Iconoclasm.

ing menaced by the Lombards in **739**, Pope Leo III sent an embassy to Charles Martel asking for help. Although he did not send forces at this time, a precedent had been set and soon the popes would rely on the Franks for protection.

Noble, *The Republic of St. Peter: The Birth of the Papal State*, 46-48. Brown, *The Rise of Western Christendom*, 408-410. Stark, *God's Battalions: The Case for the Crusades*, 39-44. Herrin, *The Formation of Christendom*, 352-353.

The Muslim advance into western Europe was stopped in **733** by **Charles Martel**, "the Hammer of the Infidels," at the **Battle of Tours** (also known as the Battle of Poitiers). Over the next six years the Muslims were driven out of Gaul. A bastard son of Pepin II and his successor as Mayor of the Palace, Charles Martel's victory made him a hero not only among his own Frankish people, but throughout the West. When the papacy was once again be-

Emperor Constantine V ascended the imperial throne in **741**. He had to defeat his rivals in a civil war and then confront Arab armies in Asia Minor. A severe outbreak of the **bubonic plague** broke out in **745**. It spread from Sicily and Calabria to Greece. The population in Constantinople was decimated. In its aftermath Slavs settled on abandoned lands in Greece.

Herrin, *The Formation of Christendom*, 360-361.

Pepin the Short (714-768), as Mayor of the Palace, became sole ruler of the Franks in 747. Three years later he obtained Pope Zachary's agreement that the king of the Franks should be the man who actually ruled them. However, it is incorrect to assert, as some do, that Pope Zachary "deposed" the reigning king, Childeric III. Nor is it accurate to suggest that Pepin and Pope Zachary had entered into a bargain of mutual support. In **751** Pepin was, in fact, elected king by the Frankish nobles. Childeric, the figurehead Merovingian monarch, whose royal lineage was itself suspect, was packed off to a monastery. This was the beginning of the **Carolingian Dynasty**.

Noble, *The Republic of St. Peter: The Birth of the Papal State*, 68-71. Herrin, *The Formation of Christendom*, 356-357. Ewig, *History of the Church Vol. III The Church in the Age of Feudalism*, 15-17.

By July **751** the Lombards had occupied Ravenna and expelled the exarch. Imperial rule in Italy was now limited to Calabria and Sicily. Although the Lombards had converted to Catholicism, they were determined to rule all of Italy, including Rome. The papacy, under Pope Stephen II, once again looked first to Constantinople for protection. However, imperial forces were preoccupied with defending the empire from Islamic armies from Bagdad and Alexandria.

Herrin, *The Formation of Christendom*, 352-360.

Lombard forces continued to break their treaties with the popes and to attack papal territory. The imperial forces in Italy were too weak to defend them and reinforcements were unavailable. Thus in **753 Pope Stephen II** turned to the Franks. He was the first pope to travel north of the Alps and he did so to forge an alliance with Pepin. Pepin pledged to protect the papacy from Lombard attacks and to preserve central Italy from Lombard rule. For his part, Pope Stephen consecrated Pepin as the king of the Franks at the cathedral of St. Denis in Paris in

July 754. The papal alliance with the Franks marked a new alignment of authority in the West. The axis of church and state power now ran from Rome to the northern European kingdoms rather than east to Constantinople.

Noble, *The Republic of St. Peter: The Birth of the Papal State*, 80-83. Duffy, *Saints and Sinners: A History of the Popes*, 64-68. Ewig, *History of the Church Vol. III The Church in the Age of Feudalism*, 20-25. Walsh, *Lives of the Popes*, 80-81. Herrin, *The Formation of Christendom*, 374.

Meanwhile in the East a synod of over three hundred bishops met in February **754** at the **Council of Hieria** and condemned the use of icons. What had been an imperial decree was elevated to a dogma. However, it had no support among the highest leaders of the Church. It is unclear whether the pope even knew of the calling of the council and no western delegates were present. The patriarchate of Constantinople was vacant and the patriarchs of Jerusalem, Antioch and Alexandra refused to attend. On the other hand, most of the eastern bishops and about half of the lower clergy and laity were supportive of the emperor's policies. The opposition continued to be led by the monks.

Ewig, *History of the Church Vol. III The Church in the Age of Feudalism*, 30-31. Herrin, *The Formation of Christendom*, 368-37.

After waging successful campaigns against the Lombards in 755-757, Pepin forced them to give twenty-two cities and territories to the pope and to recognize papal rule over them in perpetuity. Many of these territories, including Ravenna, had been under imperial rule before the Lombards had captured them. Pepin's action is referred to as the **"Donation of Pepin"** and is sometimes designated as the foundation of the Papal state. However, the popes had become independent rulers of their own lands some twenty years before.

Noble, *The Republic of St. Peter: The Birth of the Papal State*, 92-98. Herrin, *The Formation of Christendom*, 378-379.

SUMMARY OF CHAPTER FOUR

Authority

During the sixth and seventh centuries, the popes were in a continuous struggle with the eastern emperors over the question of authority in the Church. On several occasions the emperors were willing to sacrifice fidelity to the decrees of the Council of Chalcedon in the hope of achieving social unity in the East. Pope Vigilius (+555) and Pope St. Martin (+653) both died as a result of imperial persecution. Pope Silverius was deposed by an emperor in 536 and similar attempts were made against Popes Sergius I in 692 and Pope Gregory II in 727.

In the West, Pope St. Gregory the Great strengthened papal influence by asserting his authority over the bishops and contributing resources to local churches. Gregory gave the Benedictine monasteries papal privileges which partially exempted them from local episcopal authority. This established a pattern of papal direction of religious reform and evangelization which bound the local churches closely to Rome.

Doctrine

The effort to reconcile those Christians who maintained that Christ had only a divine nature, "monophytism," to the decrees of the Council of Chalcedon was the main doctrinal struggle of the sixth century. In the seventh century the emperor Heraclius promoted a compromise called "monothelitism" which maintained that while Christ has two natures, He only has one, divine will. This position was rejected by both the orthodox defenders of the decrees of Chalcedon in the West and the monophysites in the East. Monothelitism was condemned at the Council of Constantinople in 680.

The use of religious images, "icons," became controversial in the East beginning in the 720s. This "Iconoclastic Controversy" divided the church in the East for a century and further strained relations between the churches of Rome and Constantinople.

Pastoral Practice

The Rule of St. Benedict, with its moderate exposition of monastic life, increased the appeal of monasticism in western Europe. Hundreds of monasteries were established and became the religious, economic and educational centers in the largely rural West.

Irish monks introduced the practice of "private," auricular confession and it quickly became the most common form of the Sacrament of Reconciliation. The celebration of Baptism was also modified as most people received the sacrament as infants.

Church laws regarding clerical celibacy were codified by the end of the seventh century. The Church in the West expected all clerics to be celibate; in the East celibacy was required only of bishops and monks.

Saints

The most influential saints of this period were all monks. St. Benedict, St. Gregory the Great, St. Columban and St. Boniface each made enormous contributions in leading western Europe to Christianity. Two saints from the East, Maximus the Confessor and John Damascene, were heroic defenders of orthodox theology and practice.

Evangelization

In the West, the Church's evangelization efforts were directed at converting the various Arian tribes to Catholicism as well as bringing the Gospel to rural pagans. The British Isles were an important center for the mission to pagans. Christians from England, fleeing the Anglo-Saxon invasions of the fifth century, took the Gospel to Ireland. After Christianity largely died out in England under the invaders, missionaries from Ireland brought the Gospel message back. From England, Irish and English missionary monks set out for the Continent and brought Christianity to many rural recesses of northern Europe.

By contrast, the conversion of the minority Arian Goths of Spain and Italy was the result of their emersion in the majority Catholic culture.

State

In the West, the foundations for actual states began to emerge following the collapse of imperial administration. The Franks under the Merovingian Dynasty ruled Gaul and parts of what is now Germany. A Visigothic kingdom ruled much of Spain while the Vandals ruled North Africa. For much of this period, Italy was fought over by eastern imperial forces and the Lombards. The Emperor Justinian made a bold effort to reconstitute the old empire by winning back lost territories in North Africa and western Europe. However, his achievements were quickly undermined by wars with the Persians and then the Muslims.

From 500 to 750, the eastern emperors completely dominated Christians in the East who accepted the orthodox teachings of the Council of Chalcedon. However, there were large elements of the population in Egypt, Syria and Armenia which no longer gave their allegiance to the religious authority of Constantinople or Rome. In the West, the eastern Emperor sometimes protected the Popes from invaders. However at other times they were the papacy's greatest enemies.

In the West, the eastern emperors sometimes protected the popes from invaders. However, at other times they were the papacy's greatest enemies.

The Witness of St. Maximus the Confessor.

"God's will is to save us, and nothing pleases Him more than our coming back to Him with true repentance. The heralds of truth and the ministers of divine grace have told us this from the beginning, repeating it in every age. Indeed, God's desire for our salvation is the primary and preeminent sign of His infinite goodness. It was precisely in order to show that there is nothing closer to God's heart that the divine Word of God the Father, with untold condescension, lived among us in the flesh, and did, suffered, and said all that was necessary to reconcile us to God the Father, when we were at enmity with Him, and to restore us to the life of blessedness from which we had been exiled."
Epistle 11.

CHAPTER FIVE

"TO DEFEND HOLY CHURCH"
THE EARLY MIDDLE AGES C. 750-1050 A.D.

"It is incumbent upon us, with God's help, to defend Holy Church outwardly with weapons everywhere against attacks by pagans and devastations by infidels, and to consolidate her inwardly through the understanding of the true faith." - *Charlemagne.*

Sometime in the middle of the eighth century a document known as the *Constitutem Constantini* or *"Donation of Constantine"* was forged in Rome. It was based on an earlier legend which claimed that in gratitude for being baptized and healed of leprosy by Pope Sylvester I, the emperor Constantine the Great had given the papacy the ultimate authority over both the Church and the empire. The document specifically asserted the papacy's supremacy over the other four patriarchates. Such claims obviously served the popes, and some historians believe the "Donation" was fabricated in Rome during the pontificate of Pope Stephen II as it provided a justification for Pepin, king of the Franks, to "restore" to the papacy lands which had been unlawfully seized by the Lombards. However, while the forgery buttressed papal claims to sovereignty, there is no evidence that it was ever used for this purpose in the eighth century. Pepin had endowed the Holy See with lands captured from the Lombards. Imperial officials in Constantinople would not have been fooled by the forgery. By the 750s the papacy had been ruling in central Italy for decades and had no need to establish its legitimacy as a governing body. Noble, *The Republic of St. Peter: The Birth of the Papal State*, 134-137. Ewig, *History of the Church Vol. III The Church in the Age of Feudalism*, 60, 100-101. *Oxford Dictionary of Christian Church.* *"The Donation of Constantine,"* Internet Medieval Source Book fordham.edu

Almost as soon as the papal state emerged as the *sancti Dei Ecclesiae Republica* — the "republic of God's Holy Church" -it was fought over as a political prize by rival factions. The victors of the papal elections of 757 and 768 were both challenged by antipopes. Those contending for control of the papacy readily employed violence to achieve their ends. Duffy, *Saints and Sinners: A History of the Popes*, 72.

Baghdad became the capital of the Islamic world in **762** when the caliph, al-Mansour of the newly ascendant Abbasid dynasty, moved his government there from Damascus. This move somewhat lessened Islamic pressure on the eastern empire. At this time the territories under the rule of Islam stretched from Spain to Pakistan. Wickham, *The Inheritance of Rome*, 318-347. Harl, *The World of Byzantium*, 211-212.

Although iconoclasm had been endorsed as the official teaching of the Church in the East at the Synod of Hiereia, many monasteries continued to resist the decree banning the use of icons. In the **760s** the Emperor Constantine moved against the monks and nuns. Some were martyred and others forced to marry. The killing of monks and the destruction of monastic churches increased popular support for the promoters of icons. Many monks fled to Rome where they found refuge and thousands of lay supporters of icons also went into exile. As a result, western churchmen in general and the popes in particular grew increasingly anxious about the orthodoxy of the Church in the East.

Beck, *History of the Church Vol. III The Church in the Age of Feudalism*, 30-32. Vasiliew, 261-263. Donald MacGillvray Nicol, "The Byzantine Empire," *Britannica Online Encyclopedia.*

Charlemagne, *Albrecht Durer. c. 1512. German National Museum, Nuremburg.*

Pope Paul I (757-767) housed refugees from iconoclasm and supported the patriarchs against the emperor. Rome and Constantinople also clashed over ecclesiastical authority in southern Italy and in Illycrium on the eastern coast of the Adriatic Sea.

In August **768**, a priest-monk who had been an aide to Paul I was legitimately elected as **Pope Stephen III** (768-772). That same year King Pepin died and following Frankish custom, his kingdom was divided between his two sons, Carloman I and Charlemagne.

Noble, *The Republic of St. Peter: The Birth of the Papal State*, 113-118. *Walsh, the Lives of the Popes*, 81-82.

Pope Stephen moved quickly against the revived iconoclast heresy in the East. In a manifestation of papal-Frankish collaboration, twelve bishops from Francia joined thirty-seven Italian bishops at a synod held in Rome in **769**. This synod condemned the decrees of the Synod of Hiereia. Additionally, in response to the recent turmoil surrounding the selection of a new pope, the synod decreed that in the future only members of the Roman clergy could be papal electors. In doing so the synod eliminated voting by the nobles and the people. It also decreed that only Roman clergy who were cardinals could be elected pope.

Walsh, *Lives of the Popes*, 82-83. Herrin, *The Formation of Christendom*, 393-395.

145

In **771 Charlemagne** became sole ruler of the Franks after the death of his older brother and rival, Carloman. Charlemagne expanded the Frankish empire with wars against the pagan Saxons in northeastern Germany and the Lombards in Italy.

Pope Hadrian I, who reigned for twenty-three years **(772-795)**, had one of the longest pontificates in history. Hadrian manifested the papacy's growing independence from Constantinople by minting his own coinage and by dating his letters according to his own regnal years instead of the emperor's. However, the papacy still struggled to maintain its freedom from domination by the local Italian nobility who were enticed by the enlargement of the papal territories following the defeat of the Lombards.

Walsh, *Lives of the Popes*, 83.

Charlemagne took the title "King of the Lombards" in **774** after he defeated them in battle. He had made war on the Lombards at the request of Pope Hadrian I because they were once again seizing papal territory. By 785 Charlemagne ruled most of the western European lands which had once been part of the Roman Empire.

Noble, *The Republic of St. Peter: The Birth of the Papal State*, 113-118. Walsh, *The Lives of the Popes*, 81-82.
Wilken, *The First Thousand Years: A Global History of Christianity*, 335-336.

Out of personal piety and wishing to insure God's favor, Charlemagne was determined that every aspect of life in his empire was

correctly ordered. This included the doctrine and practices of the Church. Continuing the efforts of his father, Charlemagne imposed reforms on the Frankish church. In **779** Charlemagne systematized religious leadership throughout his realm by establishing a clear hierarchy of bishops and pastors and the authority of archbishops. He also mandated that all Christians pay the biblical one-tenth tithe to their parish. Additionally, he endeavored to improve the moral and intellectual standards of the clergy and to eliminate any pagan practices still found among the laity.

Herrin, *The Formation of Christendom*, 432-433.

In order to insure uniform **liturgical practices** Charlemagne obtained copies of the liturgical books used in Rome and mandated that they be used in all churches in the empire. However, as the Roman books were not as complete as desired, they were supplemented with Frankish elements from the Gallican church resulting in a synthesis of the different liturgical traditions. Thus, the brief and practical Roman rite was overlain with various Gallican enhancements. These included the use of a variety of prayers for different occasions, acclamations after the readings of the Scripture and the procession with the book of the Gospels. The resulting "Franco-Roman" hybrid liturgy soon spread throughout western Europe and was adopted in Rome itself.

Along with the Roman missal, Charlemagne also imported liturgical chant from Rome. These chants were taken from the psalms or other passages of Scripture. Talented monks from northern Europe began to embellish these chants by weaving multiple lines of chant together to create polyphony. They also developed a system of musical notation which allowed trained singers to learn the chants simply by reading these notes, called "neumes," on a page. Called "Gregorian Chant," in honor of Pope St. Gregory the Great, and propagated by monasteries as well as designated "choir" schools, this chant was the church music of the Middle Ages. It was a magnificent musical achievement. However, the complexity of the chants often obscured the Scriptural texts they were proclaiming. Additionally, as the chants were sung in Latin, these heavenly songs could not be understood let alone sung by the average believer. Thus, the sung parts of the Mass became the preserve of specially trained choirs. Needing their own voice, devotional hymns in the vernacular gradually developed for the laity. Meanwhile, priests were expected to offer their prayers in a low voice and the canon of the Mass, the Eucharistic prayer, was read in silence.

The rising sun had long been a natural reminder to Christians of the resurrection. So for the celebration of the Mass the priest stood on whichever side of the altar faced east. Depending on how a church was designed, sometimes the priest and people were facing the east together. In other churches, again because of their design, the priest faced the altar and the east while the people faced the altar and the priest while looking west. (The basilica of St. Peter's in Rome is arranged this way.) As altars became exclusively made of stone (Charlemagne mandated this practice in 769) and received increasing adornment, they were erected on the eastern walls of churches. With this arrangement priests and people were now facing the east together. However, for the congregation, the principle of looking to the east to the resurrection was obscured by the experience of seeing simply the priest's back.

By the seventh century, daily celebration of Mass had become common in the West. Monks in particular wanted to receive the Eucharist as often as possible and the earlier practice of receiving Communion outside of Mass was no longer observed. Prior to this time in many places Mass was only celebrated on Saturday and Sunday.

In addition to daily Masses, in some churches there were multiple Masses to accommodate requests that they be offered for the deceased. The practice of celebrating the Eucharist for the faithful departed went back to at least the second century and is well attested to over time. For example, St. Monica's last request of her son, Augustine, was to "remember" her at the altar. Having Masses offered for the salvation of the departed became a popular means of praying for the dead which Christians recognized as one of the spiritual works of mercy.

Mass in the Middle Ages.

Those with the means to do so began to arrange to have Masses offered for themselves after their passing. Offerings were made to churches and monastic communities for this purpose. In fact, some churches and monasteries were erected by wealthy patrons precisely so they could offer their Masses and other suffrages on behalf of their donors. Multiple daily Masses inevitably led to numerous altars being erected in churches.

The unintended consequence of these various developments was that by the Middle Ages most Catholics in the West attended a liturgy where they could neither hear nor see what was taking place or understand the prayers that were being offered. The practice of multiple Masses being offered simultaneously in the same church with little or no lay participation only underscored the fact that the liturgy was no longer a communal act of worship.

Foley, *From Age to Age: How Christians Have Celebrated the Eucharist,* 135-149.

Keith F. Pecklers, *S.J. Liturgy: The Illustrated History* (Paulist Press, 2012), 93-95, 104-10, 116.

Another development in liturgical practice which was institutionalized by the Frankish reformers was the use of **unleavened bread at Mass**. From the earliest days of the Church, the bread used for the Eucharist was brought by the people and was the same as what they ate at home. By the fourth century, the ordinary loaves of bread used in worship were stamped or pressed with Christian symbols. However, as reception of Communion by the laity declined, they also stopped bringing the bread. Producing altar bread became the responsibility of monks who made the bread more uniformly. Additionally, the increasing emphasis on the transcendent aspects of the Mass led to the desire for altar bread that was different from domestic bread. The use of unleavened bread at Passover and the Last Supper provided a Scriptural basis for the change.

Foley, *From Age to Age: How Christians Have Celebrated the Eucharist*, 166-167.

Under the Carolingian reforms the clergy were charged to exercise greater pastoral care of the sick and dying. Prior to this time the **Anointing of the Sick** with oil which had been blessed by a bishop was administered by lay people as well as clergy. Lay people were allowed to take the blessed oil home where they could either apply it to themselves or drink it as needed. People received anointing for all kinds of illnesses, not just fatal ones. The anointing by lay people was promoted by some bishops as a counter to various rituals that pagans had used to heal sickness. However, as the practice of confession increased, the opportunity to confess one's sins was often sought in times of grave illness. The two sacraments of Penance and Anointing thus became linked together in the Church's ministry to the dying. As confessions could only be heard by priests, they became the sole ministers of anointing as well. It is unclear if a concern for greater obedience to the words of Scripture was a part of this development. However, anointing by a priest was surely a more faithful expression of the biblical teaching as found in the letter of St. James 5:14-16. "Is any among you sick? Let him bring in the priests of the Church, and let them pray over the sick man, anointing him with oil in the name of the Lord." Eventually, a ritual for the anointing of the sick by priests was composed and included in Carolingian sacramental texts. Once in written form, the new ritual was distributed throughout the western Church.

Martos, *Doors to the Sacred: A Historical Introduction to Sacraments in the Catholic Church*, 373-378. J. P. McClain and J. M. Donohue, "The Sacrament of Anointing of the Sick I & II," *New Catholic Encyclopedia*.

Charlemagne also made efforts to ensure that the faith was taught correctly and moral behavior instilled in the clergy and people. To further these goals Charlemagne imposed on cathedrals and abbeys in his empire the obligation to establish schools. Additionally, he promoted the recovery of the heritage of the Latin Church Fathers. These efforts were carried out by monks and clerics and led to the "**Carolingian Renaissance**."

Brown, *The Rise of Western Christendom*, 431-461.

During the reigns of Charlemagne and his successors, numerous classical and Christian texts were reproduced. Carolingian scholars were also responsible for innovations in writing techniques. Prior to this time, Latin was written using only capital letters. There were no spaces between words and no punctuation. Monastic scholars of the Carolingian era were the first to introduce uniform script— "Carolingian minuscule," which made use of lower case letters, spaces between words, and punctuation marks, thus greatly facilitating the practice of reading.

Wilken, *The First Thousand Years: A Global History of Christianity*, 342-343.

Charlemagne was not an educated man himself. He relied on a circle of advisors from all parts of western Europe to advance his religious and educational reforms. Among these, none was more important than **Alcuin of York** (c.735-804). Alcuin, a deacon, established his reputation as an educator while directing the cathedral school in York. On a journey to Rome in **781** he met Charlemagne and was invited to direct the palace school at the imperial capital of Aachen. A gifted administrator, the curriculum of Alcuin's school would serve as a model for other schools in the empire.

The Wars of Charlemagne, *Jean Fouguet. c. 1460.*

Alcuin's intellectual contribution to the Carolingian renaissance was to produce accurate reproductions of the Bible and the writings of the Church Fathers. This was important work as over the centuries copyists had left many errors in the texts. For the liturgy Alcuin compiled a new edition of the lectionary and a revised sacramentary based on Roman liturgical books. Alcuin recorded that by this time Saturday was a day of special devotion to the Blessed Virgin Mary. In addition, Alcuin appears to have been the actual author of many of Charlemagne's decrees. Charlemagne rewarded Alcuin for his service by making him abbot of the historic monastery of St. Martin of Tours even though the scholar was neither a priest nor a monk. Alcuin is often called "blessed" and his feast day is kept in some Benedictine monasteries on May 19th.

Ewig, *History of the Church Vol. III The Church in the Age of Feudalism,* 70-76, 317. Thurston and Attwater, *"Bl. Alcuin," Butler's Lives of the Saints.*

A trusted member of Charlemagne's court circle, Alcuin was not afraid to challenge the emperor regarding some of his policies. For over twenty years Charlemagne waged a relentless war against the pagan Saxons who he saw as a threat to his empire. The Saxons were organized as a loose federation of tribes and their lack of identifiable leadership and population centers made them difficult to defeat. To accomplish this goal, Charlemagne was not above using brutal tactics. In 780 his forces massacred 4,500 Saxon prisoners after a Frankish defeat.

The pacification program directed at the Saxons included their forced conversion to Christianity. Believing coercion to be contrary to the Gospel, Alcuin objected to these practices. In a letter to Charlemagne Alcuin stated, "…faith arises from the will, not from compulsion. You can persuade a man to believe, but you cannot force him. You may even be able to force him to be baptized, but this will not instill the faith in him." Eventually Charlemagne mitigated the coercive tactics being used on the Saxons to bring about their conversion.

Wilken, *The First Thousand Years: A Global History of Christianity,* 336-337. Edward James, *"The Northern World in the dark Ages,"* in *Medieval Europe* ed. by George Holmes (Oxford University Press, Oxford, 2001), 74-75.

 **The Second Council of Nicaea**, the seventh ecumenical council, was held in **787** at the behest of Constantine VI in order to end the iconoclast heresy in the East. Three hundred and fifty eastern bishops attended while the only westerners were delegates of Pope Hadrian. Pope Hadrian's representatives brought with them a theological treatise justifying the veneration of images. This document was accepted by the Council and the iconoclast heresy was condemned. Although iconoclasm was suppressed, the battle over icons was not over as many were still opposed to the use of images in prayer and worship.

The Second Council of Nicaea also issued twenty-two canons dealing with church discipline. These canons included the condemnation of simony, i.e. the selling of clerical appointments and the charging of fees for spiritual goods. The canons also decreed that the election of bishops, priests and deacons by secular authorities was invalid and that clerics were forbidden to leave their dioceses without their bishop's permission. The Council additionally called all clerics to simplicity of life, forbade the practice of women staying in the houses of bishops or in monasteries of men, and banned the establishment of double monasteries of men and women. The Council of Nicaea of 787 had seemingly resolved the schism between East and West over the use of icons. However, the West, under the leadership of the popes and the Franks, no longer deferred to Constantinople but rather leaned on each other for mutual support. This was the last council to be recognized as "ecumenical" by the eastern Church.

Timothy Ware, *The Orthodox Church* (Penguin Books; London, 1997), 30-35. Beck, *History of the Church Vol. III The Church in the Age of Feudalism*, 32-33. Duffy, *Saints and Sinners: A History of the Popes*, 74. *Oxford Dictionary of Church History*.

The Calling of the Vikings, Viktor Vasnetov.

 In **793 Vikings** attacked the important monastery of Lindisfarne off the coast of northern England. A monastic and missionary center had been established on the "holy island" by St. Aidan in 635. Numerous Irish and English saints had lived on the island as monks and traveled from there to evangelize Britain and the Continent. One of the great artistic treasures of the early Middle Ages, the **"Lindisfarne Gospels"** was transcribed and decorated there around 697. The attack on Lindisfarne inaugurated centuries of Viking plundering of Britain and Ireland that greatly impeded developments in religious and political life.

Oxford Dictionary of the Christian Church. Wickham, *The Inheritance of Rome*, 455-457.

 The Council of Frankfurt of **794** was called by Charlemagne with Pope Hadrian's approval to deal with the heresy of "Adoptionism." The heresy arose through the attempt of the Archbishop Elipandus of Toledo to defend the distinction between Christ's human and divine natures. His solution was to assert that in his divinity Christ was God's true Son. However, in his humanity Christ was God's adopted son. Although this position had already been judged heretical by the pope, Archbishop Elipandus had supporters in Spain. The Council, which was attended by bishops from the Frankish kingdom as well as Italy and England, condemned Adoptionism. Alcuin, relying on texts from the Church Fathers, provided tracts against the heresy. While Elipandus and his supporters never renounced Adoptionism, it died out with them. This same Council, displaying an unexpected assertiveness, also condemned the decrees of the Council of Nicaea of 787 which allowed for the veneration of icons. However, their condemnation was the result of using mistranslations of the decrees of the council.

S. J. McKenna, *"Adoptionism," New Catholic Encyclopedia.* Herrin, *The Formation of Christendom,* 437-439.

Charlemagne crowned emperor by Pope Leo III. *Jean Fouguet. c. 1460.*

By the 790s Charlemagne's dominance of Europe and status as a leader had generated comparisons with heroic figures of the past. Imitating Charlemagne's own rhetoric, his court followers called him the "new David." For others he was the "king and father of Europe." For many, including himself, Charlemagne was unequaled in authority. Using the royal, second person plural, he wrote to Pope Leo III in **795** of their mutual but unequal responsibilities.

"It is incumbent upon us, with God's help, to defend Holy Church outwardly with weapons everywhere against attacks by pagans and devastations by infidels, and to consolidate her inwardly through the understanding of the true faith. It is your task, Holy Father, like Moses to lift up your arms in prayer and so to aid our army that by your intercession the Christian people, under God's guidance and guarantee, may always be victorious over the enemies of his holy name, and the name of our Lord Jesus Christ may be glorified in the whole world."

Ewig, *History of the Church Vol. III The Church in the Age of Feudalism,* 86-89.

In **797** the mother of Emperor Constantine VI, had her incompetent son deposed and blinded. Then, in an unprecedented break with imperial tradition, Irene claimed direct rule for herself. Irene's claim to imperial authority may have contributed to the proclamation of Charlemagne as emperor, for women had never before been allowed to reign over the empire in their own names but only as regents for their sons.

Harl, *The World of Byzantium,* 226, 245. Herrin, *The Formation of Christendom,* 430-431.

On Christmas Day **800 Charlemagne was crowned emperor** by Pope Leo III. Charlemagne's first biographer maintained that the coronation was solely the pope's doing in recognition of Charlemagne's accomplishments. However, even before this date, Charlemagne's scribes were referring to his domain as the "Christian empire." Additionally, Charlemagne had presided over a synod in Rome shortly before his coronation. According to

Charlemagne's empire.

a contemporary account of the synod, preserved in the "Annals of Lorsch," the assembled demanded that, since the imperial throne in Constantinople was vacant after the emperor was deposed by his mother, Charlemagne should be recognized as the new emperor. Besides they maintained, he already ruled over Rome and the other regional capitals of the West. It is sometimes mistakenly said that Charlemagne's coronation was the beginning of the "Holy Roman Empire." However, the empire was not given that title until the thirteenth century.

No emperor had ever been crowned by a pope before. Einhard, Charlemagne's secretary and biographer, wrote that Charlemagne never would have entered St. Peter's if he had known Pope Leo was going to crown him emperor. However, it wasn't the crown or the title he resented. What Charlemagne did not care for was the suggestion that he was subordinate to the pope. During Charlemagne's lifetime there was no question who was the leading partner in the relationship.

Noble, *The Republic of St. Peter: The Birth of the Papal State*, 294-295. Ewig, *History of the Church Vol. III The Church in the Age of Feudalism*, 90-95.

Some historians maintain that in being crowned emperor Charlemagne was asserting a claim to rule over Constantinople as well. These scholars note that Charlemagne hoped to buttress his claim by marrying Empress Irene and so he entered into negotiations with her. However, after she was deposed and exiled in 802 the wedding was off. Whatever his aspirations may have been, the coronation of Charlemagne as "emperor of the Romans"

153

antagonized the imperial authorities in Constantinople who continued to assert claims to all the lands of the old Roman Empire. To them, Charlemagne's crowning suggested a rebellion and they were concerned that he might actually march on Constantinople. Additionally, they were annoyed at the impertinence of someone they regarded a mere barbarian chieftain being declared an "augustus." However, subsequent eastern emperors had to accept the reality, if not the principle, that there was an authority in the West that asserted an equal claim to the legacy of imperial Rome. The coronation of Charlemagne also solidified the realignment of governing powers in the West. Church and state relations in the West would increasingly be determined by the papacy's interactions with the emerging kingdoms of western Europe.

Vasiliev, *History of the Byzantine Empire Vol. 1*, 266-269. Whittow, *The Making of Byzantium*, 600-1025, 304-305. Harl, *The World of Byzantium*, 244-245. Ware, *The Orthodox Church*, 45-46.

While Charlemagne and his son Louis were intent on using Catholicism to unify the various peoples of their empire, including pagans, they were remarkably tolerant toward **Jews**. The seventy-two years of their combined reigns (768-840) are considered a golden age for Jews in medieval Europe. A Jew, known to history only as "Isaac," was included in the delegation sent by Charlemagne to the caliph in Bagdad in 797.

The six to eight thousand Jews living under Carolingian rule were regarded as essential to the commercial life of many towns. Jewish merchants were especially valued for their instrumental role in long-distance trading as they were successful in bringing many luxury goods into the empire. To facilitate trade, the imperial authorities granted Jewish merchants certain privileges and exemptions. The imperial government even included an administrator, the "magister Judaeorum," whose job it was to see that Jews were not mistreated. Reversing long-standing precedent, Louis appointed Jews to government positions and allowed Jews to publicly promote their religious views.

Slavery was accepted under the Carolingians and some Jews were involved in the slave trade. Slavs, from whom the word "slave" comes, and other conquered "heathens" were transported from eastern Europe and traded in the markets of Mainz and Verdun. Slaves were also transported south to Spain and to other Muslim territories. The sale by Jews of Christian slaves and of slaves that might become Christians was actively opposed by the clergy. Church leaders were also incensed that Louis allowed Jews to convert their slaves to Judaism.

When a deacon from the imperial court converted to Judaism in 838 and then became an apologist for Judaism, those Christians who were opposed to the Carolingians' tolerant attitude toward Jews saw it as the inevitable result of the emperors' misguided policies.

Glick, *Abraham's Heirs: Jews and Christians in Medieval Europe*, 41-57, 69-70.

 In **807** Benedictine monks in Jerusalem introduced the **"Filioque"** clause into the chanting of the Creed during the Mass. Eastern monks in Jerusalem immediately protested this innovation. The term, "Flioque," is Latin for "and the Son." It is a dogmatic statement of the "double procession" of the Holy Spirit from the Father and the Son. This teaching on the double procession of the Holy Spirit was held by a number of Church Fathers from both the East and the West, including St. Cyril of Alexandria, St. Ambrose and St. Augustine. The first to use the specific term "filioque" to indicate that the Holy Spirit proceeds from both the Father and the Son was St. Fulgentius (462-527), bishop of Ruspe in North Africa.

Raniero Cantalamessa, *Come, Creator Spirit: Mediations on the Veni Creator* (Liturgical Press, 2003), 371-372.

The insertion of the filioque in the Creed began in Spain in the sixth century probably as a counter to Arian views which denied the equality of the Son with the Father. Eventually the profession of the filioque spread through the Frankish empire. While based on Scripture, it was not part of the Creed approved at the Councils of Nicaea and Constantinople. Its introduction into the Creed without being approved by an ecumenical council was strongly opposed in the East as an assault on the Church's central creed. Pope Leo III, while supporting the teaching, agreed with Eastern churchmen about its improper adoption. To mollify easterners he even had the Creed in its original form without the filioque engraved on silver plaques and mounted on the tombs of Saint Peter and Saint Paul. However, its use continued to spread in the West and the modification of the Nicene Creed through the insertion of the filioque continues to be an obstacle to union between the Orthodox and Catholic Churches.

Benz, *The Eastern Orthodox Church: Its Thought and Life*, 56-58. Ware, *The Orthodox Church*, 50-52. Herrin, *The Formation of Christendom*, 462-464. Ewig, *History of the Church Vol. III The Church in the Age of Feudalism*, 82-84.

St. Theodore the Studite.

In a ceremony whose significance no one could mistake, Charlemagne had his son, **Louis the Pious crowned emperor in 813**. Historians disagree on how to interpret reports of the event. Some say Charlemagne put the crown on his son's head. Others assert that Louis crowned himself. Either way, the coronation of the new emperor took place without papal assistance.

Ewig, *History of the Church Vol. III The Church in the Age of Feudalism*, 101. Noble, *The Republic of St. Peter: The Birth of the Papal State*, 297.

Upon his death in **814**, Charlemagne was succeeded as ruler of the Franks by **Louis the Pious** (778-840). As his nickname suggests, Louis was very much interested in church affairs. He continued Charlemagne's reform efforts aided by **St. Benedict of Aniane** (751-821). They began by focusing on monasteries and under their direction a great reform council met in 816. The council decreed that all monks and nuns must observe the *Rule of St. Benedict*. They were to strictly observe the rules of enclosure in their monasteries and be faithful to manual labor. Additionally, monastic schools could no longer accept students from outside the community. Prior to this time many monasteries and convents had been following their own, often rather lax rules.

Ewig, *History of the Church Vol. III The Church in the Age of Feudalism*, 103-108, 115-118.

 In **815**, after several defeats at the hands of the Bulgars, who even threatened Constantinople itself, **Emperor Leo V** (813-820) launched another campaign against the veneration of icons. The Church was once again divided by **iconoclasm**. The Patriarch of Constantinople, Nicephorus, refused to comply and was deposed. After his deposition, a synod was held in Constantinople that overruled the Second Council of Nicaea and reimposed decrees against the use of icons.

Vasiliev, *History of the Byzantine Empire Vol. 1*, 283-285. Beck, *History of the Church Vol. III The Church in the Age of Feudalism*, 41-48.

 A new defender of the use of icons emerged at this time, **St. Theodore the Studite** (759-826). Following the example of his uncle and mentor, St. Plato, Theodore became a monk and was ordained a priest. Theodore quickly gained recognition as a monastic reformer and his monastery of Studios in Constantinople became an influential spiritual center. In his writings Theodore called for a renewed dedication to the evangelical counsels of poverty, chastity and obedience. His enthusiasm and holiness inspired large numbers of men to enter his monastery and lay people sought him out as a spiritual advisor.

 Twice Theodore was exiled for his opposition to immoral behavior at the imperial court. However, his greatest trial came in **815**. Theodore publicly denied the authority of the emperor to issue edicts on doctrinal matters. Theodore was arrested for leading his monks in a public procession with icons on Palm Sunday. He was imprisoned, scourged and then exiled to Asia Minor.

Against the iconoclasts, Theodore argued that by becoming flesh, the Second Person of the Holy Trinity, Jesus Christ, had sanctified the created world. Therefore, the veneration of icons was an appropriate way to celebrate the wonder of Christ's incarnation. The campaign against the use of icons was relaxed in 820 when Emperor Leo V was murdered by his comrade and successor, **Emperor Michael II.** However, Theodore was not welcome in Constantinople and he died in exile. His feast day is November 11th on the Byzantine calendar.

Pope Benedict XVI, *"St. Theodore the Studite" Church Fathers and Teachers*, 105-110. *Oxford Dictionary of Christian Church*. Thurston and Attwater, *"St. Theodore the Studite" Butler's Lives of the Saints*.

 In **824** the Constitutio Romana was implemented by Louis the Pious. The *Constitutio* imposed certain requirements upon the inhabitants of the Roman "republic of God's Holy Church" as subjects of the Frankish emperor. Some of its regulations were intended to protect the rights of the pope as well as the papal election process. The *Constitutio* also required that the Frankish emperor be informed of the election of a new pope and that the pope-elect must make an oath of allegiance to the emperor before being consecrated. While the *Constitutio* established the emperor's temporal sovereignty in papal territories, it did not assert supremacy over the pope's spiritual authority.

Ewig, *History of the Church Vol. III The Church in the Age of Feudalism*, 112-113, 141, 146, 156, 209.
Walsh, *Lives of the Popes*, 86, 88-89. Noble, *The Republic of St. Peter: The Birth of the Papal State*, 315-322.

The Martyrs of Amorion.

Empress Theodora. She brought about the triumph of orthodoxy with the final acceptance of icons.

Muslim forces from North Africa invaded Sicily in **827.** From Sicily they menaced both southern and central Italy and disrupted communication between Constantinople and the West.

Thomas Brown, *"The Transformation of the Roman Mediterranean," in Medieval Europe ed. by George Holmes,* 17, 30.

In **831** Pope Gregory IV made **St. Ansgar (801-865)** archbishop of Hamburg and appointed him the papal legate to the Church in Scandinavia. A Benedictine monk from Picardy in France, Ansgar had made missionary efforts in Denmark and Sweden prior to this time and would continue to do so in spite of much opposition from local pagans. He eventually succeeded in convert-

ing the kings of Denmark and Sweden. St. Ansgar was revered by his contemporaries for his preaching, charity, and administrative abilities. His feast day is February 3.

Thurston and Attwater, *"St. Ansgar," Butler's Lives of the Saints.*

Danish Vikings intensified and prolonged their raids on Frankish territories as well as Britain and Ireland during the 830s and 840s. Rather than returning to Denmark following the raiding seasons, they began to winter along the coasts of their targets, the better to resume raiding in the spring. Local leaders who could not ward off these attacks began to pay gold to the Danes, "danegeld," to keep them from pillaging their communities. These Viking attacks disrupted life and undermined social organization along the coasts of western Europe from Scotland to Spain.

Daileader, *The Early Middle Ages*, 60-62. Wickham, *The Inheritance of Rome*, 454-455.

In **838** Muslim forces targeted and captured the city of Amorion in Asia Minor. Amorion was native city of the imperial family reigning in Constantinople. Forty-two of those taken prisoner by Caliph Mutasim, many of whom were imperial officials, were executed for refusing to convert to Islam. They are known as the "Martyrs of Amorion."

Herrin, *The Formation of Christendom*, 468.

 The Synod of Constantinople in 843, called by the Empress-regent, **Theodora**, finally put an end to the fight over icons. The legitimacy of icons was reaffirmed and the unity of the Church in the East was restored. The end of the iconoclast heresy was commemorated with a new liturgical celebration, the "Triumph of Orthodoxy" which is observed in the eastern Church on the first Sunday of Lent.

Benz, *The Eastern Orthodox Church: Its Thought and Life*, 1-3. Ware, *The Orthodox Church*, 269-272.

The end of the battle over icons unleashed a new missionary energy in the East. Like the Church in the West, Constantinople now looked north of the Mediterranean basin for fertile mission fields, specifically the Balkans. The use of icons and the celebration of the liturgy in the vernacular languages were very effective in evangelizing the peoples of eastern Europe. That the synod which brought about these developments had not included any representatives

from the West was symptomatic of the increased separation between the Church in Constantinople and the Latin rite Church centered in Rome.

Ware, *The Orthodox Church*, 73-77. Beck, *History of the Church Vol. III The Church in the Age of Feudalism*, 32-33.

The Treaty of Verdun in **843** ended the civil war waged among the Franks by the three sons of Louis the Pious. The Carolingian empire was divided among them into West Francia, which would emerge as the nation of France, and East Francia, which was comprised of the German-speaking lands. The third kingdom, "Lotharingia" was established between the other two but was quickly absorbed by them. By the time of the treaty the Franks of the western and eastern kingdoms already spoke the distinct dialects that over time became the French and German languages. The gradual demise of the Carolingian empire brought to an end the cultural and religious renaissance that it had ushered in.

Wickham, *The Inheritance of Rome*, 395-396, 427-431. Keene, *Medieval Europe*, 34-37.

In **845** an imperial decree, aimed at suppressing Christianity and Buddhism, banned all foreign religions from **China.** Christianity had only shallow roots in the capital and quickly disappeared. However, some among the tribes of the north continued to practice Christianity.

Charbonnier, *Christians in China A.D. 600 To 2000*, 64-67. Jenkins, *The Lost History of Christianity*, 65-66.

In **846** Muslim raiders plundered St. Peter's and St. Paul's in Rome. The following year Pope Leo IV began restoring the churches. He also rebuilt and expanded the walls of the city of Rome.

Walsh, *Lives of the Popes*, 89. Stark, *God's Battalions: The Case for the Crusades*, 22-23.

 **Pope St. Nicholas the Great** led the Church from **858-867**. An aggressive advocate of papal primacy in both spiritual and temporal matters, Nicholas asserted that the rulings of synods or councils must receive approval from the pope. Likewise, bishops could not be deposed without his approval. Challenged by some bishops who thought he was interfering in the affairs of their local churches, Nicholas was successful in getting them to submit. Pope Nicholas also forced Emperor Louis II to back down when the latter marched on Rome in an effort to force the pope to recognize his brother's divorce and remarriage.

Duffy, *Saints and Sinners,* 79-81.

 The **Photian Schism** between Rome and Constantinople occurred in **863** after the eastern emperor, Michael III, deposed the Patriarch of Constantinople, Ignatius. He then replaced him with an imperial official, **Photius**. Further, in defiance of canon law, Photius, a layman, was elevated through all clerical orders in five days time. Pope Nicholas refused to recognize Photius or the authority of the emperor to appoint him. Nicholas declared Photius deposed and excommunicated him. When Emperor Michael protested his actions against Photius, Pope Nicholas responded that "the privileges of this see existed before your empire, and will remain when it has been long gone."

Ware, *The Orthodox Church,* 52-54.

 **Boris I of Bulgaria** was baptized by missionaries from Constantinople in **864.**

Pope St. Nicholas the Great.

Boris sought to have a separate, independent patriarchate established in his kingdom. When the Patriarch Photius refused this concession, Boris began talks with **Pope Nicholas.** In 866 Pope Nicholas sent legates to Bulgaria to help establish the Church there. They carried with them the pope's written replies to questions that Boris had submitted to him about Christian practices in regard to marriage, morality and other matters. The pope's responses preserve an interesting example of evangelization in the ninth century. They also indicate the intense competition that existed between Constantinople and Rome for the loyalty of the Bulgarians.

The fasting regulations were discussed in detail. On the question of receiving Holy Communion, Nicholas offered instructions which may shed light on practices in Rome at the time. "You ask whether you should communicate with the body and blood of the Lord every day during greater Lent. We humbly pray to omnipotent God and exhort you all most vehemently that you do so…" But they should only receive "the body and blood" every day during Lent when "we give tithes of our flesh to God, we imitate the Lord Himself in abstinence, and we rightly cut from ourselves not only illicit things, but also many things which are allowed…" *(Chapter IX)*

In reply to Boris's questions regarding marriage, Pope Nicholas wrote that couples did not have to wear crowns for their marriage ceremony. It was their consent to the marriage that was essential. Widows and widowers could marry again but a man could not have more than one wife at a time. The second wife would have to be let go. And no, married couples could not have relations on Sundays "since the name 'the Lord's Day' shows clearly that the Christian should do nothing on this day except what is the Lord's."

Boris apparently had a lot of questions about the proper exercise of power by a Christian. The pope replied that fighting should be avoided on feast days, pagans should not be forced to convert nor should widows be coerced into entering convents. As to more day-to-day concerns, the pope said that the "Greeks" were wrong in saying one could not bathe on Wednesdays and Fridays. Citing Gregory the Great, the pope asserted that they could bathe on any day they liked.

Appropriate attire for women was another issue for Boris. Nicholas, quoting St. Paul's admonition to the Corinthians, insisted that women have their heads veiled in church. However, he had an open mind about them wearing pants.

"We consider what you asked about pants to be irrelevant; for we do not wish the exterior style of your clothing to be changed, but rather the behavior of the inner man within you, nor do we desire to know what you are wearing except Christ…. But since you ask concerning these matters in your simplicity…we declare that in our books, pants are ordered to be made, not in order that women may use them, but that men may….but really do what

Saints Cyril and Methodius, the Apostles to the Slavs.

you please. For whether you or your women wear pants or do not wear pants neither impedes your salvation nor leads to any increase in virtue." (Chapter LXIIII)

One of Boris' last questions was "how many patriarchs there truly are." Pope Nicholas responded that there were only three, those in Rome, Alexandria and Antioch. The pope stated that each of these sees could be traced to the Apostles. These three alone qualified. "For as regards the church of Constantinople, none of the apostles founded it, nor did the synod of Nicaea, which is more venerable and celebrated than all other synods, make any mention of it; rather its bishop was given the title of patriarch more through the favor of princes than by reason, since Constantinople was called 'New Rome'." Although Pope Nicholas did not hesitate to assert papal primacy, he rather amusingly referred to himself as "his mediocrity." (Chapter XCII) *"The Responses of Pope Nicholas I to the Questions of the Bulgars A.D. 866 Letter 99)* Translated by W. L. North from the edition of Ernest Perels, in MGH Epistolae VI, Berlin, 1925, pp. 568-600. www.pravoslavieto.com/history/09/866

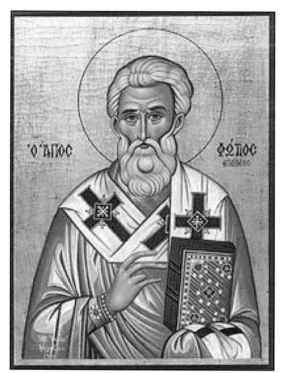

Photius. Patriarch of Constantinople who excommunicated Pope Nicholas.

 **In 867 Saints Cyril and Methodius** were warmly welcomed in Rome by Pope Hadrian. The "Apostles to the Slavs" had begun their missionary work in Moravia, which is now part of the Czech Republic. Christian missionaries from Germany had been there before but could not overcome the language barrier. The two Greek-born brothers taught the faith to the locals in their own Slavic language. They also labored to train a native clergy. As a sign of his support for them against their critics, Pope Hadrian approved their use of the Slavonic language in the Mass. He also ordained Methodious a priest. St. Cyril died in Rome in 869. Following his death, Methodius resumed the mission to the Slavs until his own death in 884.

Ewig, *History of the Church Vol. III The Church in the Age of Feudalism*, 149-151. Harl, *The World of Byzantium*, 245-247.

Pope Nicholas' remarks concerning matrimony indicate that all the Church required for a valid marriage was the consent of the couple. The various marriage rituals and even the presence of a priest were nice but not essential for a legal marriage.

Martos, *Doors to the Sacred: A Historical Introduction to Sacraments in the Catholic Church*, 424-425.

Sadly, as mentioned earlier, not everyone was interested in evangelizing the Slavic people. For some, since the Slavs were pagans they were subject to enslavement. Many captured Slavs were forced into bondage and sold throughout Europe and the Mediterranean region. Christians continued to accept the practice of human bondage as a consequence of sin, particularly the sin of warfare. However, Christians were not supposed to enslave fellow Christians. So as more peoples were evangelized, there were fewer potential slaves and slavery was gradually disappearing in Europe. It continued to exist mainly in regions that bordered pagan territories.

C. Verlinden, *"Slavery," The New Catholic Encyclopedia.* Philip Daileader, *The High Middle Ages, The Great Courses,* Course Guidebook, 8.

The **Danish Vikings** amassed a great army in **865** and in thirteen years overran the divided Anglo-Saxon kingdoms of England. The sole surviving king and the only one to defeat them in battle was Alfred the Great (849-899).

Daileader, *The Early Middle Ages*, 70-72. Wickham, *The Inheritance of Rome*, 456-457.

 Meanwhile, an eastern synod, presided over by Photius and with the Emperor Michael's tacit support, **excommunicated Pope Nicholas I and declared him deposed**. The synod also **condemned the filioque clause in the Creed** and denounced the presence of Latin rite missionaries in Bulgaria. Photius, and the eastern Church in general, saw authority in the Church as being exercised by the five semi-autonomous patriarchates of Rome, Constantinople, Jerusalem, Antioch and Alexandria. The five patriarchates were to collaborate with each other under the supremacy of the eastern emperor. This understanding was completely at odds with the Roman view of the primacy of the successor to St. Peter over the whole Church. These contrasting understandings of authority in the Church continue to divide East and West to this day.

Ware, *The Orthodox Church*, 46-49. Ewig, *History of the Church Vol. III The Church in the Age of Feudalism*, 174-180.

Within months of Photius' condemnation of the pope, a new imperial dynasty came to the throne in Constantinople. **Basil I,** a former wrestler and horse trainer, murdered his patron, Emperor Michael III, and then proclaimed himself emperor. Basil deposed Photius in November of 867 and reinstated Ignatius as Patriarch of Constantinople. Under Basil and his successors the empire in the East experienced a military, economic and cultural revival.

Whittow, *The Making of Byzantium*, 600-1025, 310-357. Vasiliev, *History of the Byzantine Empire*, 300-311.

The **Fourth Council of Constantinople** held from October **869** until February 870 is considered the eighth ecumenical council in the West. The calling of this Council

King Alfred the Great of England. *Winchester.*

was at the behest of Emperor Basil I who was trying to end the Photian Schism. The Council condemned Photius and deposed from office all clerics that had been appointed by him. These depositions created a strong sentiment against the decrees of the Council among many of the eastern clergy. Opposing the iconoclasts who still divided the Church in the East, the Council upheld the practice of venerating images. It also asserted that lay authorities were not to be involved in the election of bishops. The canons of the Council in turn called upon the bishops to be diligent in their work for the Church and to cease being involved in secular affairs.

Ewig, *History of the Church Vol. III The Church in the Age of Feudalism*, 180-181.

While undoubtedly pleased that Photius was deposed, the papal legation was surprised when the Council declared that the church in

The Trial of Pope Formosus, Jean Paul Laurens. *1870.*

Bulgaria would be under the jurisdiction of the patriarch of Constantinople. Unbeknownst to the pope's representatives, this maneuver had been prearranged by King Boris and Emperor Basil. With the king's support the Church in Bulgaria quickly founded its own institutions. From these foundations Christianity was carried to other Slavic peoples.

Whittow, *The Making of Byzantium,* 283-285. Harl, *The World of Byzantium,* 246-247.

Emperor Basil I initiated the re-conquest of southern Italy from the Muslims in **875.** In doing so he also stifled Muslim attempts to capture more of Italy.

Whittow, *The Making of Byzantium,* 307-309. Harl, *The World of Byzantium,* 254.

Photius was reappointed patriarch in **877** by Basil following the death of Ignatius. A synod held in Constantinople in 879 annulled the decrees of the Fourth Council of Constantinople which allowed for the veneration of icons. Since this time, the Fourth Council of Constantinople and its canons have been rejected in the East. Photius was deposed a third and final time in 892. However, because of his battles with the papacy, Photius, later became a heroic figure in the East and is recognized as a saint by the Orthodox Church.

Ware, *The Orthodox Church,* 55-56. Beck, *History of the Church Vol. III The Church in the Age of Feudalism,* 174-193. Harl, *The World of Byzantium,* 245-247.

Alfred the Great, who had become king of Wessex in 871, **defeated the Danes in 878,** thus preserving Anglo-Saxon England. As a scholar-king who had visited Rome as a child, Alfred was ardently loyal to the Holy See. In his youth Alfred had also visited the court of the Frankish king, Charles the Bald.

Once his kingdom was secure, Alfred set about trying to restore order in his lands. For, after decades of fighting, the cathedrals and monasteries had been devastated, many bishoprics were vacant and the clergy and monks had been scattered. Like Charlemagne, he gathered the best and the brightest scholars together and sought to restore the religious and cultural life of his people. Alfred had some of the notable works of Augustine, Gregory, Boethius and Bede translated into Anglo-Saxon. He also provided a law code for his kingdom and established schools. Alfred's efforts laid the foundation of the English nation and by the time of his death he was hailed as king of all the Anglo-Saxons.

L. A. Lehtola, *"Alfred the Great," New Catholic Encyclopedia.* Ewig, *History of the Church Vol. III The Church in the Age of Feudalism,* 136-139. Wickham, *The Inheritance of Rome,* 456-457.

Muslim forces from North Africa took control of Sicily away from the eastern empire in **878.** They then used the island for launching attacks on Italy itself.

Vasiliev, *Hisory of the Byzantine Empire, Volume One,* 278-279.

By the late ninth century the Carolingian empire was collapsing. Without a strong imperial ruler, governance of what was the Carolingian empire passed to numerous strong men at the provincial level. Government, such as it was, became a system of protection based on power and personal loyalty. Successful warriors became "noble men" who protected the "knights" under them in exchange for their pledges of loyalty and material support. The nobles used their private armies of knights to bring lands and villages under their rule and to exact support from them. The basis of all wealth in this emerging "feudal system" was land, and the nobles were in a never ending quest to place more of it under their rule.

In addition to governance being imposed by violent internal factions, the Frankish kingdoms was battered by Viking, Muslim and Maygar attacks.

Maurice Keen, *Medieval Europe* (Penguin Books, Oxford, 1968, 1991) 34-40, 47-60. Daileader, *The Early Middle Ages,* 66-67.

As the Carolingian empire declined, it was no longer able to protect the papacy. Following the death of Pope Nicholas in 867 a series of weak popes were nominated by competing factions among the Italian nobility. The greatest scandal of this period was **the "trial" of Pope Formosus.** Not content with trying him posthumously, his vindictive opponents actually dug him up, put him on trial for alleged crimes, condemned him, and then threw his body into the Tiber River. Prior to becoming pope, Formosus had been a zealous missionary in Bulgaria and was thought of as a holy man. He did nothing to deserve trial let alone the barbarities that were inflicted on his corpse.

The battle to control the papacy devolved from a regional contest to a local one early in the tenth century when three powerful Roman families with one common ancestor, **Theophylact,** began to dominate papal elections.

This was the darkest era in the history of the papacy. For approximately 150 years, beginning in 904, the papacy was controlled by one or another of these families. Sometimes they succeeded in placing their own relatives on the throne. These were among the worst papal reprobates. But more often they controlled the papacy by securing the "election" of a compliant non-entity. Only ten of the forty popes of this period reigned for as long as five years. Many of them died under suspicious circumstances and it is all but certain that five were murdered.

Surprisingly, while the moral character of many of the popes of this period left much to be desired, the papacy was able to exert its authority effectively outside of Rome. At times these popes were even successful in promoting genuine reforms in other places.

Walsh, *Lives of the Popes*, 92-108. Duffy, *Saints and Sinners*, 81-86. Noble, *Popes and the Papacy*, 27-29.

Around the year **900** Abbot Regino of the monastery of St. Martin's in Trier (Germany) compiled a collection of guidelines to be used by bishops on their visitations to parish churches. These guidelines, called "Libri duo de synodalibus causis et disciplinis ecclesiasticis," and similar compilations prepared by various synods provide a glimpse of what parish life was like, or was supposed to be like, at the time.

Parish priests were obligated to maintain the property and the cleanliness of the church. They were also expected to take care of the liturgical vestments and vessels. The guidelines expressed the importance of priests living upright lives and providing good example for their parishioners. Thus, priests

were not to have women living with them nor were they to carry weapons. They were not to spend their time raising falcons or visiting taverns. Priests were always to wear clerical attire, to show special care for the poor and hospitality to travelers.

A parish priest was to rise early and begin his day by praying Lauds (Morning Prayer). He was also to keep the other hours of the Divine Office. Mass was to be offered around 9:00 a.m. Fasting was to be observed until the noon meal. The priest was exectd to visit parishioners who were ill and administer the sacraments of Penance, Anointing, and Holy Communion to them.

Books that the priest was expected to have included; the missal, a lectionary with the Scripture readings and an antiphonary, which had the chants for Mass. He was also to have a book of homilies to preach from and it was recommended that he have the forty homilies of St. Gregory the Great. He was supposed to know the unchanging parts of the Mass by heart and to commit the Psalms to memory. The priest was also expected to be able to read the Latin prayers of the Mass without making mistakes.

On Sundays and feast days, he was to explain to the people in their vernacular language something about the epistles and Gospel passages that had been read. Priests were also expected to preach on the Holy Trinity, the Incarnation, the Resurrection and

St. Ludmilla with her grandson, St. Wenceslaus, King of Bohemia.

on which sins could lead to damnation.

As for his parishioners, on Sundays and major feast days, they were to come to Lauds, Mass and Vespers (Evening Prayer). It was the priest's responsibility to see that they knew the Creed and the Our Father by heart in Latin. They were to be taught these prayers as children by their parents and godparents. To be sure that his parishioners learned their prayers the priest was to test them by requiring their recitation at the time of their Lenten confession. At the same time, parishioners were to be asked about their faith in the Holy Trinity and in the resurrection of the body for judgment.

G. May, *"Regino of Prum, Collection of,"* New Catholic Encyclopedia. Josef Jungmann, *History of the Church Vol. III The Church in the Age of Feudalism,* 300-317.

The **Abbey of Cluny** in Burgundy was established in **909** by William the Pious, the Duke of Aquitaine. Well endowed by its founder, Cluny was free from control by the nobility. Later it was placed under the direct authority of the papacy to insure its freedom from temporal rulers. Its first abbot, Berno (909-927), established Cluny's reputation for strict observance of the Benedictine Rule and its emphasis on the monks' personal spiritual growth.

David Whitton, *"The Society of Northern Europe in the High Middle Ages,"* in *Medieval Europe* ed. by George Holmes, 128-129.

Conrad I was the elected King of East Francia in **911** succeeding the last Carolingian ruler, Louis the Child. In choosing Conrad, the nobles of the Germanic lands returned to the ancient practice of electing the king from among their number rather than having the crown pass through hereditary right. This created problems since at times the succession remained uncertain and some elections were contested. Following Conrad, they chose **Henry I of Saxony (r. 919-936)** as their king. He was succeeded by his son, **Otto I (936-973).** His forty year rule began the **Ottonian dynasty,** as he was followed by two more Ottos. In contrast to devolution of governance in West Francia or France, the reigns of these Saxon kings brought much needed stability to the German-speaking lands. Church officials welcomed their success in controlling the nobility. However, these kings exercised great influence over the Church as well.

Wickham, *The Inheritance of Rome,* 430-435. Keene, *Medieval Europe,* 40-43.

In **911** Vikings ("Northmanni" in Latin) agreed to stop attacking West Francia in exchange for being allowed to settle in northwest France. Their leader, Rollo, was recognized as the Duke of Normandy.

Wickham, *The Inheritance of Rome,* 439-441.

 Beginning in **914** the **Irish** endured a century of relentless Viking attacks. These Vikings from Norway established the fortress towns of Dublin, Wexford, Waterford, Cork and Limerick. Irish monastic communities suffered a great deal at the hands of the Vikings.

Kempf, *History of the Church Vol. III The Church in the Age of Feudalism*, 221-222. Whitton, *"The Society of Northern Europe in the High Middle Ages,"* in *Medieval Europe* ed. by George Holmes, 99-108.

 The influence of the **Abbey of Cluny** over other monasteries was furthered by its second abbot, **St. Odo (879-942)**. The reform measures at Cluny included emphasizing the solemnity of the Mass and the divine office. Additionally, Cluny and the monasteries affiliated with it maintained their independence from lay control. Soon several neighboring monasteries were under the rule of the abbot of Cluny. The influence of Cluny continued to grow until the middle of the twelfth century when over a thousand monasteries in Europe were under its leadership. The effects of the Cluniac reforms were not limited to monks. They were much admired by many among the secular clergy and inspired others to reject simony, the purchasing of church offices, and to observe a more faithful adherence to celibacy.

Wickham, *The Inheritance of Rome*, 528. *The Oxford Dictionary of the Christian Church*. Duffy, *Saints and Sinners*, 88-89. Pope Benedict XVI, *"St. Odo of Cluny" Church Fathers and Teachers*, 129-134.

While at war with the Eastern empire, **Czar Symeon I** declared the independence of the Bulgarian church. Ten years later, in **927,** Constantinople recognized the Bulgarian patriarchate.

Otto I, "the Great."

 **In 929 St. Wenceslaus** (907-929), the twenty-two year old king of Bohemia was murdered. Wenceslaus had been taught the faith by his maternal grandmother, **St. Ludmilla**, (c.860-921) who had been baptized as an adult by St. Methodius. Ludmilla was known for her gentleness and care for the poor. At the time, the Bohemian nobility was divided into pagan and Christian factions. Resenting her influence over Wenceslaus, the non-Christian faction had her strangled to death in 921. She was immediately hailed a martyr by the people. Wenceslaus, who emulated his grandmother's Christian virtues, suffered a similar fate when he was murdered by his own brother eight years later. He too was immediately proclaimed a martyr although it appears his killing was more of a political act than an attack on Christianity. In any case, St. Wenceslaus has remained a figure of ethnic pride in Bohemia, the modern day Czech Republic.

Thurston and Attwater, *"St. Wenceslaus"* and *"St. Ludmilla,"* Butler's *Lives of the Saints*.

Pope Leo VII was elected to the papacy in **936.** A promoter of reform, Leo invited Odo of Cluny to Rome to foster improvement in monastic discipline there. Leo is also remembered for a decision he made regarding the treatment of **Jews.** Contrary to some erroneous accounts, Leo did not order the expulsion of the Jews from Germany. In reality, Archbishop Frederick of Mainz requested papal permission to tell the Jews of his city they must be baptized or be expelled. Leo replied that they could not be coerced into baptism although they could be expelled if the archbishop believed it was necessary. Apparently the archbishop chose not to follow this course as the Jews of Mainz were not expelled.

Duffy, *Saints and Sinners, A History of the Popes,* 83. Glick, *Abraham's Heirs: Jews and Christians in Medieval Europe,* 63.

Prince Vladimir of Kiev. *The Baptism of Prince Vladimir. Viktor Vasnetov. Kiev Cathedral.*

Around **950** a heresy called **"Bogolism"** appeared in Bulgaria. Named for its founder, Bogomil, this heresy, like Manicheism before it, maintained that the material world is evil. Accordingly, Christ didn't really have a human body, the sacraments were false and the institutional church corrupt. Adherents were to abstain from sexual intercourse, meat and wine. Nor were they to have possessions. As a populist movement Bogomilism was favored by artisans and peasants. Part of the attraction of the movement was its opposition to the dominance of Greek-speaking clergy over the church in the Balkans.

Jennifer Kolpacoff Deane, *A History of Medieval Heresy and Inquisition* (Rowan and Littlefield Publishers, Inc. 2011), 30-31. Rosemary Morris *"Northern Europe Invades the Mediterrean, 900-1200,"* in *Medieval Europe* ed. by George Holmes, 128-129. A.V. Solviev, *"Bogomilism,"* New Catholic Encyclopedia.

At the Battle of Lechfeld in **955, Otto I the Great, king of Germany**, defeated the Hungarians and ended their century of success as horse-borne raiders in Central Europe. In **962** Otto was **crowned as emperor in the West** by Pope John XII. As when his predecessor had crowned Charlemagne, Pope John hoped that his alliance with the German kings would protect the papacy from Italian nobles. However, John and Otto had a major falling out and the emperor had the pope deposed. Still, the alliance formed between the papacy and the German Ottonian dynasty would endure. During this period no popes could be consecrated without imperial approval. In exchange for imperial protection, the popes would pledge their loyalty to the emperor as their temporal ruler. Like the Carolingian rulers, the German emperors saw the Church as an instrument for organizing the empire and they took an interest in promoting reform.

Keene, *Medieval Europe,* 40-42. Walsh, *Lives of the Popes,* 102-104. Ewig, *History of the Church Vol. III The Church in the Age of Feudalism,* 200-207.

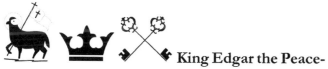 **King Edgar the Peaceful** became the Anglo-Saxon king in England in **957**. During the course of his eighteen year reign he worked zealously for the reform of the Church in his realm. Edgar had three reforming monks, **Dunstan**, **Oswald** and **Aethelwold** named as bishops of the important sees of Canterbury, York and Winchester, respectively. Together these four men did much to reestablish ecclesiastical and social order in England following another era of Viking attacks with its accompanying dissolution. Dunstan and Oswald are both recognized as saints.

Kempf, *History of the Church Vol. III The Church in the Age of Feudalism*, 224-228.

At this time there were twenty to twenty-five thousand **Jews** living in northwestern Europe, most of them along the Rhineland valley. They called this region "Ashkenaz," and they became known as Ashkenazi Jews. Here they began speaking their own dialect of German which evolved into Yiddish. The fact that they developed their own language is indicative of both their independence and isolation from the prevailing Christian culture. While Jews continued to enjoy toleration and in many ways prospered, they were still discriminated against. They also suffered indignities because of their religion. For example, in some towns in the region Jews were subject to both verbal and physical abuse on certain feast days, like Palm Sunday.

While this persecution was certainly unjust and contrary to Christianity, according to one Jewish scholar, "Jews themselves were intentionally exclusive and self-segregating in ways that could be perceived as mean and burdensome." Some Christians resented the fact that Jewish butchers tried to sell them meat which Jews themselves considered unfit to eat. Also, Jewish law forbade drinking wine that had been touched by a non-Jew. So Jewish vintners kept wine which could only be sold to Jews and other batches for Christians. This practice too raised suspicions that Jews were somehow cheating their Christian customers.

Glick, *Abraham's Heirs: Jews and Christians in Medieval Europe*, 62-75.

The important island of **Crete** was recaptured from the Muslims in **962** and their fleet was destroyed. Imperial armies in the East followed this conquest with a series of victories recapturing the island of Cyprus and the Syrian city of Aleppo.

Wickham, *The Inheritance of Rome*, 307-309.

After imperial authority was reestablished in northern Syria the patriarchates of both Antioch and Jerusalem gradually adopted the liturgical practices and the church laws of Constantinople. Prior to this time they had used the West Syrian liturgical rites.

G. A. Maloney, *"Patriarchate of Antioch," New Catholic Encyclopedia.*

Catholicism came to **Poland in 966** when **Prince Mieszko** was baptized. Soon after, a bishopric was established at his residence of Poznan. The Poles would be the most important Slavic people to pledge their loyalty to the Church of Rome rather than that of Constantinople.

Kempf, *History of the Church Vol. III The Church in the Age of Feudalism*, 238-240.

By **976** imperial forces were in a position to recapture much of Syria and Palestine that had fallen to the Muslims three centuries before. However, with the accession of a new emperor to the throne, Basil II, the eastern oriented policy of Constantinople was reversed and her efforts were refocused on Europe.
Harl, *The World of Byzantium,* 256-261.

The last Carolingian monarch, King Louis V, died in **987** after falling off his horse. To succeed him, the nobility of the West Franks elected Hugh Capet, Duke of Paris, as their king. This was the beginning of **the Capetian dynasty**, which ruled for over three hundred years. Hugh and his successors gradually obtained sovereignty over neighboring lands. Thus began the kingdom of France.
Whitton, *"The Society of Northern Europe in the High Middle Ages,"* in *Medieval Europe* ed. by George Holmes, 153-154. Keen, *Medieval Europe,* 46.

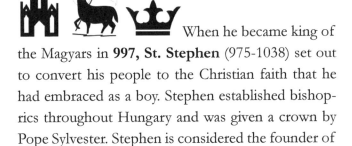 Pope John XV canonized St. Ulrich of Augsburg (890-973) in **993**. Ulrich was a beloved bishop known for his preaching and charity to the poor. This was the first formal canonization by the Holy See. Previous saints had been proclaimed by local, popular acclamation.
Thurston and Attwater, *"St. Ulrich,"* Butler's Lives of the Saints. Noble, *Popes and the Papacy, A History,* 29.

 In **989, Prince Vladimir of Kiev** (956-1015) was baptized into Orthodox Christianity. Vladimir's baptism was part of a military alliance with the eastern emperor, Basil II, which included marrying the latter's sister, Anna. This alliance brought the Russian people under the influence of the Church in Constantinople as Prince Vladimir led his people, sometimes by force, to accept baptism. Vladimir was declared a saint by the eastern Church in the twelfth century.
Ware, *The Orthodox Church,* 78-79. Whittow, *The Making of Byzantium,* 371-373. Harl, *The World of Byzantium,* 249. *The Oxford Dictionary of the Church.*

When he became king of the Magyars in **997**, **St. Stephen** (975-1038) set out to convert his people to the Christian faith that he had embraced as a boy. Stephen established bishoprics throughout Hungary and was given a crown by Pope Sylvester. Stephen is considered the founder of **Hungary.**
The Oxford Dictionary of the Church.

Gerbert of Aurillac (940-1003) was elected pope in **999** and took the name **Pope Sylvester II.** A Benedictine monk, he was the first pope to come from France. The most accomplished western scholar of his day and advisor to emperor Otto III, Pope Sylvester hoped that he and the emperor could collaborate together on reforming the Church. Pope Sylvester vigorously opposed simony and promoted clerical celibacy. He also supported the establishment of the Catholic Church in Poland and Hungary in the year 1000.

However, the pious Otto III, who actually ruled his empire from Rome, died of malaria in 1002 at the age of twenty-two. The death of Otto, followed by that of Pope Sylvester in 1003, enabled the Roman nobility to once again dominate the papacy.
Noble, *Popes and the Papacy*, 29. Ewig, *History of the Church Vol. III The Church in the Age of Feudalism*, 212-217, 247-249.

King Olaf I (968-1000) is called the "Apostle of Norway and Iceland." In his youth, Olaf was a Viking warrior. He spent a few years living in the British Isles where he was baptized in his early twenties. The great-grandson of a Norse chieftain, Olaf returned to Norway in 995 and was recognized as king. Olaf was a devout Christian and his zealousness for the faith at times led him to heavy handedness in imposing Christianity on others. He died in battle in 1000 while fighting an army of Swedes and Danes.
Brown, *The Rise of Western Christendom*, 471-472., 480-481. H. Bekker-Nielsen, *"Olaf I Tryggvesson, King of Norway,"* New Catholic Encyclopedia.

Christianity became the official religion of **Iceland** in **1000** by the vote of its assembly of leading men. Irish and German missionaries had evangelized the island some twenty years before but with little success. Eventually, Norwegian missionaries sent by King Olaf were able to convert a few Icelandic chieftains. This in turn led to widespread conversions with mass baptisms taking place in the island's hot springs. Another factor in the conversion of Icelanders was the importation of Irish slaves who were Christians. More missionaries came, churches were erected and by the middle of the eleventh century a native born priest, Isleifur Gizurrarsson, was consecrated as Iceland's first bishop. However, certain pagan practices, including the killing of female babies, continued even after Icelanders had declared themselves to be Christians.
Brown, *The Rise of Western Christendom*, 472-473. M.P. Jakobsson, *"The Catholic Church in Iceland,"* New Catholic Encyclopedia.

In **1009**, at the command of the caliph, Hakim, the ruler of Egypt and a persecutor of Christians, the church of the Holy Sepulcher over the tomb of Christ in Jerusalem was demolished.
Jonathan Riley-Smith, *The Crusades: A Short History* (Yale University Press, 1987), 44.

The beginning of the eleventh century saw new developments in western European society. Increases in population and agricultural production brought new wealth and higher standards of living. The culture in general was maturing, moving upward from the early to the high Middle Ages. These changes were accompanied by greater intellectual achievements and higher moral expectations.
Keene, *Medieval Europe*, 61-69.

Indicative of these new expectations was the **"Peace of God"** movement. Since the demise of the Carolingian empire there had been no strong central government in western Europe. The ruling nobles were little more than warlords utilizing knights to oppress peasants and attack each other. In the eleventh century local synods of bishops tried to curtail the

St. Romuald.

There were also reform movements within the Church. These included the call for limiting the nobility's control of Church appointments and its companion ill, simony. Clerical concubinage, especially among the rural clergy was also increasingly identified as a source of corruption in the Church. Influenced by the winds of reform, increasing numbers of clergy and consecrated religious pursued greater heights of spiritual asceticism.

Some of the reformist efforts took a heretical turn among small, isolated groups. In 1022 a group of heretical clerics and nuns was uncovered in Orleans (north central France). Among its members was the former priest confessor of Queen Constance. The group also included some members of the nobility. They professed a form of dualistic Gnosticism which rejected the incarnation and resurrection of Christ. They also dismissed the sacraments and the institutional Church. After being tried they were given the opportunity to recant and make a profession of faith. However, they defiantly refused and were burned at the stake. In 1025 heresy was discovered among a group of illiterate peasants in Arras (northern France). They followed the teachings of a mysterious teacher named Gundolfo. Confronted by their bishop, they recanted and were let go without punishment. Three years later another small group of lay people holding similar dualistic views was exposed in the town of Monteforte (northern Italy). The members of this group included a countess, skilled laborers and peasants. Some of these accepted the opportunity to recant while others bravely endured execution. Around the same time heretics were active in the province of Aquitaine (southwest France). As their teachings included the rejection of marriage and sexual intercourse, they were labeled "Manichees" by the authorities.

violence by demanding that the nobility refrain from attacking the Church and the peasantry. This movement quickly spread from France into Spain and Italy. Bishops enforced the peace by placing under interdict (i.e. suspending church services) territories whose leaders had violated the peace. The movement spawned the **"Truce of God"** which bound knights not to fight on Sundays and other holy days. The Peace of God movement successfully limited the constant fighting among the nobility. Some bishops even raised peace militias to enforce the "war on war." The idea that "holy wars" called by churchmen could and should be fought to insure justice was widely accepted.

The Abbey of Lessay in Normandy. Romanesque style.

While no link between these heretical groups has ever been established, they shared some views in common. They all seem to have propounded a dualistic cosmology to explain the existence of good and evil. In reaction to the laxity they perceived within the institutional Church, particularly among the clergy, these groups emphasized strict morals and pious practices. They put a strong emphasis on reading the Gospels and personal prayer experiences. At the same time they rejected the sacraments and other rites, including marriage.

These, as well as a few other smaller heretical outbreaks, quickly dissipated once they were exposed and confronted by civil and ecclesiastical authorities. Their emergence was symptomatic of the more general desire for reform of the Church and the rising expectations of the laity for personal religious experiences.

Macolm Lambert, *Medieval Heresy: Popular Movements from the Gregorian reform to the Reformation* (Barnes & Noble, 1992), 3-32. Deane, *A History of Medieval Heresy and Inquisition,* 1, 17. Kempf, *History of the Church Vol. III The Church in the Age of Feudalism,* 339-348.

 **St. Henry II** (972-1024) succeeded his cousin, Otto III, as king of the Germans. In **1014** he was crowned Holy Roman Emperor in Rome by Pope Benedict VIII. Henry was an active promoter of the reform movement initiated by the Abbey of Cluny. He also protected papal territories from attacks by the Byzantines. It was under Henry's influence that the Nicene Creed was introduced into the celebration of the Mass in Rome and thus throughout the West. Canonized in 1146, St. Henry was honored as a model Christian ruler.
Keene, *Medieval History,* 64, 67. *The Oxford Dictionary of the Church.* Pecklers, *Liturgy: The Illustrated History,* 93-94.

At the Battle of Clontarf in **1014** the Irish high king **Brian Boru** decisively defeated the Vikings, athough it cost him his life. Following their defeat, the Norsemen retained colonies in the

173

coastal towns. As they settled permanently in Ireland they intermarried with the Irish and were gradually Christianized.

In **1015** Muslims from Spain captured Sardinia. The following year a combined force brought together by Pope Benedict VIII freed the island.
Ewig, *History of the Church Vol. III The Church in the Age of Feudalism*, 250-251.

During the years **1012-1015 St. Romuald** (952-1027) founded the Abbey of Camaldoli in the central Italian province of Arezzo. Romuald had entered a Benedictine monastery when he was twenty years old and for decades sought a form of monastic life which combined both the communal aspects of monasticism and the austerity practiced by hermits. This was achieved at Camoldoli by having hermits living alongside a community of monks with all of them under obedience to an abbot. In Romuald's vision, which he derived from St. Benedict, the communal monastic life was to prepare at least some of the monks for the solitary life of hermits. Romuald's community., "the Camaldolese," would become a new monastic order under the leadership of his successors. His feast day is June 19.
B. Hamilton, *"St. Romuald," and A. Giannani, "Camaldolese," New Catholic Encyclopedia.*

Knut, a Danish nobleman, became **king of England in 1016.** Two years later he took the throne of **Denmark** and in 1028 he was recognized as king of **Norway**. A wise and pious ruler, England enjoyed peace under his reign. Un-

fortunately his death was followed by thirty years of instability for both the Church and the government. Bishops were installed and removed by the nobles at will and simony was flagrant.
Kempf, *History of the Church Vol. III The Church in the Age of Feudalism*, 228-229.

Following the death of Henry II in **1024**, the crown of the western empire passed to the Frankish people known as the Salians. The **Salians** produced four kings, Conrad II, Henry III, Henry IV, and Henry V. They ruled the German lands for a century. Like the Ottonian emperors before them, these kings partnered with the Church to organize their kingdom and evangelize their peoples.
Keene, *Medieval Europe*, 43-46. Kempf, *History of the Church Vol. III The Church in the Age of Feudalism*, 248-257.

Meanwhile, the death of the emperor Basil II in **1025** led to the long term instability of the government in Constantinople. In the fifty-six years from 1025 to 1081 there were 13 emperors. Instability led to military weakness and by the end of the century, the empire in the East would be fighting to survive.
MacGillvray Nicol, *"The Byzantine Empire,"* Britannica Online Encyclopedia.

Norman knights came to **southern Italy** in the early eleventh century. They fought as mercenaries at various times for and against the eastern emperor, the Lombards and the papacy. Before long they were taking lands for themselves and became the dominant force in southern Italy. Eventually, under Robert Guiscard (1015-1085), they took the provinces of Apulia and Calabria away from the eastern empire.
Harl, *The World of Byzantium*, 286-287.

In **1028** Duncan was consecrated the first bishop of **Dublin**. Prior to this time bishops in Ireland were associated with monasteries and answered to their abbots. The new diocese was placed under the supervision of the Archbishop of Canterbury. The establishment of the Diocese of Dublin brought the church there within the normal hierarchical structure of the Church. Accordingly, Bishop Duncan ministered to the local community with the assistance of secular priests who served as pastors of parish churches. The boundaries of the diocese and its parishes were defined geographically and the local church was governed by Roman canon law.

As the governing authority of Dublin expanded into surrounding regions so did the Roman form of church organization. This brought some conflicts with the traditional **Irish monasteries.** However, by the eleventh century the Celtic monastic system was badly in need of reform. Following Celtic family traditions, the lay founders of the monasteries had claimed the right to have members of their families elected as the abbots. Over time this devolved into a hereditary right to install whomever they wished as abbot and often those chosen were laymen. In effect, "lay abbots," were appointing monk bishops and through them they exercised almost complete authority of the Church in Ireland. Since Irish monks had brought Christianity to the Picts of Scotland, the same system of church governance prevailed there as well. During the course of the 11ᵗʰ century, as the power of the government in England increased, so did the authority of the archbishop of Canterbury. Under the leadership of

Pope Leo IX. A leader of Church reform in the eleventh century.

the archbishops of Canterbury, the Church in both Ireland and Scotland was gradually placed under the governing norms of Rome.

Kempf, *History of the Church Vol. III The Church in the Age of Feudalism*, 222-224.

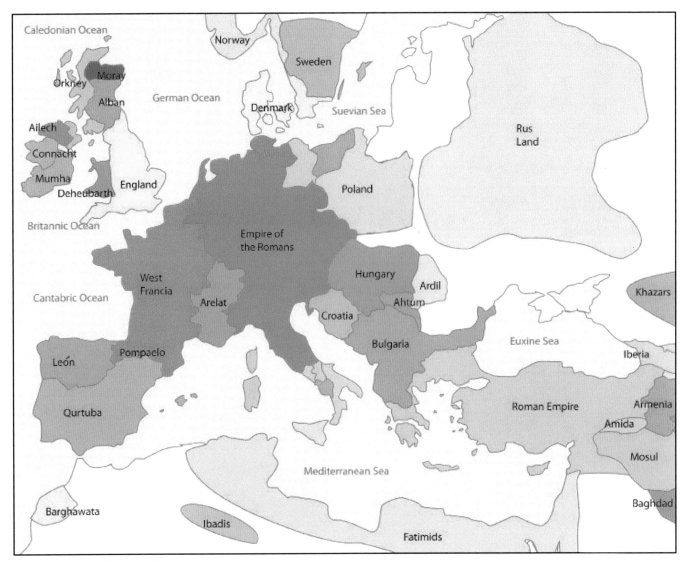

Europe in the mid-eleventh century.

Romanesque architecture in the construction of churches and monasteries flowered in the middle of the eleventh century. Based on the Roman rounded arch, this building style allowed for the erection of larger churches featuring high vaulted ceilings. Appearing first in northern Italy around 950, the style soon spread throughout western Europe and was a manifestation of the optimism which followed the passing of the first millennium of the Church. Larger churches encouraged grander liturgies. An unintended consequence of this development was that the laity was further removed from the liturgical action and their participation in the Mass increasingly diminished.

S. Edwards, *"History of Church Architecture-Romanesque," New Catholic Encyclopedia*. Pecklers, *Liturgy: The Illustrated History*, 110-114.

St. Peter Damian (1007-1072) a noted scholar, retired to the monastery of Fonte Avellana near Ravenna in **1034**. There he wrote a life of St. Romuald. A few years later he was elected prior of the monastery. Peter then wrote a Rule for the Camaldolese hermits which combined the Rule of St. Benedict and spirituality of St. Romuald. For Peter Damian the hermetic life was the highest state of life for it allowed one to be free of all distractions so as to better commune with God.

St. Peter Damian was very concerned with both monastic reform and Church reform in general. He was a fearless crusader against corrupt clerics whose perversities were denounced in his "Book of Gommorah." His writings on the subject of reform gained him many enemies among the clergy who feared scandal more than the rot of corruption. Peter Damian's reform efforts led to his ordination as a bishop. Later Pope Stephen IX forced him to accept appointment as a cardinal.

As an emissary for the popes, St. Peter Damian labored to reconcile various factions in the Church.

These duties required Peter Damian to leave his beloved monastery and the life of a contemplative which he sought. He was the most important mystical writer of the eleventh century and wrote often of the mystery of the Cross. His "canonization" as a saint was by popular acclamation. He was declared a doctor of the Church in 1823 and his feast day is February 21.

Pope Benedict XVI, *"St. Peter Damian" Church Fathers and Teachers*, 135-140.
St.Peter Damian, *Selected Writings on the Spiritual Life* translated with an Introduction by Patricia McNulty (Harper & Brothers, New York, 1959)11-52, 147-158.
Pope Benedict XVI, *"St. Peter Damian," Church Fathers and Teachers*, 135-140. O. J. Blum, *"St. Peter Damian," New Catholic Encyclopedia*.

 **St. Edward the Confessor** (1003-1066) became king of England in **1042**. Raised in Normandy, the land of his mother, the pious king was regarded by many as more Norman than Anglo-Saxon. During his reign, his court was sharply divided into Norman and Anglo-Saxon factions. Edward initiated the restoration of the **Westminster Abbey of St. Peter** which was dedicated in 1065. He was the last king of England of Anglo-Saxon lineage.

Kempf, *History of the Church Vol. III The Church in the Age of Feudalism*, 228-229. *Oxford Dictionary of the Christian Church*.

 The Roman nobility lost its hold on the See of Peter in **1046** when King Henry III of Germany deposed the legitimate pope, Benedict IX and two pretenders, Sylvester III and Gregory VI. Henry then succeeded in placing on the papal throne first, Clement II and then, Damasus II. Both of these men were German bishops and friends with Henry. They both also shared Henry's interest in church reform. However, neither one was pope for long. Clement died after nine months as pope and Damasus after less than one.

Walsh, *Lives of the Popes*, 112-113. Duffy, *Saints and Sinners*, 88-89.

In **1049 Emperor Henry III** arranged for the election as pope of his distant cousin, Bishop Bruno of Toul (1002-1054). As a bishop in Alsace, Bruno had promoted clerical reform and argued for the freedom of the Church from secular interference. Indicative of his commitment to the Church's independence, Bruno refused to become the pope unless he was elected in the traditional manner by the clergy and people of Rome. Bruno walked to Rome as a pilgrim and once there was elected by acclamation.

 The new pope took the name **Leo IX** and assembled a like-minded group

of reformers to assist him. Leo IX presided at many reform synods and, breaking from tradition, traveled around Europe in order to make his influence felt. Like other reformers, Leo saw simony and clerical concubinage as the greatest causes of corruption in the Church. To fight the latter abuse, which was common among the lower clergy, Leo forbade the laity in his diocese to have anything to do with priests who were known to be unchaste. Pope Leo and his collaborators were even more fervent in their fight against simony which they viewed as a heresy that undermined the sacraments. Leo publicly exposed bishops who had obtained their offices through simony and deposed those who refused to confess. No pope before him had ever exercised authority to discipline bishops in so direct a manner. Although his attempt to have all "simoniacal" ordinations declared invalid did not succeed, he did have many such clerics admit their wrong doing and be "re-ordained."

Kempf, *History of the Church Vol. III The Church in the Age of Feudalism*, 351-358. Duffy, *Saints and Sinners*, 89-91.

♛ In spite of his initial successes, Pope Leo's papacy ended in disaster after his attempts to deal with the Normans and to bring about reconciliation with Constantinople both failed. By the time he ascended to the Chair of Peter, the Normans had supplanted both the Muslims and the forces of Constantinople as the greatest threat to the papal authority in southern Italy. In **1053** Leo led an army against the Normans but was quickly defeated and then held prisoner for nine months.

🔑 One of Leo's closest advisors, **Humbert,** Archbishop of Sicily, went to Constantinople to seek reconciliation between the churches and military help against the Normans. Unfortunately, the Patriarch of Constantinople Michael Caerularius (c.1000-1058), who prior to becoming a monk had imperial aspirations, was fanatically anti-Latin. The Patriarch resented the very presence of the Latins in the previously eastern controlled territories of southern Italy and Sicily. Additionally, for some time, Constantinople had been in a war of words with Rome over the insertion of the filoque into the Creed and the use of unleavened bread at Mass. Each side had also been suppressing the other's rites in territories under their control.

🔑 With Leo imprisoned, the curia chose to send Humbert to Constantinople to negotiate on behalf of the papacy despite the fact that he had been leading the polemics against the Greeks. The bad blood between Michael and Humbert, combined with their intemperate dispositions, enabled misunderstandings to become hostility and eventually violent denunciations. Each side accused the other of various heresies and then excommunicated the other. This was the **Great Schism of 1054.** However, as Pope Leo had already died and the Greek excommunication was aimed only at Humbert and his fellow papal legates, the excommunications did not mean much at the time. But the episode did accelerate the already growing estrangement between East and West.

Beck, *History of the Church Vol. III The Church in the Age of Feudalism*, 351-358, 409-417.

♛ In **1055** Turkomen tribes under the leadership of Tughril Bey, the first "great sultan" or "protector," invaded what are modern day Iran and Iraq and seized Baghdad. Tughril successfully married his daughter to the Sunni spiritual leader of Baghdad, the caliph. Together, the sultan and caliph would unite **Sunni Muslims** against the **Shi'ite Muslim** rulers of Egypt whom they considered to be heretics. The fact that these "heretics" controlled the holy cities of Mecca and Medina and were allied with the eastern empire necessitated their destruction. In pursuit of their goal the Turks began attacking the eastern empire which was allied with the Shi'ites in Egypt.

Harl, *The World of Byzantium*, 288-289. Donald MacGillvray Nicol, *"The Byzantine Empire," Britannica Online Encyclopedia.* Jonathan Riley-Smith, *The Crusades: A Short History,* 1-2.

Although his pontificate lasted only five years and ended on a low note, by his own fearless example, Pope Leo IX had transformed the papacy into the driving force for reform in the Church. Leo's three immediate successors, Victor II (1055-1057), Stephen IX (1057-1058) and Nicholas II (1058-1061), continued his reform efforts during their own brief pontificates. Behind their efforts, giving continuity and determination to the reform movement, was Leo's protégé, Hildebrand. A monk from Rome, Hildebrand would carry the reform movement and papal authority to new heights as Pope St. Gregory VII (1073-1085).

Duffy, *Saints and Sinners: A History of the Popes,* 91-99.

SUMMARY OF CHAPTER FIVE

Authority

From the middle of the eighth century to the beginning of the tenth, popes contended with the eastern emperors over the issue of iconoclasm. During this period there were two ecumenical councils called by the emperors to settle the controversy, at Nicaea in 787 and Constantinople in 869. After much struggle, the traditional position on the permissibility of images upheld by the popes was vindicated. But the controversy permanently strained relations between East and West. Both the emperors and the patriarchs resented papal claims of primacy. On their part, the popes and their supporters grew more alarmed at the emperors' willingness to sacrifice doctrinal orthodoxy for political expediency.

With the emergence of the Carolingian empire under Charlemagne, the popes gained both powerful allies and rivals for authority over the Church in western Europe. Following the demise of the Carolingian empire, German emperors asserted themselves as protectors of the Church in the West. And like their predecessors, they too challenged popes over the exercise of authority within the Church.

Doctrine

Iconoclasm, which was the attempt to suppress the use of images in Christian devotion, remained the foremost doctrinal issue in the eighth and ninth centuries.

The heresy of Adoptionism was for a brief time a problem in Spain. However, after being condemned at the Council of Frankfort in 794 it quickly faded away.

In the middle of the tenth century a heresy known as Bogolism appeared in Bulgaria. Like the earlier Manichaean heresy, Bogolism had a dualistic view and regarded the material world as evil. Similar heresies appeared about seventy years later in France but were successfully suppressed.

Pastoral Practice

The desire of Charlemagne and his successors to standardize liturgical and sacramental practices led to greater uniformity. Roman practices supplemented by Frankish additions began to dominate all the local churches in the West. Further, as Benedictine monasticism spread, aided by popes and kings, monastic spirituality exerted a profound influence over all aspects of church life. An unintended consequence of these developments was the physical and spiritual distancing of the laity from the celebration of the Eucharist. There were also developments in the way that sacramental reconciliation and anointing of the sick were administered.

Saints

The most influential saints of this period were all monks, and in the West they were all Benedictines. Some were reformers and others missionaries. Among them were Benedict of Aniane, Odo of Cluny, Romuald, Peter Damian, and Ansgar.

Three eastern monks also made their mark on the Church in this period. Theodore the Studite was the leading voice against iconoclasm. Cyril and Methodious, Greek-speaking brothers, brought the Gospel to the Slavic peoples.

Several kings from this era are remembered for their piety and for leading their people to accept the Christian faith. Perhaps most notable among these are Wenceslaus of Bohemia and Stephen of Hungary. Vladimir of Kiev is honored in the eastern Church for bringing the Gospel to the Russian people. However, his accomplishment had more to do with his military prowess than his personal piety.

Evangelization

From 750 to 1050 the most important evangelization efforts in the West took place among the Scandinavian peoples as well as in Bohemia, Poland and Hungary.

In the East, missionaries were successful among the Bulgarians and other Slavs in the Balkan region. The conversion of the Russian people to eastern Christianity a century later was of monumental importance in shaping the whole culture of Eastern Europe.

State

Both eastern and western rulers sought to use the Church as an instrument in achieving their political and social objectives. In addition, having been given lands in central Italy, the popes became increasingly immersed in the often violent struggle to hold on to them.

In the West, the passing of the Carolingian empire in the middle of the ninth century resulted in political chaos, with the nobility competing for power on the local level.

The Witness of St. Peter Damian.

The mystery of Christ is unchangeable and immovable, for there is manifold witness to it. The witness of men and women, of those in the prime of life and of the aged, of things earthly and heavenly, of Gentile and Jew, of ancient times and of His own day; the witness of light and of darkness, of the Law and the Prophets, of kings and of the multitude, of living and dead... The multitudes bore witness, for the Gospel tells us that they said: 'We have seen strange things today,' and 'If this man were not God, he could do nothing.' And because of this they wanted to take Him by force and make Him king. Living men bore witness, for the two who were travelling to Emmaus came and told all that had befallen them. Dead men bore witness, for 'many bodies of the saints which slept arose and appeared to many.' The brute beasts bore witness: 'The ox knoweth his owner and the ass his master's crib.' The sun bore witness when it was darkened. The earth and the elements bore witness in the great earthquake. The air bore witness when a cloud received him out of the sight of his disciples....Since then, brethren, the mystery of the Cross had the witness of all that I have mentioned...let every tongue confess that Jesus Christ is Lord, to the glory of God the Father. And may our Lord Jesus, who is the splendor of lights, the flower of flowers, the life of goodness, the school of virtues and the crown of the saints, and who reigns over the choirs of angels for ever and ever lead us to that glory. Amen.

From a sermon By St. Peter Damian on the Feast of the Epiphany

CONCLUSION

From the day of Pentecost until the mid-eleventh century, millions of men, women and children had accepted the promise of eternal life through Jesus Christ and been born again by water and the Holy Spirit. Over the course of those thousand years they gave witness to Jesus Christ by **evangelization** beginning in Jerusalem and then to the known ends of the earth—Ethiopia in the south, China to the east, Norway in the north and Iceland to the west.

Although the number of commonly recognized **saints** for the Church's first thousand years is relatively small, among the millions of Christian believers there were undoubtedly hundreds of thousands who followed the teachings of Jesus in exemplary fashion. Then of course there were many, not unlike ourselves, whose witness to Jesus Christ was undermined by their attachment to the things of this world. Still, by God's grace, even these less than stellar Christians have found a place at the supper of the Lamb. Regrettably, there were also those who bore the name of Christian but who for all appearances were enslaved by the "ruler of this world." Their infidelity undermined the witness of the Church but could not destroy it.

Within a century of Pentecost a well-defined order of **authority** was operative in the Church and it quickly became universal. The hierarchy of bishops and priests under the supreme authority of the popes was established well before the Church was given legal status under Constantine. It is true that papal primacy was challenged at times. But it is also true that the Church was most effective in her mission when popes were strong in fulfilling their divine charge to "strengthen the faith" of their brothers and sisters.

The formulation of correct **doctrine** based on both scripture and tradition was a major concern of the Church in these centuries. The factionalism was ugly and sometimes violent. The enduring divisions tragic. However, as distressing as the doctrinal battles were, they resulted in a creed regarding the nature of God that most Christians have continued to agree upon into the third millennium even while continuing to have our differences over the nature of the Church.

The **pastoral practices** of the Church, founded on the proclamation of the Word of God and the celebration of the sacraments, remained largely consistent with those of the first Christians. This consistency in pastoral practice is particularly remarkable considering the diverse times and cultures the Church lived in. The way that Christians worshiped developed over the centuries and the elaboration of the liturgy may have unintentionally complicated the average believer's experience of Christ's presence in the sacraments.

However, in both the East and in the West, the celebration of the Eucharist continued to be the "source and summit" of the Church's life. It would remain so for virtually all Christians until the schisms of the sixteenth century.

No other aspect of the Church's history in the first millennium, or in the following centuries for that matter, scandalizes contemporary readers as much as her relations with the various temporal powers

I have called the **state.** Far removed from a world which saw the union of altar and throne as logical, twenty-first century Christians often find it incomprehensible that their fourth-century co-religionists, just recently relieved from imperial persecution, actually requested that the Emperor Constantine involve himself in the Church's affairs. The subsequent history of emperors and kings manipulating the Church for political purposes and churchmen pursuing political goals only increases the sense of outrage and spirit of cynicism. However, we need to bear in mind that for all its blessings, the "separation of church and state" brings its own evils, the most damaging being moral relativism.

Jesus Christ is quite forthright that each of His followers and His Church as a whole must share in His temptations, suffering and cross. However, while our trials are mutual, our salvation must be worked out individually "with fear and trembling." The chasm that often exists between Christ's universal invitation to salvation and our varying personal responses will always be the scandal of the Church's history. While lamenting the individual and collective failures of believers to be faithful witnesses to Jesus Christ, we should not forget that the Church of Christ is contending not only with the flesh and blood of her members but also against "the principalities, against the powers, against the world rulers of this present darkness." Let us also remember that in Jesus Christ, the Son of God, we have a high priest who is able to sympathize with our weaknesses. For though He did not sin, He was tempted as we are. And He has promised that all who draw near to Him in their time of need will receive mercy and grace.

BIBLIOGRAPHY

Aquilina, Mike. *The Mass of the Early Christians.*
    Huntington, IN: Our Sunday Visitor Press, 2007.

Aquilina, Mike and Christopher Bailey. *Mothers of the Church: The Witness of Early*
    Christian Women. Huntington, IN: Our Sunday Visitor Press, 2012.

Aumann, Jordan, O.P. *Christian Spirituality in the Catholic Tradition.*
    San Francisco: Ignatius Press, 1985.

Bacchiocchi, Samuele. *From Sabbath to Sunday: A Historical Investigation of the Rise of Sunday Observance in Early*
Christianity. Rome: Pontifical Gregorian University Press, 1977.

Barnett, Paul . *Jesus & the Rise of Early Christianity: A History of New Testament Times.*
    Downers Grove, IN: InterVarsity Press, 1999.

Bauckham, Richard. *Jesus and the Eyewitnesses: The Gospels as Eyewitness Testimony.*
    Grand Rapids, MI: Eerdmans, 2006.

Benedict XVI, *The Apostles.* Huntington, IN: Our Sunday Visitor Press, 2007.

_____. *Church Fathers and Teachers: From Saint Leo the Great to Peter Lombard.*
San Francisco, Ignatius Press, 1985.

Benz, Ernst. *The Eastern Orthodox Church: Its Thought and Life.*
    Garden City, NY: Doubleday, 1957.

Bradshaw, Paul and Maxwell E. Johnson. *The Eucharistic Liturgies: Their Evolution and Interpretation.*
    Collegeville, MN: Liturgical Press, 2012.

Brown, Peter. *The World of Late Antiquity AD 150-750.*
    London: Thames & Hudson, 1971.

_____. *The Rise of Western Christendom: Triumph and Diversity, A.D. 200-100.*
    Malden, MA: Blackwell Publishing, 2003.

Cameron, Averil. *The Later Roman Empire, AD 284-430*.
Cambridge, MA: Harvard University Press, 1993.

Catholic Encyclopedia.
New York: Robert Appleton Company.
New Advent: http://www.newadvent.org

Chadwick, Henry. *The Early Church*.
New York: Penguin Books, 1967.

Charbonnier, Jean-Piere. *Christians in China A.D. 600 To 2000*.
San Francisco: Ignatius Press, 2007.

Cochini, Christian, S.J. *The Apostolic Origins of Priestly Celibacy*.
San Francisco: Ignatius Press, 1990.

Cohen, Mark R. *Under Crescent & Cross: The Jews in the Middle Ages*.
Princeton: Princeton University Press, 2008.

Cross, F.L. and E.A. Livingstone, eds. *The Oxford Dictionary of the Christian Church*.
Oxford: Oxford University Press, 1990.

Daileader, Philip. *The Early Middle Ages*. Great Courses Gide Book
Chantilly, VA: The Teaching Company, 2004.

Danielou, Jean and Henri Marrou. *The Christian Centuries* Vol. One *The First Six Hundred Years*. Mahwah, NJ:
Paulist Press, 1983.

Davis, William Stearns ed., *Readings in Ancient History: Illustrative Extracts from the Sources,* 2 Vols. (Boston: Allyn
and Bacon, 1912-13), Vol. II: Rome and the West, Scanned by: J. S. Arkenberg, Dept. of History,
Cal. State Fullerton. Prof. Arkenberg has modernized the text. This text is part of the Internet
Ancient History Sourcebook.

Dawson, Christopher. *The Making of Europe: An Introduction to the History of European Unity*. New York: Sheed
and Ward: 1932.

Deane, Jennifer Kolpacoff. *A History of Medieval Heresy and Inquisition*.
Lanham, MD: Rowan and Littlefield Publishers, Inc., 2011.

Duffy, Eamon. *Saints and Sinners: A History of the Popes*
New Haven, CT: Yale University Press, 1999.

Eusebius. *The Church History*. Translation and commentary by Paul L. Maier,
Grand Rapids, MI; Kregel Publications, 2007.

Frediksen, Paula. *Augustine and the Jews: A Christian Defense of Jews and Judaism*.
New York: Doubleday, 2008.

Foley, Edward. *From Age to Age: How Christians Have Celebrated the Eucharist.*
    Collegeville, MN: Liturgical Press, 2008.

Glick, Leonard, *Abraham's Heirs: Jews and Christians in Medieval Europe.*
    Syracuse, Syracuse University Press, 1999.

Groeschel, Father Benedict C.F.R., *I Am With You Always: A Study of the History and Meaning of Personal Devotion to Jesus Christ for Catholic, Orthodox, and Protestant Christians.*
    San Francisco: Ignatius Press, 2010.

Herrin, Judith. *The Formation of Christendom.*
    Princeton: Princeton University Press, 1987.

Hogan, Richard M., *Dissent from the Creed: Heresies Past and Present.*
    Huntington, IN: Our Sunday Visitor Press, 2001.

Holmes, George. *Medieval Europe.*
    Oxford: Oxford University Press, 2001.

Jedin, Hubert. Editor *History of the Church Vol. I, From the Apostolic Community to Constantine.*
    New York: Crossroad, 1987.

_____. *History of the Church Vol. II The Imperial Church from Constantine to the Early Middle Ages.*
    New York: Crossroad, 1987.

_____. *History of the Church Vol. III The Church in the Age of Feudalism.*
    New York: Crossroad, 1987.

Jenkins, Philip. *The Lost History of Christianity: The Thousand Year Golden Age of the Church in the Middle East, Africa, and Asia and How it Died.*
    New York: HarperOne, 2008.

Johnson, Maxwell E. *The Rites of Christian Initiation: Their Evolution and Interpretation.*
    Collegeville, MN: Liturgical Press, 2007.

Johnson, Timothy Luke. *Early Christianity: The Experience of the Divine.*
    Great Courses, Chantilly, VA: The Teaching Company, 2002.

Josephus. *The New Complete Works of Josephus.* trans. by William Whitson. Commentary by Paul Maier.
    Grand Rapids, MI; Kregel Publications, 1999.

Jungmann, Josef S.J. *The Mass: An Historical, Theological and Pastoral Survey.*
    Collegeville, MN: Liturgical Press, 1975.

Justin, St. *Dialogue With Trypho,* EarlyChristianWritings.com

Justin, St. *First Apology,* Translated by Marcus Dodds and George Reith. From Ante-Nicene Fathers, Vol. 1. Edited by Alexander Roberts, James Donaldson, and A. Cleveland Coxe. Buffalo, NY: Christian Literature Publishing Co., 1885. Revised and edited for New Advent by Kevin Knight. <http://www.newadvent.org/fathers/

Keen, Maurice. *Medieval Europe.* Oxford: Penguin Books, 1968.

Lambert, Macolm. *Medieval Heresy: Popular Movements from the Gregorian Reform to the Reformation.* New York: Barnes & Noble, 1992.

Leithart, Peter J. *Defending Constantine: The Twilight of an Empire and the Dawn of Christendom.* Downers Grove, IN: IVP Academic, 2010.

MacMullen, Ramsay. *Christianizing the Roman Empire A.D. 100-400.* New Haven: Yale University Press, 1984.

Mango, Cyril. *Byzantium: The Empire of New Rome.* New York: Scribners, 1980.

Martos, Joseph Martos. *Doors to the Sacred: A Historical Introduction to Sacraments in the Catholic Church.* New York: Doubleday, 1981.

Mazza, Enrico. *The Origins of the Eucharistic Prayer.* Collegeville, MN: Liturgical Press, 1995.

McGinn, Bernard, John Meyendorff, and Jean Leclerq, editors, *Christian Spirituality: Origins to the Twelfth Century.* New York: Crossroad, 1985.

Mitch, Curtis. "Introduction to the Gospels," *Ignatius Catholic Study Bible New Testament.* San Francisco, Ignatius Press, 2010.

New Catholic Encyclopedia. Volumes I-XV. Second edition, 2003.

Nichols, Aidan, O.P. *Holy Order: Apostolic Priesthood from the New Testament to the Second Vatican Council.* Dublin: Veritas, 1989.

Thomas F. X. Noble, *The Republic of St. Peter: The Birth of the Papal State, 680-825.* Philadelphia: University of Pennsylvania Press, 1984.

Pecklers, Keith, F. S.J. *Liturgy; The Illustrated History.* Mahwah, NJ: Paulist Press, 2012.

Pelikan, Jaroslav. *Jesus Through the Centuries: His Place in the History of Culture.* New Haven, CT: Yale University Press, 1982.

_____. *Mary Through the Centuries: Her Place in the History of Culture.*
New Haven, CT: Yale University Press, 1996.

Riley-Smith, Jonathan. *The Crusades: A Short History.*
New Haven, CT: Yale University Press, 1987.

Ruffin, C. Bernard. *The Twelve: The Lives of the Apostles After Calvary.*
Huntington, IN: Our Sunday Visitor Press, 1997.

Sommer, Carl J. *We Look For A Kingdom: The Everyday Lives of the Early Christians,*
San Francisco, Ignatius Press, 2007.

Sordi, Marta. *The Christians and the Roman Empire.*
Oklahoma City: University of Oklahoma, 1986.

Stark, Rodney. *Cities of God: The Real Story of How Christianity Became an Urban Movement and Conquered Rome.*
New York: Harper Collins, 2006.

_____. *The Triumph of Christianity: How the Jesus Movement Became the Largest Religion in the World.*
New York: Harper One, 2011.

Thurston, Herbert, S.J. and Donald Attwater, eds. *Butler's Lives of the Saints* Vols. I-IV.
Westminster, MD: Christian Classics, 1988.

Vasiliev, A.A. *History of the Byzantine Empire* Volume One.
Madison,WI: University of Wisconsin Press, 1952 & 1980.

Walsh, Michael J. Consultant editor *Lives of the Popes: Illustrated Biographies of Every Pope From St. Peter to the Present.* New York: Barnes & Noble, 1998.

Ware, Timothy. *The Orthodox Church.* Oxford, Penguin Books, 1997.

Westermeyer, Paul. *Te Deum: The Church and Music.*
Minneapolis, MN:Augsburg Fortress Press, 1998.

Whittow, Mark. *The Making of Byzantium, 600-1025.*
Berkeley: University of California Press, 1996.

Wilken, Robert Louis. *The Christians as the Romans Saw Them.*
New Haven, CT: Yale University Press, 2003.

_____. *The First Thousand Years: A Global History of Christianity.*
New Haven, CT: Yale University Press, 2012.

INDEX

abortion 28, 52

Acacian Schism, 109

Adoptionism, 58, 150-151, 180

Advent, 88

Alaric, 100

Alcuin, 150

Alemanni, 129

Alexandria, 26, 73

almsgiving, 37, 65

Anointing of the Sick, 102, 149

Antioch, 17-18, 73, 84, 130

anti-pope, 62

apologist, 42

Apostles 8-12, 15-17

Arians, Arianism, 77-81, 90-92, 94, 98, 111-112, 127

Arabia, 17, 40, 63, 70, 84

Armenia, 23, 70, 85, 108, 142

Attila the Hun, 107-108

Balkans, 158

Baptism, 12, 19, 39, 44, 53, 87, 121, 141-142

barbarians, 64, 100-102, 108, 116, 127

Bible, 48,61,70,86,91,94,98,113,137,150

bishop (office of), 30, 66, 83, 109

Blessed Virgin Mary 8, 11, 46, 50, 79, 97, 104, 112, 129, 150

Bogolism, 168, 180

Britain, 63, 71, 101

Bulgaria, 159, 163, 167-168

canon, 48, 94

Carolingian, 148-149, 150, 164, 170-171, 180

Cassiodorus, 126

Catholic, 33, 96

celibacy, continence of clergy 59, 93, 108, 112, 119,134-135, 142, 167, 171

Charlemagne, 146- 155, 164, 168, 180-181

Charles Martel, 139

China, 62, 84, 106, 112, 125, 131, 158, 183

clergy, 67, 89-90, 112

Christmas, 88

Church of Rome, 67, 73

Cluny, Abbey of, 166- 167

Communion, reception of, 88-89, 156

Confession (see also Penance), 119-120, 127, 141, 149, 166

Confirmation, 89, 102, 121

Constantinople, 81, 91, 92, 107, 127, 131, 133

Coptic, Copts, 131

Council of Carthage in 411, 103-104

Council of Chalcedon in 451, 107, 112, 119, 130, 138-139

Council of Constantinople I in 381, 94

Council of Constantinople II in 553, 125

Council of Constantinople in 680, 133, 141

Council of Constantinople in 869, 162, 180

Council of Elvira in 304, 72

Council of Ephesus in 431, 106, 112

Council of Frankfurt in 794, 151

Council of Hieria in 754, 140

Council of Jerusalem in 49, 18

Council of Nicaea in 325, 777, 80, 81, 89, 90, 92, 94, 111,

Council of Nicaea in 787, 151- 152, 180

Danes, Denmark, 157, 164, 171, 174

deacon, 16, 27, 29, 30, 32, 33, 39, 44, 45, 59, 60, 61, 63, 66-68,71, 73-74,80-81,93,99,107,111,127,135,150,151,154

deaconess, 36

Didache, 27-28

Docetism, 33, 39

Donation of Constantine, 144

Donation of Pepin, 140

Donatism, Donatists, 72, 77- 78,103-104, 111, 114

Dualism, 34

east, facing for prayer, 87

Easter, 52, 53, 88, 112

Edict of Milan, 76

Egeria, 94-95

Egypt, 23, 26, 40, 63, 69, 78-80, 83-84, 86, 93-94, 105,107-108, 123,129-130,133,142

Emperor Basil I, 158-159

Emperor Constantine the Great, 76-87,90, 113-114

Emperor Constans II, 132

INDEX

Emperor Diocletian, 70

Emperor Domitian, 29, 34

Emperor Heraclius, 132

Emperor Julian the Apostate, 99

Emperor Justin I, 109, 117

Emperor Justinian I, 117- 118, 121- 122

Emperor Leo III, 136-138

Emperor Louis the Pious, 155

Emperor Michael III, 159

Emperor Nero, 16, 23

Emperor Theodosius I, 71, 92, 94, 97-98, 100, 105-106

Empress Irene, 152-153

Empress Theodora (wife of Justinian) 117, 123

Empress Theodora, 157-158

England, English, 76, 121, 125, 127, 136, 137, 142, 151-152, 161-162, 164, 169, 174-175, 177

Epiphany, 88

Ethiopia, 63, 86, 108

Eucharist, 13-15, 24, 28-29, 30-31, 33, 39-40, 44-46, 50-51, 55-56,, 60-61, 65, 67, 68-69, 73-74, 86, 88, 89, 95, 121, 135, 147, 148, 181, 183

Eucharist – as sacrifice, 27, 29, 46, 51, 52, 61, 68, 74

Eusebius of Caesarea, 81

evangelization, 8, 9, 18, 21, 22, 40, 52, 74, 84, 86, 91, 96, 99, 100, 103, 106, 113, 127, 129, 141, 142, 151, 158, 159, 161, 171, 174, 181, 183,

exarchates, 126

excommunication, 54, 65

fasting, 57,65

filioque, 154-155

Formula of Hormisdas. 118

Franks, 110, 116, 133, 139, 140, 142, 144, 145, 151, 155, 158, 170

Gaul, 49, 63, 71, 83, 94, 96, 100-101, 106-110, 116, 121, 127-128, 139, 142

Georgia, 85

Germanic, Germans, 49, 62, 83, 84, 90, 91-92, 98, 100-101, 108-110, 136, 137, 142, 146, 158, 161, 168, 169, 171, 173, 174, 177, 180

Gnosticism, 33-34, 39

Gospel, 19, 21, 26

Goths, 91, 117, 122

Great Schism of 1054, 178

Greece, 20, 22, 23, 26, 84, 108, 139

Greek,12, 15-16, 17, 23, 27, 33-34, 44, 48, 49, 51, 53, 55, 58, 69, 81, 83, 84, 86, 94, 121, 128, 131, 160, 178, 181

Gregorian Chant, 128

Hagia Sophia, 123, 137

heresy, heretics, 33, 47, 51, 58, 62, 65, 73, 77, 79, 82, 98, 104, 109, 111, 112, 133, 138, 139, 145, 151, 152, 158, 168, 172, 173, 178, 180

Hildebrand, 179

Holy Orders, 89-90

Holy Week, 53, 95

Humbert, 178

Hungary, 170

Huns, 107-108

hymns, 51, 82, 86, 97

Iceland, 171

iconoclast, icons, 129, 137-139, 141, 145, 15-152, 156, 158, 162-163, 180-181

infanticide, 52

India, 23, 1106

Ireland, Irish, 106, 118, 119-121, 129, 142, 151, 157, 167, 171, 173-174, 175

Islam, (see also Muslim), 130-133

Israel, 26

Italy, 63--64, 67, 83, 93, 96, 100, 108-109, 116-117, 122-123, 125-127, 129, 133-134, 136-137, 138, 140, 142, 144-145, 152, 157, 163-164, 172, 174, 176, 178, 181

Jacob Baradaeus, 125

Jerusalem, 37, 63, 73, 84, 129, 169

"Jesus Prayer", 129-130

Jews,(Jewish) 13, 15, 19, 21-25, 33-34, 37, 39, 40, 42, 48, 52, 53, 55, 62, 87, 91, 99, 103, 121-1 to 2, 128, 129, 154, 168, 169

Josephus, 23

Judaizers 22, 33

King Alfred the Great, 164

King Boris I, 159-160

INDEX

King Clovis, 110

King Pepin the Short, 140

King Recared, 127

King Theodoric, 109, 122

Latin 58, 94, 127

laying on of hands, 16, 74, 93

Lent , 88, 95, 112

liturgical,liturgy, 227, 28, 31, 45, 47, 48, 52, 58, 61, 67, 73-74, 86-87, 88, 89, 90, 92, 94, 95, 97, 99, 102, 112-113, 119, 127, 133, 135, 146, 147-148, 150, 154, 158, 165, 169, 176, 180

Lombards, 92, 117, 126-127, 139, 140, 142, 144, 146, 174

Louis the Pious, 155, 158

Manichaeanism. 62,102

Marcion, Marcionism, 47,73

marriage, 39, 51-52, 64, 74, 78, 93, 121, 134-135, 159-160, 161, 172-173

martyr, martyrdom, 16, 23, 37-38, 74

Mass, 45,55, 86-87, 146-149, 165

Mohammed, 130

Merovingian dynasty, 110

Milan, 94, 96

modalism, 5eight

monasticism, monks, 56, 69, 92, 112-113, 126-127, 155

monophysitism, 107-108, 112, 114, 123, 125, 141

monotheletism, 131-132, 141

Montanism, 48, 51

Muslim, Muslims, (see also Islam) 130-131, 133-136, 142, 157-158, 164,, 169-170, 174, 178-179

Nestorianism, Nestorius, 105-106, 112

New Testament,12, 27, 39, 48

Nicene Creed, 80, 106, 111, 155

Normans, 174

North Africa, 664, 102, 122, 125, 132, 135

Norway, 1171, 174

Novatian, 64

Odoacer, 108

Old Testament, 45, 47, 48

original sin, 104

Origen,54-56, 63, 66, 70, 96, 98

Ostrogoths, 116, 122

paganism, pagans, 24, 25, 98-99, 103, 113, 121

Palestine, 26

papal (petrine) primacy, 17, 65, 73, 107, 111

papal state, 140

Patriarch Germanus, 138

Patriarch Photius, 159, 162-163

Peace of God,171

Pelagianism,, 104, 112

Penance, Sacrament of, 65, 119-120, 141

penitential, 65

penitentials, 119-120

Pentecost, 8, 12, 88

persecution, 16, 17, 18, 23-24, 29, 34-35, 38, 47, 54, 63-64, 67-68, 70-71, 72, 74

Persia, Persian, 62, 85, 106, 108, 128-129

Photian schism, 159, 163

plague, 64, 108, 123, 139

Poland, 169

"pope", origin as title of the Bishop of Rome, 70

Pope Clement I, 29-30

Pope Damasus I, 48, 93-94

Pope Gelasius, 109

Pope Gregory the Great, 141-142

Pope Gregory, II, 136, 141

Pope Gregory III, 137, 138-139

Pope Hadrian I, 146, 151

Pope Hormisdas, 118

Pope John I, 122

Pope Leo the Great, 107-108

Pope Leo III, 139

Pope Leo IX, 177-178

Pope Liberius, 90

Pope Martin I, 131-132, 141

Pope Nicholas the Great, 159--161, 162

Pope Silverius, 122

Pope Stephen II, 140

Pope Victor, 53

INDEX

Pope Vigilius, 122-123, 125, 141,

population – Christian, 42, 63, 71, 83-majority,

Pliny, 33-26

prayer, 13, 16, 31,36, 55,56,57, 58,59, 60,65, 68,93, 117, 119, 121, 129,130,135,147,151, 165-166, 173

priest, 32, 33, 39, 40, 45, 47, 59, 60, 61, 63, 66, 67, 73, 74, 78, 87, 151, 161, 166, 167, 175, 178, 183

Quinsext Council in 691, 134-135

Ravenna, 100, 126

Real Presence, 14-15, 38, 46-47, 50, 55, 95-96

relics, 38, 117, 129

Rome, sack of, 100-101

Rule of St. Benedict, 1117

Russia, Russian, 170, 181

St. Aidan, 151

St. Ambrose, 96-97, 102, 113

St. Anthony, 669, 82, 113

St. Ansgar, 157, 181

St. Athanasius, 81-83, 86, 90,, 92, 95, 113

St. Augustine,87, 96, 98, 101, 102-105

St. Augustine of Canterbury, 127

St. Barnabas, 18

St. Basil the Great, 92-93, 113, 115

St. Bede, 134-135

St. Benedict, 117

St. Benedict of Aniane, 155

St. Blandina, 48-49

St. Boniface, 136-137, 149

St. Brigid, 121

St. Caesarius, 1121

St. Clement of Alexandria, 50--51, 59, 65

St. Columba, 118, 125

St. Columban, 127-129, 142

St. Cyprian, 64-65, 67-68, 69, 74

St. Cyril, 161, 181

St. Cyril of Alexandria, 105, 154

St. Cyril of Jerusalem, 86, 95-96

St. Edward the Confessor, 177

St. Gregory of Nyssa, 92-93, 113

St. Gregory of Nazianzus, 92, 113

St. Gregory the Illuminator,70

St. Henry, 173

St. Hilary, 82, 89

St. Hippolytus, 60, 62-63

St. Ignatius of Antioch, 32-33, 39, 40, 56

St. Irenaeus, 37, 49-50, 54, 74

St. Isidore of Seville, 128

St. James, 21, 25

St. Jerome, 70, 94, 97-98, 127

St. John, 22, 33,37

St. John Chrysostom, 99

St. John Damascene, 138, 142

St. Justin Martyr, 442, 44-46, 74

St. Leander, 127

St. Ludmilla, 167

St. Luke, 17, 22

St. Mark, 17

St. Macrina, 93

St. Martin of Tours, 96

St. Methodius, 160-161, 167

St. Monica, 102, 113, 147

St. Nino, 85

St. Odo, 167

St. Pachomius, 78-79

St. Patrick, 106

St. Paul, 17-24, 40

St. Perpetua, 56-57, 75

St. Peter, 11-24, 27, 40

St. Peter Damian, 176-177, 182

St. Polycarp, 37-38, 41

t. Romuald, 176

St. Stephen, 16

St. Stephen of Hungary, 170

St. Theodore the Studite, 155-156, 181

St. Ulrich, 170

St. Wenceslaus, 167

Schism, 109,125, 151

    Acacian, 112, 118

Donatist, 77, 103, 111
"Great," 178
Photian, 159, 162

sign of the cross, 56, 60
simony,1151, 167, 171-172, 174, 178, 179
Slavs, 126, 139, 154, 160-161, 181
slavery,slaves, 26, 37, 54, 154, 161, 171
Synod of Arles in 314, 77-78
Synod of Constantinople in 843, 158
Synod of Rome in 382, 94
Synod of Trullo in 691, 134-135
Synod of Whitby, 133
synods, 48, 54, 67, 077, 79, 80, 89, 111, 132, 139, 140,
145, 152, 153, 156, 160, 162, 116, 165, 171, 178

tabernacle, 87
Tertullian, 51-52, 55-56, 59, 64-65
Theophylact, 164
Theotokus, 79, 105-106, 112
toleration, 76, 83, 84, 86, 112, 117, 169
Truce of God, 172

Vandals, 105, 122, 142
"Vicar of Christ", first use of title, 109
virginity, 48, 59, 92, 93
Vikings, 151, 157-158, 161, 164, 166, 167, 169, 171, 173

Made in the USA
Charleston, SC
17 April 2015